It's May and the Lilacs are Blooming

One Foot on Earth and One in Heaven

Elaina Deva Proffitt

Heart Drop Publications

It's May and the Lilacs Are Blooming

ISBN 978-0-9970639-0-5

Final Edits and Proof Reading
by Robert K. Vaughn at rkvaughn.nv@gmail.com

Cover Design, Interior Design and Typesetting
by Donna Osborn Clark at: CreationsByDonna@gmail.com

Lilac Painting of Elaina Deva
by Artist Sabrina Wheeler

Sabrina Wheeler
9/16/57 - 2/16/17
Rest in Peace

Published by Heart Drop Publications

www.heartdrops.net
www.devawhispers.com
heartdroppublications@gmail.com

Scripture taken from The Holy Bible - King James Version (KJV)

First Edition

God Whispers

This book came alive with pen and ink after counseling and sharing for so many years with those whom I have walked with through their challenging and sometimes pain-filled journeys. I quickly learned that their struggles along life's path were like my own in many ways except even more pain-filled and overwhelming than my own. Each page is filled not only with their journeys, but also my own passages and contemplations as I reflect upon what was received from each step taken upon the path of my life. Some pages are simple thoughts for you to reflect upon and add to those within your own being. Others are a specific journey I have taken in this lifetime that would, on many levels prepare me for a life-threatening experience that was yet to come. What precedes that event is also a key, unlocking a door that will also become a book at another time.

Throughout this book, I use the word "Whispers". Since I was a child I always felt that God was whispering to me whenever I received an intuitive message or someone had shared something very profound with me in a deep life-changing moment.

There are countless souls that have touched my life across myriad places in this world in both new and sometimes oh-so-familiar ways. I learned again and again that the teacher becomes the student, and that lesson has always been the message that continues to be shown to me. If we profess to be a teacher and a guide for others, then we must sit across from another without ego. It is necessary to be completely open to the essence of each soul and be ready to become a Divine Instrument of love, compassion, wisdom and grace.

One day when counseling at The Silver Sage Book Store and Metaphysical center in Reno, Nevada, the owner, Pat Gross, brought a new awareness to me. "What I see coming through you is the gift of not being afraid to teach by personal example. You share your own vulnerabilities and challenges and those who come to you seeking your wisdom soon not only find a teacher but a human being." Reflecting upon her statement I realized the truth that rested within her words. None of us is beyond nor exempt from the challenges and growth that arrives in this lifetime. It is what we do with each cycle that is the key. The strong empathic gifts that God has given to me have been a gift but also sometimes a curse. Feeling others deeply has a price, but when we learn how to use that gift for their growth we find it is ours also. It is worth the price that we pay!

Be the Light! Is the Whisper.
Elaina Deva Proffitt

This book is dedicated to those who are grieving, who carry their own pain, sickness and death or that of a loved one.

To those who are lost and forgotten…struggling in your life. I see you and you are so precious to me. All of you lonely travelers in the dark night of the Soul, have faith! Helpers do arrive and Angels will be with you, just like they were for me.

I am grateful to those who throughout the years trusted enough to reach out and take my hand, sharing their pain as we walked into the Light or into a new way of living on Earth. I am also humbled by those who took my hand in my darkest hours and continue to do so.

Those of you who are the Guardians of this planet, working tirelessly in the shadow of death daily. Walking into the heinous acts of others and the pain and suffering they cause.

The Doctors, EMTs and medical personnel who continue to work diligently to save lives.

Know this! Heaven does exist.

Acknowledgments

A Thank you

For the support and encouragement from so many of you who were with me at different stages of this writing;

Donna Osborn Clark, my dear friend and amazing graphic artist, designer, book cover design, layout and all the promo materials associated with this book.

Contributing Editor: Bob Vaughn, Rosemarie Kempton and Michaelle Van Meter who gave a fresh pair of eyes to these pages.

Artist Sabrina Wheeler who created the lilac art around my photo that is on the back cover of this book and on my website.

All those who continued encouraging me to continue with this writing despite many challenges. I appreciate you all.

Acknowledgments continued on page 323

Preface

This book is written with the hope that it will help those who are facing life-threatening illness and is also for their loved ones. May it bring a deeper understanding of what happens during those days, months and years when we or a loved one are facing a serious health crisis in our lives. It is written to remind you that you are not alone. During the course of a serious life-threatening illness there is a constant cycle of feeling better one minute then falling back into pain the next, never knowing when the cycle will repeat itself again. The hours, days and weeks blend together and decision making fluctuates between clear and clouded. The fight is so exhausting, a repetitive vicious cycle of emotional highs and lows. Serious life-threatening illness or trauma forces one to spend a lot of time reflecting, whether lying in bed, being still, or undergoing treatments and testing. Each day provides a lot of time to think about many things including what we have done with our lives. It also reveals our true relationships with family members and friends. The discovery of who steps up to support us and who does not can be hurtful; but when spirit surprises us with souls who arrive to help and support, it can be a heart-warming yet humbling experience. We become filled with deep gratitude. I also became aware that near-death experiences (NDEs) come in many ways. Since experiencing my own NDE, I have counseled many individuals who have taken the journey. I found when working hospice, for example, clients often spoke very open and deeply with me about life, death, what comes next, the Other Side. When I reflect upon these experiences, I feel that I have always lived with one foot on Earth and one in Heaven. Throughout my life my aura has seemed to project a safe zone where people whisper their life and death secrets to me comfortably, openly, and without hesitation. As the years passed, I developed an extensive background in grief and loss counseling that went hand in hand with my NDE experience. I found myself becoming a confidant to those who had experienced this mysterious event.

When a loved one is dying, there are many dialogues going on within them as they experience this mysterious process. Each person has a unique experience that is not only a physical process, it is also occurs on more hidden levels. The mind, emotions and soul are in deep inner dialogues, all part of what is called a human being upon this Earth. It is said that when you are dying your life flashes before you. While I can only speak for myself, yes, it does happen and on deeper levels each day, before leaving this body. I found this to be true for myself and many others. As each day passes, one's sight becomes different regarding what we call life. What was important in the past may not be in the present. If we survive the ordeal, we are changed for the rest of this life. There are constant waves of what I call "whispers" from many physical and spiritual levels, as one's senses see and feel from a whole new perspective. It is hard to put into words, for the rational reasoning mind has been altered, with unexplained flashes of scenes being revealed in an uncontrolled manner. At times, there is only a "knowing" that life has changed.

It took years for me to finish this book and I endured untold health problems along the way. Coincidentally or perhaps Divinely, a number of my significant health issues occurred in the month of May. Despite being knocked down again and again, I rose up and continued writing until I arrived at the last page! I knew there were so many waiting for this book to arrive. Their faith and longing kept me going. I also felt that when this project was completed a new chapter of life would begin for me at long last.

This book is also the story about life taking me into the dark world of homicide. I consulted for many years as a psychic detective on murder cases. Investigators observed the mysterious abilities I had when working as a medium: connecting with a deceased victim, reenacting a murder. Other worldly skills manifested in me as I worked through a case. A profile of the perpetrator would be revealed; the way they talked, their temperament, their fantasies, a description of their residence and favorite locations. A profile would be painted from the psychic realm like brush strokes in my mind's eye. It was as if I was playing both roles at times, becoming the victim and the killer describing what led up to the murder…even their conversations. My body would suffer various traumas in another realm. On some occasions, I would slowly open my eyes and see the investigators staring at me in complete silence…as if in shock. During one of these psychic reenactments a detective told me, "That was scary! A cop's worst nightmare! There was nothing we could do to stop it!" It would take time (usually several minutes) before I fully entered back into my body. There were times I would have to sit quietly for a while at the Division office just to make sure I could drive home.

As part of my work with the homicide detectives, I would be given a most sacred gift from them. Detectives would refer the victim's families to me with the hope that they could find some comfort after their tragic loss. They knew that the families would be safe with me and not used for personal gain. My life has been filled with many twists and turns and the work given to me has been filled with mystery, danger, intrigue and travel to faraway places. All my life people would say to me. "You need to write a book about your life!" This book is Volume One and there is so more much to tell. Sometimes Truth is stranger than fiction…and more exciting! One very important aspect to clearly understand about all the stories and work I describe throughout this book is that the vast majority of the events took place long before there was wide-spread, commercially-available broadband (or even dial-up) Internet, reality TV, or all the home-based/mobile "instantaneous everything" technology gadgets we have all come to know and love (or hate). Instead, VHS video tapes, fax machines, answering machines, and compact discs were the "high tech" of the time. Pay phones (and landlines in general) were still in wide-spread use as a primary conduit of communication. My clairvoyance and extra sensory perceptions on so many levels were my information superhighway and my psychic abilities were the search engine.

Table of Contents

One Foot on Earth and One in Heaven

Since I was a child I have always lived with one foot on Earth and one in Heaven. Looking back upon my life, it took many powerful experiences to come to this realization. Even as a child I always felt an unseen presence that walked beside me. I did not know what to do with it. I had a strong sense that part of me did not belong on this Earth…as if my life straddled two different worlds. There would come a time when my feelings were validated by others who were also spiritually gifted, who saw and felt things just as I did. In contrast, I also heard ramblings from religious community members who said it was "evil" for anyone to claim they could "see" souls on the Other Side. Even at a very young age, I did not believe the nay-sayers for I knew my God was a loving one. I questioned why a loving God would not bring us those who were given spiritual gifts, even seeing those on the Other Side. What could be evil about bringing messages from Heaven? When the road is dark and lonely, would not a loving God bring us ones who help shine the light so we will not stumble and fall?

I have oftentimes reflected upon this challenge even as an adult, not only on a personal level, but with others whose lives were fading and they would reach out to me for help. Through years of counseling others and in my travels, I learned that there are many layers of dying: emotionally, mentally, psychologically and of course physically. Death could occur in a multitude of ways, some more pain-filled, others in a more heinous manner. So many do not get to share near-death experiences with their busy doctors. How can one not wonder if these doctors knew the complete story of what happened during their time with that patient? How did they (the doctors) touch not only the patient's physical body but also how was a Higher Power working through them during that most critical time in their patient's life that they were sharing together? I have always been blessed to be able to see and experience this phenomenon with the doctors/healers that have arrived at exactly the right time. Angels have always given me signs in the most amazing ways. When the right doctors arrive and I see their eyes, I always know that Divine Source has sent the Archangel Raphael (the Angel of Healing) to watch over me and them during our time together.

I became aware at a very early age that destiny and fated events do exist. Simply stated, Destiny is something we are meant to do. And if one believes in Karma then one will also be tying up loose ends with people and the events that arrive. Once again, the choices we make will bring an action to be put into motion. Some are more avoidable than others. How we use those experiences will clear the way for a new path to materialize before us. My life was fated not only in the psychic realm but also the astrological realm. My astrology chart (a tool showing how the positions of stars and planets influence and shape our lives) revealed that many of my planets and their aspects were sitting in the house of death and violence. I walked this path since I was a child and angels constantly protected me. Years later once again, the pattern was shown to me by a woman doing a birthday reading for me. "Your soul chose to turn that darkness and pain not towards yourself, by answering the call to work in the world of death, pain and the dark night of the soul with others." It made sense recalling how others always asked me, "how can you do that type of work?" My response would always be, "how could I not?" Along with the other placements in my chart; healer, teacher, counselor, seer and warrior, it made sense as to how my life's work arrived. It did not mean there were no adventures or fun times in my life; there were many! Traveling this world, seeing so much beauty, fills me with joy and recharges the life force needed…to do the types of work given to me. While writing this book, as my eyes scanned the pages of my journey, I realized just how much of a major theme was unfolding with each event.

Looking back, it is fascinating to see how certain people arrived and what their role was in creating powerful, amazing, loving and sometimes painful events either for them or for me in what we call Life. Powerful bonds were created and to this day many are still in my life, while others have gone to the Other Side or have walked away for one reason or another. We are what I call an "Over Soul." We have a connection to a group of souls in physical body consciously or unaware of this Divine Holy Spirit, that despite the differences in their jobs or appearance, have the same feelings and desires to accomplish something in a specific life theme to which they are all drawn. We will most often have work to do together even personal lessons to learn for our own soul's growth. When we meet these people, there is usually an immediate connection, one that might not be completely clear in the beginning. As we find ourselves together for a variety of reasons, we can see and feel the destiny or fated aspect of this connection. I believe it is many times, a relationship with someone that brings a powerful learning experience, closure or a powerful purpose from another life.

If we want to make changes in this world, we cannot do it alone. That is what the Over Soul does: it brings us together to learn, create and make changes in this world and within our own hearts. For some of us, they appear in more dangerous or life-threatening ways, creating powerful bonds whether near or far that last forever.

Destiny and fated events occurred yet again when I began this project. Ill health impacted me numerous times and I wondered if I would even be able to complete this book let alone live. It took all my inner strength to climb the mountain once more, spending most of the past six years alone and writing. I became the "monk in the monastery." Ironically, the time I spent in an actual monastery long ago paid off because I knew self-imposed isolation can be a dangerous walk. I now understood the words that a powerful Buddhist monk Rhosi Ju (old teacher old master) Roshi Houn Jiyu-Kennett, founder of Mt. Shasta Abby, known as the "Order of the Buddhist Contemplatives" spoke to me so long ago, "This will prepare you for what is to come."

At some point, I discovered that I had four potential books in one file. I realized I had been lost in time in another world. This time has been a more serious, introverted cycle with very little fun or times of seeing family and friends, and forgetting even the dream of a loving relationship arriving in my personal life. All I knew was that I was guided to walk this path. I struggled to keep the faith that I would be free to live once again when I had completed listening to those insistent whispers within: "Keep writing, all will be given." When I started to sense the book was at the end, life seemed to shift and doors opened again. I experienced brief periods of relief seeing family and dear friends, and I could feel that I was getting closer. I felt like Phoenix rising from the ashes once more. I have lived, grieved and died in so many ways with each stroke of the keys, bringing this book into being. I became aware of how so many had left this Earth-some more tragically than others, bringing closure and a final goodbye. Intense soul psychotherapy had arrived once again, knowing the healer must be healed, the counselor must be counseled.

I felt as if I was racing a time clock because so many people who had a life-threatening illness or lost a loved one were waiting for me to finish this book. There was pain on so many levels and my life path was to comfort them in their suffering…work that continues to this day.

I read parts of this book to my dear friend, Irene Morros who was dying of lung cancer. Irene was a client who quickly became spiritual family to me. We had a strong, spiritual connection. I called her "Goddess Peace" and she called me "Ms. Gypsy." There were times when she counseled me and there was always laughter spilling all over us when we got together. She "got me" and knew…it was not an easy path I was walking. During Irene's final days, she asked me to come see her to help get her spiritual life back on track before crossing over. I quickly booked a flight to Reno. While I was packing my bags I heard the inner voice whisper "take the manuscript with you." When I arrived, I was to share it with Irene upon my daily visits to her home because I knew it would be the last time we would see each other on the earth plane. Irene was one of my Angels on Earth, urging me to hurry to get this work completed knowing there were many who would not live to read it. I can still see her sitting there, so frail and full of grace, quietly listening as I read the chapters of my search for a doctor and the agonizing pain I suffered. Her words brought powerful confirmation of the reason I was compelled to write this book. "I don't think it is by accident that you just read to me about how much you suffered. I am also hanging by that thread right now just like you were. I have to go see that doctor this week to poke me too." With tears in her eyes she added, "I am so sorry honey that you hurt so badly too. I know how you felt." We both had tears falling as I helped her back to her bedroom.

From that day forward, I knew her remaining time was short and now it seemed I was being guided to share the chapters that were important for her own passage. On another visit, taking a deep breath, I shared my last agonizing moments leading up to arriving in the emergency room, into the operating room, and then out of my body into a beautiful heavenly place. As I was reading, the room was filled with an angelic presence and we both knew she would be gone soon. We fought back tears as it took every ounce of strength to get my voice to read the passage about going into the Light. There was a powerful silence in the room with us after those last words. We both silently knew we had come to the end on many levels. The two of us had a couple of weeks to prepare for what was to come. There would be a few more days to visit and spend the afternoons with her laying on the bed just talking and preparing her for the journey. At one point in a moment of silence between us I would find her arm around me with my head gently near her shoulder hearing her soft voice as she lovingly ran her hand down my head, side of my face, shoulder and arm. It was light as a feather and with it arrived what appeared to be a white wisp of mist coming out of her fingers then outlining my body. I could feel Goddess Peace was flowing through her and with each word spoken. "Few really see you Elaina, or what your world is like when you are helping those of us who are suffering or when we need you to sort us out." As she continued to speak about my private world, tears came to my eyes with this most sacred gift she was giving to me at that moment.

There is nothing that cuts the heart so deep nor as bittersweet as knowing when you give someone a final hug and words of love, and walk out the door, that you will never see each other again on this Earth. There was a smile on her face after staring at me for such a long time, suddenly her words broke our silent communication.

"Oh Honey, this book is going to help so many people"
I pray it so Dear Irene, I pray it so!
Irene Morros
8/19/1933 - 11/4/2010

The Story of My Life

There are so many books and pages needing to be turned to tell this story. So many years ago, while sharing some of my travels, adventures and the fascinating people that have come in my life, my mother handed me a cup of tea and shared some powerful words: "When you write the story of your life you must classify it as fiction as no one will believe it!" All her life, my mother was an avid reader of a variety of subjects: Science Fiction, Ray Bradberry, the Classics. She had a strong interest in Polynesian Culture. I always thought that was from a past life because her knowledge was so in depth she could have done lectures on the subject. I remember one time opening her bedroom clothes closet and seeing that it was stacked neatly up to the ceiling with pocket books! There was a time she worked at the Portland Library and later a career change found her working for a big law firm for many years. When my siblings and I were children living by the Oregon Coast, she would read the classics to us as we sat by the fireplace on a cold, rainy day or eve. There was always a cup of tea and cookies or a cup of hot chocolate. The book list was very large including *Jungle Book, Kim, Captains Courageous, Wee Willie Winkie* and all the books by Rudyard Kipling, who was an ancestor. We also played a card game called "*Authors.*" Books are a major part of daily life, when your mother is a Bibliophile. Her comments about me writing the story of my life that day in the kitchen were quite appropriate, and throughout the years we both had good laughs over and over again about it. Little did we know this book would arrive. I often hear her voice and those words that would become another prophesy coming true in my life.

Some of us seem to live many lives at a time. We have lots of traffic in our lives. There is constant travel, moves and changes, bringing many faces and places into our lives. Some folks do not understand this lifestyle, and even condemn it because they are locked into a narrower life experience. All my life, if I started to share news about an exciting event I was invited to, or someone I had met and worked with, some people would think that I was telling stories or bragging. No, that was not the case. It was simply part of my life. And then, there were the darker worlds in which I walked, which must be kept silent, so as not to compromise a criminal case.

To this day, I have continued to live so many lives in just this one and I must say, in exciting and unusual ways that people find it hard to comprehend. So now, it seems my mother's prophetic words so long ago have come true and have been repeated over and over by others in this lifetime.

"When you write the story of your life you must classify it as fiction as no one will believe it" and Shirley Proffitt, I reply to you in Heaven:

"Yes, Mother Dear, it came true and here is just one of those chapters. I know you remember this one." My life is filled with such bittersweet stories; I guess I must write of these things to not only help others but to heal my own heart and soul…as we all must do.

"Beginnings and endings are one and the same! All paths rejoining I've know them by name."-Gary Eubanks

Signs

There was a book written many years ago, by Manley P. Hall entitled *"The Ways of the Lonely Ones"* and it has always been one of my favorites. I guess because I can identify with so many of the stories about mystical experiences given to regular people whose lives were changed because of things that happened to them, lifting them to a higher vibration of spiritual life and awareness. To this day when reading these stories, there is a comfort and a peace with who I am in my own unusual way. Not many people know what my life has been like, including two sisters who have rarely spent time with me in our adult lives. I found that my spiritual gifts were passed down to me through my father's mother, Grandma Proffitt, and his oldest sister, Auntie Lavelle. They were first born daughters as I am. It is common in families who have relatives who walk the spiritual path to have a mix of compatibility because it is an unusual life that many just don't understand or even fear. And there are others who just follow a different road. The Bible says, *"A prophet will not be honored in their own town"* and it is true for those of us who have a variety of intuitive, clairvoyant and psychic abilities. Often, we are known as the "black sheep" of the family.

There were times not even I comprehended who this woman was (me) or what comes to me in this life! Looking back at all the amazing journeys I have been taken on in so many ways, I realized that most of my adult life has been without the siblings I shared the first part of life with. I often found myself in the role of their protector as a young girl, a heavy weight put upon my shoulders at a very early age. I carried my baby sister around so much that for a while our new neighbors even thought I was her mother. Many years later I also became aware of an unseen responsibility placed upon my shoulders: to carry into the Light of understanding the pain of my ancestors, and others who often were not treated kindly.

I found myself in the media at times, and I knew I must be grace-filled and act in a respectful manner because my gifts were a tool I could use to reach so many who were suffering. It was an opportunity to send out hope and information that could lift people up and empower them. I also had a strong feeling that there would be serious work to do not only for myself, but for my own ancestral family. Other people would also arrive at my doorstep at times bringing sacred work into my life. Their reasons would vary; physical pain, emotional pain, lost in life. I have also been given great "gifts" in the form of supportive people who have given me unconditional love. I am so grateful because we have become family. They are the ones that have been by my side when serious medical issues have arrived, even for the holidays and in my daily life.

In this life I have been in many ways a curiosity. And let's face it, mine is not the "normal" career or life path. My clients or students saw and received the gifts that flow through me; energy of deep empathy, strength, vision and empowerment. We had unforgettable mystical experiences together. Other souls who are in my private inner circle see the woman who is not always that strong, wise one. She struggles just like everyone else. It is also hard for some family members to understand who and what I have become in this lifetime. My path has not been easy for me to accept at times. I have had a lot of traffic in my life; those on the Earth plane and those on the Other

Side. After years of denial that I was not like everyone else (in their normalcy that I wanted so much), there finally came the time of acceptance and love for the path that had been given. Looking back, there were always signs along the way but only pieces of a puzzle that would be revealed many years down the road. Recalling a prayer I regularly uttered since the age of seven asking God to "make me a divine instrument to help others," I should have realized that something was happening right then and there because that is not the normal thing that a little child would whisper in their prayers. For some reason I always "felt" things about people and they were not always good feelings. There was a time when I attended a PTA meeting at the grade school with my little sister Janice and my mother. I was sitting between my mother and a lady on the other side of me. The lady looked quite nice and pretty much the same as everyone else. But the longer I sat there, the more I kept leaning towards my mother, as if trying to get away from the lady sitting to the right of me. I felt a surge of energy rush through my body (like an electrical charge) getting more intense and bringing me an enormous amount of emotional sadness and pain. There was a deep sense of grieving coming from this lady as if she could not handle much more pain in her life. I was trying not to look at her because it frightened me and I kept trying to scoot closer to my mom who would gruffly whisper to me "stop it!" I was overwhelmed with the empathic bombardment of feelings and I wanted to get out of there but I was trapped!

I was sitting there all alone in a room full of people that had no clue as to what I was experiencing inside. These feelings brought emotions that nearly made me cry out loud. I also felt confusion and fear, knowing that I would probably get into trouble when we got home for distracting my mother. Even at that early age I saw what appeared to be people that no one else could see. Maybe living by the rugged Northern Oregon Coast in my younger years enhanced those abilities. I was drawn to Mother Ocean, the sound of her waves coming to shore and all the gifts that she gave us.

Hunting for agates, shells and other treasures was so much a part of my private time. After a storm, my dad would have us all go down to the beach to gather driftwood for the fireplace. While we were there, other treasures would be left by the sea; shells, sometimes pieces of pottery and worn glass. I was and continue to be an ocean gypsy. I was very connected to the Earth, sky and water and the wildlife that also called this place home. There were times I saw what appeared to be forest spirits and fairies. These experiences all felt so natural for me. Janice and I would play in the forest behind our house exploring all day. We would make forts from tree branches. We learned which berries we could eat. We were like salt and pepper in appearance. She had dark straight hair that my mother would braid. Mine was very blond with tight thick curls that my mother brushed constantly to straighten but to no avail. All of Nature's elements were very much a part of us. They enhanced my sensory perceptions as we played in the peaceful forest and instilled in my sister a love for gardening and caring for wounded wild birds that would arrive at her doorstep.

"Signs" continued later in life. At my 20-year class reunion when it was revealed my path was to become a psychic or seer, my classmates' responses were quite the surprise to me. "Proffitt, it does not surprise us, you were always talking about seeing ghosts!" Their reactions astonished me as I did not recall ever saying those things. More signs arriving along the way it seems. Looking back, I received one of my first messages at my eighth grade graduation assembly program. It was there that the most prophetic words would be spoken in a most unusual fashion. The valedictorian was standing at the podium going through the names of the class and saying a little something about what type of work each graduate would be doing in their life. I was very excited and could not wait to hear what they had to say about me and my friends also. I was a little Capricorn and just knew that I was going to be a doctor or nurse, since I always wanted to help sick people. Or maybe, I would be a singer or a movie star or maybe a dancer. So many choices…it was exhausting to even decide and it was not quite time to choose.

Little did I know at that moment, that later during high school I would also be drawn towards being a *Police Officer, Detective* or an *FBI Agent* when I grew up. At one time, I found myself babysitting for a couple on a nearby street, and at some point I learned the husband was an *FBI Agent*. He married a beautiful woman from Japan when he was working there. It was a major event when I could watch their beautiful child so they could have a night out when he was at home. I also spent time with them on occasion and he told me how much he appreciated my watching their child so they could go out and enjoy without worry. His wife was also proficient in martial arts and she showed me her abilities and occasionally taught me some of the *katas*. When he was gone, I also visited his wife to make sure she was okay and he appreciated my doing so to give her company. Occasionally, he pulled out magazines about investigations of crimes and say, "let's play a guessing game." Then he'd ask me questions on a variety of subjects and what I thought happened to that person who was dead in the photo. "So, what can you tell about what happened here?" My replies to his questions would be quite accurate it seemed. "You would make a good detective Elaina because you have a natural ability to see beyond the surface of a situation." He told me about the college I would need and that I would need to stay out of trouble. After many months spending time with them, one night I came to babysit and he took me into the kitchen where he showed me a gun that was on top of the refrigerator. Taking it down and emptying the chamber, he gave me a lesson on its workings and had me practice holding it. Over and over we went through the steps then he looked at me and said in a most serious voice, "there are times when it is dangerous in my work and being gone so much I always have a weapon for my wife and child's protection in the house. Under no circumstances are you to touch this unless someone is trying to get into the house. If someone is knocking on the door do not open it. If they persist, call the police, and if they break in, use it." He made me promise to do as he said. I did not know this would be a bell ringing the foretelling of part of my destiny later in life! Sweet sixteen and life turned me in the direction of a most dangerous and serious life path that would arrive many years down the road. We are always given guides as we walk through life who whisper "more is coming."

Listening to the Valedictorian speaking about my life, the thought of maybe even being a Nun or a servant of God, helping the poor and sick also ran through my little mind, although I was not Catholic. Sitting there, the anticipation was high! At last, it was my turn and my girlfriends sitting on both sides of me were smiling and waiting to hear what was given for me. Suddenly, this young man's voice changed and was not a man or a woman's voice. I would learn later that when this happened it was a message or what I call a whisper from Spirit.

Now standing on the stage before us his words would change my life, "We see Elaina Proffitt sitting at a table wearing golden earrings with a crystal ball and cards telling the futures of people." The auditorium burst into laughter and I hung my head in shame fighting back tears as my face turned red with embarrassment. Everything was in slow motion and I had chills running through my body which I would learn later would signify that truth had been spoken. I was in shock! How could this be? It was quite hard to accept because I was a devout church going Southern Baptist girl and in my church, they believed soothsayers and astrologers were demons and all were going to hell. I prayed constantly for guidance regarding this subject asking for answers. Spirit revealed the truth in many ways, but many years down the road. I couldn't know in that graduation ceremony that later in life there would be times some of those same types of hell fire and brimstone preachers would be sitting across from me asking for counseling. When I asked them, "what would your congregation think about you sitting here with me?" their response would be, "Oh the sheep would never understand." Priests, Dominican Nuns, Rabbis, a known Guru and others of just about every faith knocked on my door from time to time seeking guidance.

But at this moment I was just a little girl who had hopes and dreams like all the rest of my classmates even though I was not from a rich family and had very little parental support.

It would be many years down the road, later in life, that many things would be revealed by my Auntie Lavelle and my cousin Karen to whom Auntie would pass down the genealogy of our people and what it all meant. Karen took me to the South, and we toured cemeteries and searched for our lineage. We found ancestors including very inspirational and uplifting ministers. Others were pharmacists making and dispensing things to make people feel better and to heal. There were also those on that tree of life that had unusual abilities like I did. I never thought about the first sign given to me when I was born and my last name upon the birth certificate. I learned many years later that a name change was made when my first great grandfather arrived in this country. Our last name was originally thought to be Proudfoot, a Scottish last name pronounced Prophet or Proffitt. At some point our name was recorded as Proffitt. Sitting in my eighth grade graduation, why was I being told I would become what the church preached so darkly against? It would take many years to see that I would get to have all my heart's desires but just in a different way. In my Bible that I earned in a Sunday school contest, memorizing verses, one passage would constantly appear when I prayed. It would reveal itself-bringing new understanding of God's amazing and most mysterious plan for me. That verse as well as many others are underlined on those now well-worn pages. It is a strange feeling when I look back at my youth because it reveals a deep understanding of this ancient book, an understanding that was far beyond my age and religious education. These are the verses that would walk with me, haunt me and whisper to me repeatedly when I prayed. There would arrive in the future a deep spiritual awakening that would answer why my Bible would always open to this section.

1Corinthians 13:2 KJV
2-and though I have the gift of Prophecy and understand all mysteries, and all knowledge; and though I have all faith so that I could remove mountains, and have not charity I am nothing.
1Corinthians 14:1 KJV
*14-Follow after charity, and desire spiritual gifts, but rather that ye may prophesy.
1Corinthians 14:3 KJV
*3-But he that prophesieth speaketh unto men to edification and exhortation and comfort.

Heavenly Seeds Planted

Let's face it, there must be a Divine Plan and Gardener for each of us with those constant nudges and whispers throughout our lives, not to mention the people who help activate our sleeping internal abilities and desires. We realize at some point that we can't avoid trying them any longer. When we step back and look at the signs along the way, we suddenly see those common threads resting within each step upon the path of life. One of my steps verified and confirmed what in ways I always had believed, that there is another place that we go to after dying. Since I was a young girl, I could always see souls who were on the Other Side and it was verified by people on this Earth plane who were connected to those souls. I did not know those who had passed, did not know how they died, did not know what relation they were to the person sitting or standing next to me. I also did not know then, that there would come a time when I would have a childhood friend die. It would be a moment in time that would unknowingly shape my life, just as the lilacs in my grandparents' yard would many years later bring a new understanding about life and death. It was not yet time, though, to know how my friend's death would guide me ever so quietly. It was not yet time to know how her crossing over would be a Heavenly seed planted within me waiting to bloom, thus becoming a deep spiritual awareness about my life's work. Looking back, I can see how this subject seemed to follow me in unusual ways and there was always a deep spiritual revelation that would be given to me.

My first experience with someone crossing over was when my childhood friend Kathy Wood died of leukemia at the age of thirteen. I couldn't visit her at her home because she was not able to have company at that time. Saddened, I prayed hard that I would be able to see her. I sensed a deep feeling that I may be able to take away some of her pain. My poor Grandma Jenny was overwhelmed with my insistent demands to call Kathy's house to see if she was feeling better. I was anxious to have Grandma drive me up the road to see her. God finally granted me that nonstop request. One day it was finally announced in Sunday school that Kathy would be able to come to our group the following week. She was feeling better and wanted to come to church because it would be the way she could see everyone at the same time. We were instructed that if we were sick we could not attend that day because Kathy's immune system was very fragile. I made it my mission not to get a cold and to mark each passing day on the calendar until Sunday arrived. I arrived early that morning just so I could save a seat next to me for Kathy telling the Sunday school teacher it was to be Kathy's seat…placing my Bible on it! With a smile and her eyes filled with compassion the teacher nodded permission to do so.

It seemed like forever before my friend arrived and was gently guided to her seat next to me. At last, I could relax and I was finally getting to see my friend who I could see and feel was very ill. Giving her a gentle hug then saying quietly "Kathy! I have tried to see you but no one would let me come to visit you! I am so sorry, know that I did try so hard." With a smile, her words comforted me, letting me know that she knew and had just been feeling sick and it hurt so bad. As I looked at her ever so pale skin, the spiritual gifts resting within me whispered that my sweet friend had *"one foot on Earth and one in Heaven."* It was as if a bucket of cold ice water was thrown upon my whole being. God whispered gently that this would be the last time I would see my beautiful friend on Earth. Trying my best to deny what became a familiar foreboding feeling of things to come, I struggled to smile and stay happy. Turning my head and looking behind us at the others that had arrived I saw a variety of emotions upon their faces in each row. Many were uncomfortable, did not want to look at her or me. And then there were the others trying to appear normal but I could feel their waves of fear and sadness rolling towards us. I do not remember what the teacher chose for our Bible lesson that day but I do remember God's lesson for me that has walked with me from that day forward. Overwhelming compassion filled me when I reached for my friend's hand and saw her smile as I did so. Suddenly I could feel a familiar warmth pouring through my hand into her cold one without knowing that others would arrive in my life in the future to receive the same. Soon, what I was dreading arrived; Sunday school was over and it was time to say goodbye. There was a sickening feeling in my solar plexus and deep sadness in my heart and I did not want to let go of Kathy's hand. Others left while we remained just a few precious moments longer. There were promises I would come soon to see her and I would continue to pray for her to be well soon. I reminded her that she needed to make it her goal to ride her horses. Looking back at us that Sunday, at some point in my life, I would understand that her family brought her to church that day for a variety of reasons, not just to say hello but also, it had been so lonely for her being that ill with no friends to keep her company. This visit was also her goodbye and so she could have a blessing in God's house. As she was guided out the door it would be the last time I would see her alive. Kathy Wood died of leukemia on July 27, 1959 at the tender age of thirteen just as she was beginning to blossom into a beautiful young lady with that beautiful black hair and dreamy eyes. The whole world was waiting for her to explore and she was taken away before it all would arrive.

One day the wall phone in Grandma's kitchen would ring loudly and from the dining room I would hear her speaking quietly saying, "Oh dear! I am so sorry to hear this, if there is anything you need please call me. I will write this on the calendar. Yes, I will tell her, so heartbreaking, again my condolences to you all." Hanging up the phone, she saw me standing in front of her with a demanding look upon my face. I looked at my grandmother's perplexed eyes. She did not know how to approach what I was already having a sickening feeling about. "What Grandma?" I said in a strong brave voice. In what seemed like an eternity, she gently put her hand on my shoulder and her words flew into my heart. "Honey, I am so sorry, that was Kathy's mother on the phone wanting you to know that Kathy has gone to Heaven." Since that day in Sunday school I had known that she was leaving but in those days and weeks to come I tried to deny all of that!

Running out the door, tears started to fall as I sat on the lawn looking up the quiet country road in the direction of Kathy's house. The small community known as Bonny Slope was now filled with a deep sadness with the loss of one of its children. And young people lost a part of their innocence with the realization of the meaning of death. So many emotions ran through me and the days prior to her service are a blur, except for the battle to go to her funeral. Death was a quiet and uncomfortable subject for most people in those days and even more so if it was a child who had died. I found myself having to demand, insist nonstop, that my grandmother take me to my friend's funeral. "Are you sure you want to go dear?" she gently asked while stirring the fried apples in the pan hoping they would make me feel better. Defiantly, I replied that I was going even if I had to walk! I needed to say goodbye and to see her! Just to make sure she was okay.

What I meant was that I needed to see her, to accept that she was dead. At last, I got my way and soon found my grandmother driving us to the funeral service. Entering the room filled with people, the scent of so many flowers and the wave of sadness enveloped me. We found ourselves being seated on the right side and I remember looking up front at the open casket with just a peek of her dark hair. Her parents were sitting in the front huddled together and I could feel their pain. It was grief revealing itself to me and when I bowed my head there was such a strong overwhelming desire to ease their suffering. Such a helpless feeling to have at such a young age. Turning away, I glanced across the aisle at the other kids all dressed in their best. I remember boys in dress shirts and suits with solemn faces. Even more of our innocence was now being taken away and it was overwhelming for us all. I don't recall the full service and the words spoken, just the part about Kathy, her love of horses and her colt named Star. She had wanted to win the blue ribbon at the Washington County Fair on her 13th birthday. Her birthday would have been August 29th. Many tears were falling.

At the end of the service it was announced that we could pay our final respects to this Angel. I remember watching adults walk up to the casket, pause for a moment and then walk on. Some of the young people were also brave enough to do so, quietly passing by her fighting back their tears. At last I stood up and walked slowly towards her resting place feeling my heart pounding in my chest. It was the first time I would see someone who had died. As I turned to face the casket, I looked to the left where her parents were sitting in the front row. Looking at me, their tears falling, I was silently saying to them, "I wish I could fix this so you would not be in so much pain but I can't." Then, taking a breath, I walked up to her knowing I needed to just stand there for a moment. She looked so beautiful and peaceful as if she was sleeping. Her dark hair and white skin made her look as if she was Snow White waiting for the Prince to kiss her so she could wake up. Just for a second I thought she was breathing, that she was alive and I was remembering our last conversation that day in Sunday school. Without thinking I placed my hand gently upon her chest. Then I knew, she was gone, and what remained was just a shell of this young girl, my friend. Leaning over the casket and looking down at her with tear filled eyes, I whispered, "I am so sorry you were in so much pain. I wish I could have taken it away from you and you didn't have to go. But you are Heaven now and I will see you again." Just for a second, suddenly there was a shimmer of light and her smiling at me standing next to the head of the casket. Inside my heart, I heard her whisper "It's okay, I am here." Time stood still and it did not matter if others were behind me, they lovingly and patiently waited their turn. There was no fear as I found my hand softly touching her hair as I leaned closer giving her a kiss on her forehead hearing my last words "Goodbye Kathy, I will love and miss you always."

As I slowly walked away with tears falling, I looked at her family a final time carrying their weeping with me back to my seat next to my grandmother. It was a solemn walk back to the car and I felt as if I was out of my body. It did not seem fair to me that my friend had to die. On the way home, it seemed as if at times I was counseling my grandmother about this sensitive subject as she tried to comfort me. Her newborn son died so many years ago, and I know that it was on her mother's heart that day. There is always a huge hole that is left within us each time in our life when someone dies, especially when it is a child.

That day was my first experience with the reality that time is precious and there are no guarantees how long we will be here. I had a fear that someday my grandparents would die also. Little did we both know that many years down the road this would be part of the work that would be given to me in a variety of ways.

Kathy would become one of those Heavenly Career Guidance Counselors in my life.

My dear friend Kathy Wood who died at the age of 13.

The first funeral I went to demanding my Grandmother take me...

God showed me what my work would be that day...

Kathleen M "Kathy" Wood

Aug. 29, 1946 - July 27, 1959
Portland Oregon, USA

Death July 27, 1959
Portland
Multnomah County
Oregon, USA

AMBITION of Kathy Wood was to have colt, Star, win blue ribbon at Washington county fair on her 13th birthday.

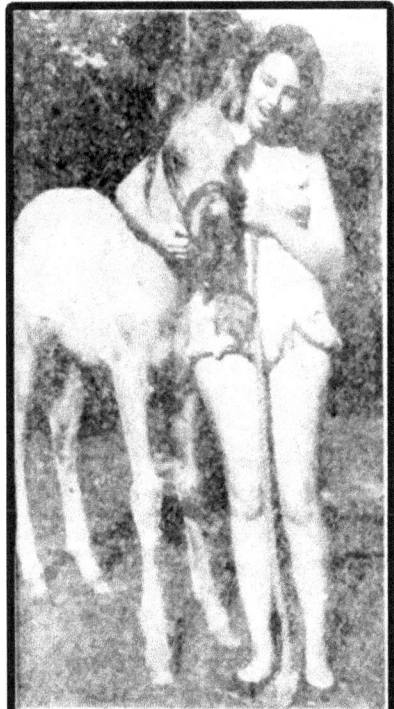

Wounded Warrior

Dedicated to our Vietnam Vets and all those warriors who have come into my life throughout the years and who have taken this NDE journey in a variety of ways as we walk together through the shadow of death.

Throughout the years, people arrived in my life in strange ways needing to share their deep emotional pain and grief. Most times, it would be a surprise to them not knowing why they could share their secrets with me. It made no difference where I was working or what I was doing, even socially they arrived and still do to this day. There have been numerous times I found myself speaking with a grieving stranger on an airplane sitting next to me, in a coffee shop, at a party, and even in a doctor's office while having some tests. Many times, there was no specific place. It just seemed to be anywhere I happened to be at that moment. To this day, I can still see many of their faces, feel their deep grief and see their tears as they searched desperately for peace, understanding and even forgiveness over the loss of a friend. It is always a blessing to be a part of seeing some peace in their eyes, knowing they had moved to a more comfortable place in their life.

It was the end of the Vietnam war and the return of our weary soldiers to a country filled with unkind behavior and lack of compassion towards them. I received an unexpected lesson about the danger and darkness of a warrior's silent pain. On a typical cold and rainy day in Portland, there was the troubled man who came into the bar of the nice hotel where I was working the day shift in the Show Room Bar, while going to college in my twenties. While there could be busy afternoons, there was usually no one else in the place except an occasional waitress with an order from the dining room or a well-known band playing a concert at the arena. It was a slow day when this stranger came in from the rain, sat down at the bar and ordered a whiskey. The minute I placed his drink in front of him I could feel an overwhelming sadness and edginess that concerned me. His eyes were filled with sadness, and while I wanted to keep my distance, I was compelled to casually start a conversation with him. "Another rainy day in Portland," I said with a smile as he took a cigarette from his pack of Marlboros. I reached for my lighter and gave him a light. The long bar became wrapped in an intense energy and I felt overwhelmed for a moment. It was just him and me in another world and it seemed as if time had frozen. After a "thank you" and a few sips of his whiskey, he seemed more relaxed. After a while, what I thought would be a casual conversation became serious and he opened up and told me about his life. He was a Vietnam Vet, and as he sipped his drink with his head bowed, he began quietly telling me about his pain, hopelessness, and the killing of so many people. "It was a rough road for us in a living hell we thought we would never get out of," he said quietly as he took a puff off his cigarette, blowing the smoke into the air. I shared briefly what it had been like as a young Army wife overseas during those times. I tried to be ever so still as he described what he had seen and felt; his friends dying in battle, the overwhelming sounds, the rat-a-tat of bullets, the yelling and the chaos. With his head down, he whispered some of what he and others in his unit had done and seen and the eyes that still haunted him. Part of me felt calm as I listened silently. His story sounded so familiar; it was also echoed by my friends who had returned alive from the nightmare.

Their identity had been the same no matter how many surrounded them and it seemed as if they all were…"the last man staring into the depths of hell!"

The air in the room was becoming more intense with each word spoken. "I can't believe I am telling you these things and you haven't kicked me out of here. Especially with the homecoming shame we've received," he said taking a last sip of his whiskey. Suddenly, a gut feeling told me that I was not to let this man leave at that moment and the words seemed to be whispered to me what must be said to him. "Well, maybe it is time to share all of this instead of keeping it inside of you," I said softly, placing a clean ashtray upon the bar in front of him. "I am glad that you felt comfortable enough to tell me these things. Not good to try to hang on to all that darkness. As I told you, I was an Army wife and we had our own nightmares going on here with you guys over there. So, keep talking and keep me company while I clean this big bar up for the night shift." Taking his empty glass, I said with a smile, "Let me buy you a "welcome home" drink, soldier, even though it has been a couple of years since you arrived. I am so glad that you and some of my friends made it back home!" Without thinking, I found my hand on the top of his hand, heat was pouring from mine into his cold hand, "Soldier, we will get through all these messes, so you must have faith and know that your angels were, and are now, with you." In that moment, the wounded warrior lifted his head up and with tear-filled eyes he whispered, "Thank you, Miss." Passing him some cocktail napkins for his tears, I took the glass on the bar and placed it in the sink. I then heard what would become familiar words I've heard for the rest of my life: "Sorry, I don't know why I am crying in front of you and telling you about all this pain and death," the man said gruffly. Dropping ice into the fresh glass then reaching for the whiskey bottle, I paused, my eyes meeting his, "Hey, it's okay to do that and I can't figure out why yet, but for some reason people do that a lot when spending time with me," adding with a little smile, "when they do, they seem to feel better." Pouring the amber liquid over the ice cubes, I said a silent prayer for this soul and put the glass down in front of him with a smile. With the bottle still in my hand, I poured a small splash in a rock glass for myself and lifting my glass to his, "To better days and better ways, Soldier!" A small smile came upon his tear stained face as he lifted his glass to mine. Taking a sip of the whiskey, I was compelled to say, "Now! You know with your grieving so deep and rightly so, you can't be drinking a lot nor doing drugs. I want you to promise me you won't do that. Get yourself into a support group where you can also get some help with other guys and get stronger!" With a nod of his head and a "Yes, Ma'am," the energy in the room shifted to a lighter level. I felt guided to have this stranger stay awhile longer so, while placing oranges, lemons and limes on the cutting board, I said, "I am going to get all this prep work done and you can keep me company…unless you have some place you have to go." With a small smile on his face he replied, "I can do that."

We spent three hours together that rainy day and not a customer showed up at the bar except for an occasional drink order from the restaurant. Looking back, I knew that was meant to be and there was a reason for the stillness. Before he left, he dropped a tip on the bar then he said with a goodbye, "Something made me come in here today. I've been having a rough week, and it was in a very dark place that I thought I was not going to get out of this time. To tell you the truth, I had planned on coming in here for one last drink and then killing myself." At that moment, I understood the reason why I felt such fear upon his arrival and yet was compelled to keep this stranger sitting with me all that time. Seeing the concern in my eyes with those words he quickly added, "You changed that by being here and listening to the nightmares of my dark world and in some way, you understood what I told you. Somehow you took that weight off my shoulders and eased a lot of that ache inside." In a serious voice, he added, "I am going to do as you suggested, go to the VA and see if I can get some counseling and try to turn a corner."

With a small smile upon his face and a flicker of hope in his eyes he said, "Looks like there are those angels out there you were telling me about, and you happened to be mine today and I thank you so much for being my angel today."As he turned to leave I called out, "Hey Soldier! Remember, you know where to find me." He turned and smiled at me and I felt tears in my eyes and hope in my heart. Although I did not totally understand all of what had happened, there was the feeling that something powerful had occurred for both of us. Going forward, many warriors whose days and nights were filled with the nightmares of what they had seen and done on a battlefield in Vietnam or other wars would arrive in my life. Police officers who have experienced and seen horrific things that haunt them for life would find me as well.

From that moment on, I found that near-death experiences come in many ways and that danger and the grim reaper would bring me work to do in that dark world. Little did I know, years later all those heavenly seeds that were planted in so many ways would start to grow. I believe that if we get out of our own way, allowing our destiny to arrive, we will be shown the work we are meant to do. It seemed this was the direction I was to take at that time and I did not resist it; but I would discover, "How can you do that type of work?" would become a popular question. Once again, each time I would hear the silent whisper from my heart reply, "How could I not?" In the years to come, those heavenly seeds multiplied and a pattern was revealed. So many souls appearing at my doorstep had reached the end of their road with their traditional counseling and support groups and wanted to dive deeper into a more spiritual level. When working on these levels, I am always mindful of each client's state of being. If I feel they need more work with a psychologist, I will suggest that or assist them in finding someone to monitor their emotional wellbeing. If I have an intuitive question or feeling about how a loved one died or if foul play may be involved, I will also contact a police investigator to speak with them. Being very much grounded in this work has led to having contact with professionals that I can refer the client to for a variety of needs. It took me years of consistent and accurate work on a myriad of levels to establish a credible relationship with authorities.

When you have been through a life-threatening trauma or illness that brings you to death's door, it brings new awareness on deeper levels about this taboo subject. Whether others believe it or not, something remarkable does happen to those who undergo what is called a near-death experience. How this mysterious event occurs and the level of having this experience is all unique and yet it is the same.

I remember talking with my beloved grandmother about the month of May, as I watched her place beautiful lilacs from her garden into a vase, their intoxicating scent filling the room. There would be an echo from the past that would arrive many years later in my life.

Lilacs & the Gypsy in the Tea Room

"I see you dying around the age of forty. It has something to do with a large loss of blood but you may survive as you have two life lines. It is not known clearly now but I feel you will have a choice which way to go. You will always have the ability to leave your body at any time. I see you with one foot on Earth and one in Heaven in your travels."
-Palm Reader in a Tea Room

When I was a little girl, my grandmother's yard had big lilac bushes that I just loved. Grandma would cut fresh purple and white lilacs and place them in an old-fashioned vase on her dining room table. The memory of their perfume filling the house is still with me. My mother also loved Grandma's lilacs, and after a visit she would cut some and bring them back to our house as well. Later in life she would be living in that same house on that country road with those lilac bushes and little did we know that this house would become a part of a most sacred journey. There were times growing up when my sisters and I would live with our grandparents. As a young girl, I loved spending time by those purple and white flowers breathing in their fragrance and day dreaming about where life would take me someday. One time while watching my grandmother place each of those purple blooms into the vase, I suddenly yet calmly told her, "When I die it will be in May so I can have lilacs at my funeral." I did not know how prophetic those words would become or the meaning of those lilacs, which would transform me in the years to come with one of the most powerful experiences in my life!

In my early twenties, my dear friend (Fran) and I decided to go to a Russian Tea Room and have our futures told by a woman who was known as a Palm Reader. Many people claimed that she performed very accurate readings. In my teens, I use to babysit for Fran and spent a lot of time at her house. We became avid readers of spiritual books and she studied astrology; so it did not surprise us when years later we found ourselves heading for that Tea Room before one our favorite past times, which was hitting the book stores. The "Reader" was from Europe, a beautiful woman with dark, flashing eyes that looked deep into my mine as she said "Hello." As I sat across the table from her, my heart was pounding as she took my hands looking at the lines in each palm with her captivating eyes. As she studied my hands, she told me many things about myself that were true. I could feel intense energy almost like electricity running through my body as her fingers touched various areas of my hands. Then, suddenly she pointed to a place in my hand with her finger still locked in position. She gazed at me very intensely and I could tell she was disturbed about something. After I asked her numerous times what she was seeing, reluctantly she said, "There is danger! Something will happen that could cause your death at an early age." It was apparent that this woman was very uncomfortable with what she had said, and I had a sick feeling inside me. I found myself quickly asking her, "When?" then firmly asking her to tell me the details and my age at which this would event would happen. "Tell me what causes this. Just tell me! A car accident? Illness? Tell me how old I will be!" Pausing for a moment as her dark, flashing eyes scanned my palm again, she whispered, "Something to do with loss of blood, I see lots of blood!" Then, after a moment she said softly, "It looks like around the age of 40 but wait! You will have a choice to come back if you want to." I was shocked, frightened, and my head began filling with scenes of how the tragic event would happen. Being a young mother, my first thought was of my child and my husband who did like to drive too fast. My voice was quivering asking, "Is it a car accident?" My eyes were like a hawk watching each expression upon her face. Shaking her head still staring at my palm replying, "No, it is something else!"

"See this mark in your palm?" she asked softly. "It means that you have great spiritual gifts and protection. There are two lifelines!" Her eyes had a touch of amazement as she whispered, "You will always have the choice to very easily leave your body whenever you desire to visit to the Other Side." She stared at my palm and then turning her focus away from my hand, she gazed into my eyes once again. "I see you always with one foot on Earth and one in Heaven…all this lifetime. Part of you travels between two worlds. Should you live, you will have strong gifts that will bring many suffering people to your doorstep. I see pain-filled souls needing advice and healing. They will arrive all your life in many places in the world and in many ways." Letting go of my hand she said, "Our time is up. God be with you." My head was swimming with questions but she looked away from me, saying, "no more." Leaving the Tea Room, I felt very dazed and disoriented; my hands were hot from her touch. Exiting the Tea Room, I prayed that what the beautiful palm reader had whispered to me would not come true. There was a silent Knowing between us; it was destined for her to speak of these things.

From that day forward, life would take me to so many places, and in the years to come, the doors to my spiritual path would open rapidly. It would also bring the ending of my marriage, which I discovered is quite common when one partner decides to step upon the spiritual path. When our mind and soul becomes thirsty for understanding, if there is not a similar goal, life can separate. It was a painful transition for not only me but for my son. Each journey brought new teachers and lessons, preparing me for the day when I would be fighting for my life and standing at death's door. Years of meditation, discipline and expanding awareness activated the tools that I would use for this pain-filled journey. I discovered quickly that everything and everyone has a purpose. Each is a piece of the intricate patterns woven into the tapestry of our lives. I didn't know at the time that years later when I was thinking about the past, I would discover an unusual pattern of events: the repetition of numbers and dates with the same theme all bringing…what could be serious consequences.

The first event occurred before the Russian Tea Room and the beautiful gypsy. It would be in Paris. November 22nd would be a recurring date later in life when I would have yet another close call with death.

Bonjour Paris

On November 22, 1964, a grey cloudy day in Portland, Oregon, I boarded my first plane ride heading for New York City, JFK. Upon arrival at JFK, I headed for the TWA Flight Center and boarded a Boeing 707 (TWA Flight #800) bound for Paris, France. I was going there to marry my high school sweetheart! A whole new life and world was beginning for me. Looking down at the New York City lights, I was in awe. This little Northwest country girl was on another airplane with her new life waiting across the ocean. As I looked out the window, I saw what appeared to be flames coming out of the engine. I nervously mentioned it to the flight attendant who was serving cocktails. There was an immediate concerned look in her eyes as she leaned over me to look out the window. With a smile, her soft voice comforting me, "Oh don't worry about that, Honey, that is what it looks like at night." I told her these were my first flights. She patted my arm and said, "let me get you a drink." I remembered what my Auntie Lavelle had said about drinking a cocktail, "A good martini or a scotch on the rocks is always a good choice for a lady." So, I ordered a Johnny Walker Black "scotch on the rocks" and soon was feeling my big girl boots on. It would be a long night heading across the pond to Paris. There was also a very unsettling feeling that I had carried with me when boarding the plane. No matter how excited I was about my trip, there was that last conversation with my grandmother the night before that confused and concerned me. Prior to my leaving, my Grandmother Jenny stopped by the house to say goodbye a second time. She would not come in the house because my father was there and they did not get along. Standing outside on that cold, dark night at that moment I did not know her words to come would soon haunt me. Her visit was unexpected as she usually did not drive at night. When I asked her the reason, she just said, "I just had to come by and see you one last time before you leave tomorrow." There was deep sadness in her eyes and I became concerned. I told her not to worry about me, that I would be just fine and she would see me again in a couple of years. It was so cold that November night and our breath looked like fog as she said softly, "I don't know why, but I just don't think I will ever see you again." Shock and confusion ran through me as I tried to think of something to say to her. I gruffly replied, "Why would you say that, Grandma?" She shook her head and repeated, "I don't know, but I am afraid I won't see you ever again is all I know. I had to come by one last time honey to tell you I love you." There was a worry and sadness in her eyes as she hugged and kissed me saying, "Goodbye Elaine, remember I love you so much." As she slowly turned away, and walked towards her car, I did not know at that time that her feelings would be prophetic.

I would understand her words a few years later when we returned to the United States. Our Mustang that was bought in Paris would be waiting for us at the docks in New York City. We would drive our new car across the country and stop to visit my husband's relatives in Nebraska. As we were driving, there was a dark ominous cloud that was following us across the plains. Upon arriving in Nebraska, we stayed at my husband's grandmother's house for a few days to rest. We each called our family saying we had arrived safely and would be heading for Oregon in a couple of days. Two days later the phone would ring loudly in the afternoon. For some strange reason, I was guided to pick it up. This was not my house nor my phone but an ominous feeling fell upon me as I found my hand suddenly reaching out to answer it. I knew this call was for me, one I did not want to answer! Tears were coming to my eyes as I said in a shaky voice, "Hello?" On the other end of the line was my mother, telling me that my grandmother had been admitted to the hospital and had died from a blood clot. Prior to the phone ringing, while lying on the bed for a nap with new baby Michael, I had been thinking of my Grandmother Jenny that she soon would see her great grandson. Suddenly, I saw her face and that phone rang! It would not be the last time my grandmother would appear to me. Many years down the road I would see her eyes again. Just in a different way!

I did not know while sitting on this plane, that there would be cruel tragedies in my future that were the reasons for my "unknown uneasiness," including the engine outside my window with those flames. There also was a pain-filled cocktail of unseen fated dark events that was being prepared for me as I was drinking that second scotch in the dead of night, on my first airplane ride to Paris. Passenger overhead lights were being turned off as many were preparing to catch a nap. Others were reading a book as they sipped their drinks. I was too wrapped up in excitement to rest and there were those feelings that I had to stay awake. I must force myself to keep an eye on that wing for some reason. Eventually, the flight attendants invited me to their private area to spend some time with them and distract me from my engine concerns. They were happy for me, now taking on the role of "big sisters" telling me stories of their first times leaving the United States just like me. I was captivated with their stories about living in Paris, traveling in Europe and how romantic it was to be getting married in Paris. Nevertheless, I had an uneasy feeling I could not shake off whenever I went back to my seat; I just did not want to stay in that seat. I had not felt comfortable there since we took off and when I looked across the aisle at the sleeping passengers, that side felt even more uncomfortable! Time passed and soon we were again talking in the back of the plane. These beautiful young women were giving me snacks and fussing over me. At some point, the Captain called needing to know what their plans were when they landed in Paris. I can still see them in a semicircle as I listened to them discuss their plans for their days off, talking about going to Rome and then heading for Greece. There was a lot of indecision and I remember one of the women saying she did not feel like going to either place. The others tried numerous times to persuade her to join them for some sun and fun. "Oh, come on, we can go to Greece for three days and get some sun by the water or hang out in Rome." I could tell she did not want to go, but at last she gave in saying "I will see when we land and decide from there."

Time was literally flying and I could feel the shift of the plane's altitude. It was time to go to my seat and for them to get back to preparing passengers. There were hugs and excited good wishes for me as we all headed back to the cabin. As the wheels touched down I was filled with anticipation of what my life would be like in this country. In high school, I had always said I would go one day to Paris even though others in high school laughed at me saying that would never happen. I was now silently laughing at them. Taking a deep breath, I said a "thank you" prayer. Despite my excitement, I could not stop feeling that there was something horribly wrong with the engine. I also wondered if the flight attendant had felt something was not quite right; she also seemed unsettled.

Soon, I was stepping off the plane at Paris Orly Airport, now being greeted by my fiancé's beautiful brown eyes and a delicious kiss. I would find out there was a delay at the airport as my baggage had not made the flight with me. The airport gave us a nice complimentary breakfast in the restaurant overlooking the tarmac. Once the luggage arrived, it was time to head for the "City of Light." As we drove through the city streets, tears began to fall as for some reason it felt like I was finally home again! It seemed so familiar and there were stirrings within me that I had experienced this place before. Each mile brought amazing views of what would become my new home. Arriving at our little apartment as we entered the gate, my new life would begin.

We found out the next day that I'd had a very close call. The next evening my fiancé came home with a newspaper in his hand which he placed upon the table. "My boss asked me this morning how my new wife felt about flying and then he handed me this paper." On the front page was a photo of the airplane I had stepped off at the Paris stop. It was in black flames and it would be revealed my bad feelings about the engine were accurate.

My plane had taken off heading for Rome's Leonardo da Vinci Fiumicino airport. On the last leg for Greece it crashed, killing fifty people including crew members when trying to abort the flight due to engine failure. The cause of the accident was, "an inoperative No. 2 engine reverse thrust system, even though indications in the cockpit were that the reverser had deployed. This was caused by the disconnection of a duct with resulting lack of pressure in the pneumatic clamshell door actuating mechanism. This malfunction allowed the development of considerable forward thrust by No. 2 engine even though the thrust levers for all four engines were in the 'reverse' position. No. 4 engine struck a pavement roller and the aircraft caught fire." (Aviation Safety Network Accident Summary)

The instruments in the cockpit were not reading correctly! Malfunction of a part and fuel flow was occurring that finally revealed itself in a most disastrous way. This crash had evidently been a disaster in the making for a long time and there were no lights indicating this was starting to happen. This flight should have never left New York City or Paris!

During the years I spent in Paris and all the fun times, I tried not to think about the fact at some point in time, I would have to get back on a plane and go back to the States. Especially since the next year, we now had a beautiful son who was born at Paris American Hospital. His name would be Michael and as I spoke this out loud, I asked this most powerful Archangel to bless and protect our son. To this day, I call upon Archangel Michael to watch over him. I did not know it at the time but there would be many times in the years to come this Archangel would appear in many powerful ways. We took our boy to his home, the top floor of an old Victorian home. It was not far from the hospital. I held him in my arms and looked out our bedroom window. In the distance was the Eiffel Tower. "Look my little boy, that is the Eiffel Tower, you are Mommy and Daddy's little Parisian." Wrapped in my arms, his little eyes were looking straight ahead; his father came into the room and joined us at the window. A precious moment in time...never to be forgotten. The next year, weeks before we were to return to the States, I had a dream our plane had crashed and we were in the water. I had a life jacket on and was holding my baby up high so he did not get into the cold water. When the actual day arrived, holding baby Michael in my arms walking towards that plane, my legs froze. It took a lot of coaxing to get me inside but I made it. That day and to this day, when flying I am always looking at the wing and the engine surrounding it in white, blue light of protection. Sometimes we are truly flying by the seat of our pants!

I will never forget my first overseas flight and my premonition of things to come. I had fussed about that engine and the flames coming out if it when I looked out the plane's window into the night sky. I could feel it in my bones, all the way across the ocean to Paris. Something was horribly wrong with that plane despite the assurance from the flight attendants that everything was okay. I carried that memory with me throughout my life. I also wondered if one of my flight attendants had died on that plane. Many times I searched online for my airplane and could never find all the details.

It was just a few years ago, I was compelled to do a search once more and everything would come up.

Note: after years of researching to get clarity on my flight, I met on Facebook a retired TWA Flight Attendant Lynn McKinny (TWA 3/11/1966 and early retired with 25 years 4/12/1991) I sent her what I had found in my search asking for her help in finding out if any of the flight attendants that were on my plane had died. Lynn contacted a retired TWA friend and gave me the following update.

"It was Paris-based flight attendants with a New York-based cockpit crew. One of the flight attendants survived, she was based in Rome. You can rest easy, the one you were worried about was not on it."
-Lynn McKinny
Former TWA Flight Attendant

The Buddha and Michael

After our return to the States, the time came when my son, Michael, and I were on our own. Despite our sadness, we found a world that opened its doors to us. Michael and I took many spiritual journeys to many different places. We were soul travelers together in this life, embracing many cultures and spiritual beliefs. There is an ancient saying that goes: "When the student is ready, the teacher appears." In my own life, I had many "teachers" that arrived…in many different disguises…a Healer, Doctor, Homicide Detective, Catholic Priest or even a high-ranking Zen Buddhist Roshi (old teacher or elder master). Our journeys even took us into a Zen Buddhist monastery where Michael became the first child ever allowed to stay behind such sacred walls. As I tried to spiritually and emotionally recover from my divorce, I went through a great deal of soul searching…trying to figure out who I was and where I wanted my life to go next. A friend had introduced me to the monastic life and I wondered if a monastic path could be a key to putting my life back on track. A major consideration for following the monastic path was that I would have to be separated from my son. Monasteries were not a place for kids. Nevertheless, I decided to enter the monastery for some personal reflection. I took Michael to live with my mother during this time but the separation from my son would end up taking its toll on me. Unknowingly, after my arrival the Roshi Houn Jiyu-Kennett would have some important decisions to make. She was a powerful woman from England and had become the first female to be accepted by the Soto School of Japan to teach in the West. She was also the founder of Mt Shasta Abby in 1970 known as the "Order of the Buddhist Contemplatives" whose influence would become far reaching including West Indies, United Kingdom, Netherlands, Canada and Germany. She was a large woman whose shaved head enhanced her presence even more than the power that she was given. At times, I would find my private audiences with her commanding presence instilling the counselor within me. Often, she shared the responsibilities that were given to her and that I had brought the answer to her contemplation about allowing children into the Abby. That entire time, sitting inside the temple in meditation, brought me to the realization that I missed my son who was in Portland with my mother. He needed me, even though when explaining to him where I was going and why, his brave words, "Go momma" at such a young age indicated that he had blessed my journey. Each morning in the temple I asked for enlightenment and Michael's face would come before me. I questioned my actions asking for guidance. His father had left him and now his mother was saying goodbye for an undetermined amount of time. I could not choose to remain in the monastery and upon meeting with one of the monks I expressed my need to leave. Soon an audience with the Roshi was announced and I found myself prostrate on the floor in front of her. With tears flowing, I requested to leave the monastery sharing with her about my son. After a time of silence there was her voice calmly commanding, "Sit up, please!" Wiping my tears on my sleeve, I shyly looked up finding her staring at me with a most serious look upon her face. "This is something that I knew I would have to make a decision about at some point, and you have brought the reminder to me. There is a married couple that have just given birth to twins. They are also monks and because of the 'no children allowed rule', have been preparing to leave. They are very devoted and I have been reflecting upon this issue for some time." Closing her eyes for a moment, she took some time before speaking again. "We are going to work on this, for you are not leaving. Usually, I would not respond that way, but I have a feeling that in the years to come there will be much placed upon your shoulders also and being here is part of the path to strengthen you for what is to come." With a serious look in her eyes, I was dismissed. "I will need a bit of time to see how to do this for you and this couple, as it can cause a few issues in the monastery so I will need to sort things out a bit. I will send for you again." Bowing my head, my heart feeling lighter, I returned to my quarters feeling more peaceful.

Within a matter of days, a monk approached me. "Roshi wants to see you immediately." My heart was pounding as I headed for the receiving room and my mind was racing with questions. What would be the outcome in this most powerful meeting about bringing my son into the Abby? What would be the direction my spiritual life would be heading? Upon entering the temple, I was quietly guided by a monk to the door that would open bringing the answers. The room was filled with a solemn vibration as I bowed and then sat before this high-ranking monk. Looking deep into my eyes she then spoke in a very direct manner. "My decision is made, and while it will cause quite the stir on various levels, that will be on my shoulders not yours." Her eyes twinkled contemplating what those dialogues would be with the others as she then told me her decision. "You have permission to call your mother and set things up for bringing your son here. Notify her that a monk will be calling her about making the arrangements for the dates of his travel. Michael will come by bus. He will be picked up at the bus station in Shasta and brought here to the Abby. He will be able to see you for a while then he will go to the cabin with the twins and their parents. These children will not have access to all the daily activities that we do. Children are innocent, having a purity that only fades as they grow up in the worldly realms. They do not need to see all this ceremony and silly things we adults have to do to get back to our purity."

It seemed Michael was activating change for others on their quest for spiritual growth as well as his own. Through the coming years, this role would become part of his spiritual path just like it was for me. Soon he would be on the Greyhound bus with a sticker book filled with fish that I had sent to him. It would occupy him on the long trip to Mt. Shasta. He had no idea of the powerful event that had transpired with a high-ranking Buddhist leader whose decision to bring him into the monastery would affect so many in the years to come. To this day, he still remembers the sticker book with all those fish. My son was my traveling companion, and looking back now, I see that our spiritual education would often be together. Many people and turns in the road of life have tried to separate us but it never lasts. Eventually the veil is torn from his eyes, lessons are learned, and we come together once again. We have a telepathic knowing when something is wrong with each other whether near or far. I miss those adventures we had together. My heart knows he needs to be in the spiritual world. It is where he was and is appreciated by others and respected for his wisdom and compassion. To this day, I hope those other realities that try to separate us, creating walls, will crumble and we can enjoy a few journeys together again before we leave this Earth.

Back then, I did not know there would come a most powerful time in my life when I would have to walk alone. A turn upon the spiritual path would arrive that he would not be a part of, a time when the lilacs were blooming.

Hidden Gifts Revealed

With each passing year, there was a different path to explore. I was on a spiritual journey that would take me to many mystical places. My surrendering to life would bring messengers, teachers and healers, all handing me another key to the door of a deeper understanding and the meaning of what we call life. With each new journey, my own being was getting activated and hidden gifts were being revealed. Everything that transpired led to a day in the month of May (and those lilacs) when life would not be the same. Each life experience brought all that was to be learned consciously or unconsciously, preparing me for what was coming, giving me strength and the gifts I would need for a battle between life and death. Not only for myself but for that of others.

In the late '70s I was living in Mexico City where the hidden intuitive gifts of clairvoyance, mediumship and healing abilities were strongly activated. I traveled to this country with a strong healer from California named Tao Raahn whom I had met at a metaphysical workshop. Many individuals were also drawn to this man including those working on the cutting edge of discovery in the world of the paranormal and those who were doing research in the world of healing and vibrational medicine. One of them was Steven Halpern, a musician who had been doing research creating music filled with tones, harmonics and frequencies that would release stress bringing deep relaxation and awareness. I remember to this day the two of them sitting at the kitchen table discussing energy, vibrations and harmonics. Steven influenced my life and the healing work that would find me. I played his music continuously when writing this book. I remember him sitting one afternoon talking with Tao about the toxic sound effects many of the machines in our daily lives have upon us. At the top of his list was the household refrigerator which is something that I have never forgotten and reminded him of this when we finally found one another again. His first album "Spectrum Suite" was the first New Age Album launched in 1975. I've used this album and others that he created in conjunction with the healing gifts (that come through me) on people in deep emotional and/or physical pain and with those who are dying. These harmonics are the perfect fit for the soothing energy of my voice as I guide a client to a calm, altered state.

We traveled throughout Mexico for four years, meeting with others who were gifted Shamans and Curanderos in the jungles and towns by the ocean. I would find myself at one point doing card readings that soon turned into channeling, at the Psychic Institute owned by parapsychologist Dr. Soria high up in the mountains in the town San Cristobal de las Casas. Chiapas is filled with Sorcerers, real magic and Curanderos. After reading for many hours, I would somehow be speaking in the language of the people. As people would enter the room, I would be reading them as they crossed the threshold and sat down across from me. One was an old man and I felt a strong presence sitting down with him. Suddenly, I felt myself slip away. From another place, I was observing the two of us sitting at the table and heard myself speaking another language. At some point returning to my body, I saw his eyes looking deep into mine. I did not know…he was a Sorcerer that many loved! To my surprise, he returned the next day with a gift! a pouch for my cards. Placing it in my hand, he told me that I had strong magical powers that came from many lives. "You are one of us!" he whispered. All my life I have been told by those gifted with sight, when I walk into a room...there is a strong presence that is with me. There are also many...who are "unseen".

Healers journeyed from South America, Europe, the Philippines, Haiti and other parts of the world to gather for private council meetings in seclusion. People with strong medicine, psychic surgeons and other healing gifts arrived in our lives. I also found out they were unknowingly working on me at times when they visited us at our beautiful Villa in San Angel in Mexico City. I had no clue about all the abilities resting within me until I would hear one of them speaking about their observations. One time we drove into to town at midnight because Tao was to meet with a well-known Voodoo High Priestess who had flown in for a conference. I was nervous about meeting her and then suddenly she entered the room, I caught my breath! She was a very large black woman, all dressed in white including her head wrap. In her hand was a big box of chocolates. Behind her, were three young black girls in their early twenties dressed the same way that I was told were her assistants. There was a power surrounding her with an unseen presence that could not be put into words. She must have been performing rituals because her eyes were still fixed and shiny, as if she was not seeing anything on the Earth plane. When I was introduced, she looked so deep into my eyes it felt like her energy was running through my bones. As she sat down at the table, the street lights below cast our shadows upon the wall. I listened quietly as the two of them caught up since the last time they saw one another in Bogotá, Colombia. She glanced at me on occasion and in a casual manner asked me a few questions, putting me at ease. But when she stared at me, it felt like she was scanning my whole being. My heart skipped a beat when their conversation turned to me, talking openly about their observations. I caught my breath when I heard her words as she gazed into my eyes. "You were right Tao, this one has strong gifts running through her.

She has more power in that pretty little finger than most of them." He nodded in agreement and said, "She is not aware of what all that means but she will find out soon." As we said goodbye, I felt something powerful had happened to me at that table in the wee hours of that morning. There were many questions that I needed answered and I would have another lesson in the car on the way home. "Your life is changing and there are a few things you need to know about the work that will be arriving." I was given the "Golden Rules" upon the new path that would come to me soon. "Have you noticed that most of the mediums, psychics and channels drink a lot of liquor, smoke, eat a lot of sweets, carbohydrates, and many are obese?" He then explained the common health issues they had and that I must not fall into the trap and said, "Did you notice Mambo had that big box of chocolates as she entered the room? When you work from unseen worlds, it takes a lot of energy to do so and we must refuel." He then explained how sugar, nicotine and alcohol shoot toxic energy quickly through our body. It gives a temporary "fix" when acclimating to being back in our physical bodies as the altered state slowly leaves us. "Remember the medium that was here from England? He was chain smoking day and night." I was reminded of the day we spent time with him and his physical appearance. He was very thin and his aura had a dull cast to it. His skin was pale and he did not seem clean to me.

Tao then instructed me to drink lots of water, eat healthy foods and snacks because I had the ability to go out of my body for long periods of time. I would be working with people who were suffering, and because I constantly had one foot in another realm, I would forget to nourish myself. I have never forgotten his words and do my best not to fall prey to those addictions. He also told me how to protect myself from the jealousy of others who did this work. Living in Mexico and the inner circle of the paranormal was a world to which few are exposed and my training would come in a most different way.

My son also experienced many mysterious things. Michael was like a sponge soaking up this paranormal elixir. He learned by listening and observing these gifted people. At times, he even asked questions and I would see him sitting quietly with a very respected healer or spiritual teacher having very deep conversations with them. They would tell me how they enjoyed their private talks with him. "You have a very wise boy; he has a deep understanding of the spiritual and metaphysical world that most adults do not comprehend. His eyes see into other realms easily." Michael learned quickly, recognizing when someone was a real channel or they were just pretending. His exposure to those who were the "real deal" brought him a wisdom that most of us do not have in these times. Sadly, nowadays, we find ourselves giving blind allegiance to the latest mystic or channel. Since the beginning, when people asked if they could follow me, my reply was always, "Don't follow me, follow yourself."

My world was now filled with a rare opportunity to enter the hidden inner circle of the most powerful ones who welcomed us into their lives. You do not find them on television or before large crowds. Many live in remote places and are not flamboyant in their appearance or the work that they do. You do not find them…unless they want you to do so. Traveling into the jungles while exploring many of the ancient pyramids, it was upon a visit to Chiapas, visiting Palenque the great Mayan ruins, I discovered the ability to do psychic archeology. We were allowed to sleep on the grounds of this ancient site and were drawn into the energies and people of those times. My dreams became powerful vehicles to astral travel. I learned many things leaving my body at night while resting upon this ancient soil, hearing the jaguars calling out into the night. In the daylight hours, I would come upon a spot where there appeared to be only overgrowth but I could feel underground tunnels with a room filled with objects. This vision was verified by a groundskeeper, who stated archeologists believed what I was describing was underneath that area of the earth, but they did not have the finances to excavate. I perceived faces with big eyes resting upon what appeared to be an altar; and a few days later I would see this exact same artifact in a museum. Walking through the grounds of the pyramid called Palenque, I had an intuitive knowing of what certain structures were used for without prior knowledge. This type of sight and perception would be the gift I would use later when working on murder cases, or going to crime scenes or haunted places.

Life as I knew it changed as I entered the world of the unknown. I attended paranormal conferences with healers and researchers from all over the world who gathered to speak and to demonstrate their abilities. There were also those who investigated UFO sightings and the pyramids of Mexico and Egypt including Dr. Jim Hurtak. Many who participated in these events were well known in those times for their investigative research on a variety of anomalies including Thelma Moss Ph.D., Psychologist and Parapsychologist. It was in the 1970s she led UCLA's Parapsychology laboratory where she explored many areas of the paranormal. This path would lead her to what would become the focus of her career, the research on Kirlian photography which she believed was our astral body. I would be tested with this equipment while working with a parapsychologist in Mexico City, Dr. Soria. It was there that I would see for the first time what the healing energy looked like that poured from my hands and the reason people said in my early twenties, "your hands feel so hot and soothing that my pain is leaving." Placing my hands on glass plates using Kirlian photography, I was asked to go into altered state and send the energy out through my hands. Glowing lights danced around my fingers, shooting out each time I focused deeply. At last here was validation that all that I had felt now made sense. In years to come, I would be using this strange ability in many new ways. I also found myself drawn towards the work of a woman named Elizabeth Kübler-Ross, a pioneer in near-death studies and the author of the groundbreaking book "*On Death and Dying*" which discusses the five stages of grief.

My hugs and my touch had a life of their own in a wonderful way and I could not stop this gift, even if I tried.

Black Magic in the Penthouse

During our second year in Mexico, we moved into a penthouse apartment not far from the Villa. It was also near the private school that Michael was attending. I was invited by the owner of the school to teach English to kindergarten, first and second graders. My classrooms were filled with brilliant children at the Montessori Academy. Many spoke three or four different languages and were a handful to keep up with. Some of them had fathers who worked closely with the President of Mexico. The families were very kind to me and there were times I would go to their beautiful villas for dinner. Another world had opened to me that was filled with so much love. I loved starting my morning before work or on the weekends in the kitchen. There was a nice window with its view of the volcano in the distance that always seemed to bring magical experiences when I was home alone for a long period. Our new place was not far from an ancient pyramid that had not been completely excavated. There are so many artifacts and rubble discovered in Mexico this was not uncommon. We were only thirty miles from the Pyramid of the sun and moon in Teotihuacán. The first experience occurred on a sunny early afternoon. Mexico is the land of healers, shamans and witches and I was introduced to many of them and found myself learning so much when traveling throughout this ancient country. Many of those things seemed so natural for me to do and for some unknown reason it felt so familiar. We had traveled extensively throughout Mexico when Tao was doing healings and workshops and meeting with the local Shamans. We went to the town Tepic, located in the central part of the Mexican state Nayarit. This town has the traditional old churches surrounded by fertile agricultural land and is the home of the Cora, one of the first civilizations in Mexico dating from 400 B.C. There are people today who have this bloodline.

I learned that Tepic is also filled with witches and the not so good type. While many scoff at this, it surely does exist and the spells cast affect a targeted person unless they are very strong and aware of such things and know how to deflect the energy. Not being fearful is an important key, and understanding how to use certain energies that cannot be taught in a book is also very important. I met a woman who unknowingly felt threatened by me and wanted Tao for herself. The kind young woman did not appear to be a witch, disguised by the way she dressed and her gentle words. She was there for healing that night when Tao and a medical doctor had a room filled with people looking for answers. I learned my first lesson that night in Tepic that real witches rarely broadcast their lifestyle (dressing in wild costumes with tons of jewelry on their bodies, running around calling themselves "witch"). This innocent appearing woman very quickly tried her best to harm me using her magic. This can be a dangerous test for many women and men that work in the world of traditional religion, the paranormal, metaphysical, spiritual and healing world, or even in the role of a doctor or therapist. They find themselves sometimes being tested when surrounded by those who want to follow them. Their profession creates a power of influence that can be seductive and can fill them with ego, power, control and lust. It is a fine line to walk at times and sometimes dangerous games are played.

After returning home many weeks later from Tepic, one day while I was alone in that kitchen looking out the window at the volcano Popocatépetl in the distance I felt the presence of "something or someone" with me. It felt like a female energy and I was confused as to who or what it was. I saw flashes of images in my mind's eye showing myself being cut by a knife blade along with other violent images and feelings. I felt a strong force of anger and hatred directed towards me. Asking for clarity, it was whispered/told to me that I must be very conscious during my day when working around the house or at work. And I was to surround myself with heavy protection to block this darkness at night when sleeping. For seven days and nights I was alone in the house with little sleep, flying by the seat of my pants doing psychic battle with this dark energy. I was grateful that Michael had returned to the U.S. for a family visit, but Tao was in Bogotá, Colombia for a conference. There was no contact number to call if I could. It would take all my spiritual faith and trust. All that I had been taught consciously (and unconsciously) by all those powerful healers, shamans and even a voodoo high priestess, would come to my rescue as I dealt with this dark energy. I found myself calling out at night for them to help me, praying for Archangels and the Christ Light to protect me. I was guided to put specific candles, potent incense, objects and crosses to seal off each gateway in each room. I was told by Guidance how to protect my physical body and how to cleanse each day and night. Time stood still; it felt like an eternity before the dark energy withdrew! It takes just one such experience to bring the clear realization that there are many worlds we live in concurrently; some are filled with Light and others with darkness!

And the kitchen! The kitchen would bring me another message...one that would change my life again...opening yet another new world.

Giver of Things

Shortly after my birthday one January mid-afternoon day, I had just made myself a cup of Earl Grey tea and I was standing at the kitchen sink looking out the window at the beautiful volcano Popocatépetl in the distance. I was wondering what this new year would bring to me because I felt change in the wind. I felt a move coming and that this would be my final year in this land filled with history and magic. Suddenly, I felt something behind me that brought chills running through my back and shoulders. Praying immediately for the white blue light to cover me and running a protection ritual around me, my heart was pounding as I tried to scan what was standing behind me. It seemed like an eternity before I could slowly turn around holding no fear within me. There was a slight hissing sound in the room and standing in the doorway was man dressed as an ancient one adorned with a colorful headdress, large bracelets, bead and shell necklaces wearing a loin cloth and moccasin-type boots. He had a wood staff or club in his hand that was carved and there was a fierce look in his eyes. There was a constant energy activating a shield around the room as the floor began to almost tilt. Looking across the room at him standing in the doorway, everything was turning into what seemed to be another dimension. My eyes and senses were trying to adapt. The energy in this space was occurring in microseconds with multi levels of communications happening simultaneously. The hissing sound continued to fill the room. With my heart pounding, I spoke out strongly to this apparition, "Peace be unto all who enter!" I stretched out my arm then placing my fingers and palm straight up in a "stop" motion, blocking any further entrance into the room. Calling out to this spirit, "If you come in peace, then welcome! Show me your reason for being here! But if you come with darkness, leave now!"

Time stood still and the spirit looked down at the floor numerous times and then back at me as the hissing sound became what felt like a harmonic frequency. I could see nothing in the direction that his eyes traveled on the floor but at some point, he disappeared!

Feeling light headed, in a matter of seconds my eyes were drawn to my feet. There was a long, golden line that was swaying slowly across the floor in sync with this hissing harmonic that filled the room. It had small points of reflected light moving through it like the water in a winding creek. I had no fear when a familiar voice, not a man nor a woman's, spoke to me. "It is time for you to make a choice Elaina, as to what path you will take in life. You have been given all of the gifts that will be needed if you choose to continue on your spiritual path and work." My response was filled with questions that my heart and soul needed to be answered. I knew this situation was very real and my decision would bring changes beyond my comprehension at that moment. Time stood still in front of this golden line before my feet and my final questions arrived, "How will I support myself and my son? What type of work will I do?" The reply went through my complete being! "If you choose to commit to the work and step over the line, you will not want for anything. You will be blessed for life. There are many who are waiting for you, in some faraway places. Know that you will be sent to them and all will be provided."

I had a final question to this holy presence, "What if I choose not to cross this line? What will happen to me and these abilities that you speak of?" It seemed that time stood still waiting for the answer which would seal this one way or the other. I felt a rush of energy and anticipation waiting for the reply. "Your life will be more in the earthly ways like others. You will still have some of the natural gifts but not as strong nor will they be used in the way your new path will bring." Then there was the final whisper: "Should you choose to remain where you are in this moment, this will be forgotten." At that moment, it felt as if I was in two places at the same time. Standing there on the kitchen floor with that golden line in front of my toes swaying across the room then suddenly it was as if the floor opened and I saw only darkness and the unknown. Urgency now filled me with a whisper that it was time to choose. Either remain in the world I had known all my life or to trust and jump. It was as if I was reviewing my whole life while time stood still and then there was the whisper inside me, "Do it!" Immediately, the golden line on the floor stopped moving and the floor tilted once again. I felt like I was standing on a cliff looking down into velvet darkness and all that awaited me. Saying a prayer and taking a breath, I pushed off the cliff and dove into the unknown waters of Life.

The next thing I remembered was my feet dropping back down onto the floor which now was now upright and flat. The line was gone and so was the hissing frequency. Perfect stillness was in the kitchen and within me. Life would change from that moment on because of what happened that day. Who and what had arrived was a Messenger manifesting that day in my kitchen in this ancient land. In the Nahuatl language, the word for priest was "Tlamacazqui" which means "giver of things" such as offerings, ceremonies and sacrifices. A most powerful gift was received! I had received a Light activation, filling my body, mind and soul with abilities that would surface as needed when working with others. These experiences would follow me through life, bringing messages and powerful life-changing events.

Career Changes

Upon returning to the United States, I moved to California and settled back into American life. A couple of years later, I met a man, fell in love and would find myself married again. I also found myself in the unusual profession as a psychic. I certainly had not planned on making it a career but for some reason I seemed blocked from finding a regular job. I was frustrated because it had always been so easy for me to find work. I kept asking for guidance as I went through the newspaper. One day I was looking in the phonebook to find a metaphysical bookstore. I wanted to buy some incense and candles maybe even have a tarot card reading. As my eyes scanned the pages, the Creative Awareness Center jumped out at me and soon I was driving over to the store. Upon entering, I knew this was a place that I would be coming back to many times discovering shelves filled with books, incense and a sign that said Psychic Readings by appointment. As I was exploring the variety of books, a woman asked if she could help me find something. Soon we were having a wonderful conversation about my experiences in Mexico, the clairvoyance and other strange abilities that had occurred. She also shared her knowledge of the paranormal world and that she was familiar with the powerful "Light Centers" throughout the world. "My name is Vicky Rowe and I am the owner of the store. I am looking for qualified readers to work in the store. Would you be interested in working here?" she asked with a radiant smile. Her question came as a surprise to me and I expressed some anxiety about doing so as I had not done this as a full-time career. "It is simple, I will have you fill out an application with your background and have you do a short reading on me and then we will decide if this is the direction you should be going." Seeing the surprise on my face she then added, "You have a very interesting background, even writing for that large paranormal magazine in Mexico City and South America; it is apparent you are very qualified." She went on to explain that unlike most stores who just allow people to read in their business, she required a reader to have an extensive background with their abilities. For some reason, I was guided to fill out the papers and do a reading on this nice woman. She then asked me, "When can you start working?" What started out as entering a nice metaphysical bookstore to buy a few things ended up with me being hired as a reader. At last, I found the answer to what type of work I was to be doing no matter how crazy and impractical it seemed to my more traditional Capricorn birthday.

After being surround by healers, teachers, mystics and light workers from all over the world, I recognized that Vicky Rowe was the real deal. This woman had come into my life also turning me in the direction of the path that I was to follow. Soon, I was working out of the bookstore and having very interesting people sitting across from me. Vicky remarked one day as I was waiting for the next client to arrive, "You are not what people would think of as being the typical psychic. It must be from the activation of your gifts while living in Mexico. There is a very strong energy that surrounds you. It feels very ancient seeming to make you more grounded with the work that you do. It is interesting to see the different types of people that seek you out and their requests." I questioned what she meant by the "type of clients" as I had not lived in the area for many years and did not know the locals. She then said, "You seem to draw many wealthy established people in this community. There are quite a few who are also in the medical profession even some therapists and then there are those from other cultures."

Going into my office to prepare for a reading, there was time to reflect upon Vicky's observation. I came to the realization that I was more focused on that soul's needs not on their lifestyles. There were those who were grieving and the faces appeared before me of the young teens whose parents had sent them to me. Many were going through a rough time in so many ways and psychiatry was not working. There was also a nurse who could not work the night shift because the street lights sparked panic attacks and she had no idea why they were happening. I heard a whisper within me to put her into a deep altered state and guide her back to a place and time where the reasons for her current suffering would be revealed. There were also ones who sought me out in distress, their feeling that a witch had put a curse upon them. In the quiet of my little room in this bookstore, there was a new awareness being revealed. I was using so many tools and abilities unconsciously and having amazing results. Channeling was now my vehicle to understanding those who sat with me. I also learned (while living in Mexico) there were hidden worlds to discover that few entered. The skeptical, grounded one inside me underwent mind-blowing demonstrations in these separate realities. They opened my mind and world to magic on so many levels. Closing my eyes, I drifted back to that ancient land filled with so much mystery and magic. It had only been a year since I had moved back to California. Everything was so different in this place and it felt as if part of me was still in Mexico. People even remarked that I had an accent when speaking to them. Also, it was taking me time to adjust to the types of people working in the metaphysical community, their abilities and ways they worked. Gone were those mysterious ways that had been sent to me in Mexico and the powerful events that happened while living there. Memories of faces and places passed through my mind revealing why, at times, I felt like a stranger in a strange land in this new home. The vision of that kitchen with the view of the volcano outside the window and a golden line moving across the floor came before my eyes once more with the messenger that had appeared in the doorway. It was all part of the reasons I now had another type of work given to me; a most unusual career path had rapidly arrived after stepping over that golden line. My reverie was interrupted with a knock on the door…my client had arrived.

Lights, Camera, Action

As the months passed, word spread rapidly about my abilities and the phone was constantly ringing. Television and radio stations started inviting me to be a guest on a variety of shows. Eventually, I found myself being a regular featured guest on Sacramento's KCRA CH3 "Live at Noon" talk show with Mike Boyd. Mike was a top journalist who covered all the major stories of the times including the first in-person interview with Charles Manson. Mike became my teacher each time I sat next to him and his cohost on the set waiting for the "on-the-air" countdown. One day he announced on the air that I would become part of the "Live at Noon" show as a regular guest. In a commercial break, thanking him once again for this spot on the show he replied, "I love doing these segments with you, Elaina. You make my job easy, you're always prepared and you know your stuff. Those calls keep coming in and this is fun!" That was the highlight of being a regular guest on Live at Noon! I was like a sponge, soaking up all that professional atmosphere in the studio, and his wisdom and feedback stays with me to this day. We worked together for over two years. Soon it became apparent some of us would be pioneers in the "how and where" this work was conducted. Some of us were ending up more in the spotlight, and with that came even more responsibility to use our gifts with ethics and integrity.

I have been interviewed by many hosts over the years but there's only been a few that were on the same level as Mike Boyd. They include high profile Investigative Journalist, Diane Dimond who was with Hard Copy, Court TV and now with the Daily Beast. Also, Senior Investigative Reporter Ed Pearce, KOLO CH 8 in Reno, Nevada who also covered the Secret Witness segments. He has been the only one who would be allowed to shoot video of me working on a case.

One day destiny would arrive; my husband needed to drive up to Reno because he had a business appointment at one of the local television stations. He asked if I would like to go with him. It was there that I met a petite dark haired woman named Donna who asked a question that would bring destiny once more into my life. "What type of work do you do?" My response immediately brought an interesting offer. "I can get you on the radio here to do a few shows, but then it is up to you how you handle the guest spots. If they like you, they will invite you back to do more." I took her up on the offer and soon found myself driving up to Reno doing guest appearances on a KOH talk radio, "The Lou Gutenberger Show". Lou had an extensive background in "radio land" all over the country and I was now riding the airwaves with a pro! The phones rang off the hook and Lou invited me back for a regular guest spot. From that first show Lou and I would ride the KOH airwaves together and had so much fun!

Change was in the wind, and very quickly I made many new connections and started to build a wonderful clientele in this beautiful high-mountain desert town. There was lots of love surrounding me and destiny was in the making once more! I was also about to get a most painful lesson about making wiser choices...one being who you give your heart to! In a short time, life was changing fast and so was my relationship with the man that I had married during this time frame. As each year passed, there was a growing tension coming into play that soon brought pain and darkness. My husband wanted to become an actor or be in television. He was driven to be in the spotlight and joined the local theater crowd. After a while it became clear he was uncomfortable with the path I was following. I never sought the media; it found me. But it was obvious that he was conflicted about my success and career path. It also added more tension in our relationship when, with just two phone calls one sunny afternoon, destiny steered me into the world of investigative work. Those calls would bring two powerful men back into my life.

Whispers of Danger

I picked up the phone one day and decided to call my old friend Vic Calzaretta to see how he was doing. Vic had been the Chief Criminal Deputy of the Clark County Narcotics Unit in Vancouver, Washington. I had known him since I was in my twenties and it was good hearing Vic's voice. He updated me on his life, and I was surprised to hear that he had retired from law enforcement. He had replaced the long black hair and goatee of the streets with a successful criminal law practice. He sounded happy and was pleased he had left Narcs without one of his men getting hurt on his watch. Vic was feared and hated by every criminal on the streets of Vancouver, and wherever his work would take him, danger was his companion. He walked on the edge his whole career, his life at onetime mirroring the movie about the New York City cop Frank Serpico, who also fought against the corruption in his own police force. Vic Calzaretta walked the same path in the Chicago Police Department before moving out to the West Coast. His name "Calzaretta" got out very quickly to all the dealers in the Northwest and he did not win any popularity contests. There was a saying on the streets, "When Calzaretta pays a call, it's your worst nightmare; there's no knock, the odds are the door will come down and it will not be pretty." His conviction rate was very high. When his best friend,

Detective Rod Englert from the Multnomah County Sheriff's Department in Portland, Oregon, was added into the mix, it was a done deal…in more ways than one! Hearing Vic's voice brought back all those times spent together, and I wondered how the past six years had treated him. Time had flown by in our lives, taking each of us in new directions but we always stayed in contact to see how everyone was doing, which included Vic giving me updates on Rod. We reminisced about our adventures and always enjoyed having a few laughs. There were undercover rules when I was with Vic and Rod and if ever people approached us, I was to keep my mouth shut. If they were known by a different name or gave me one, I was to go along with the program. It must have been a peek into things to come in my future, because I would find myself on some unexpected adventures with them. Looking back, those events were my own personal Criminal Justice training seminars for what would come into my life twenty years later.

Vic and I always enjoyed walking down memory lane. One of our favorites was the time I ended up going on an unexpected fast ride with him and his team around 2 a.m. on a cold winter night. I had finished my shift, shut down the bar, and stepped out into the dark empty street to meet Vic and the guys working with him that night. They were giving me a ride to where my car was parked. Hopping into their undercover car, plans changed quickly. Back in those days, it was not just marijuana that was illegal; there were other dangerous drugs being sold, just as it is across this country today. Vancouver, Washington was also the gateway for the heroin trafficking trade and its transport to and from British Columbia. That night and at that very moment, a most wanted and elusive suspect drove by us in his truck. There was no time to lose, and in a flash things changed. The decision was made that I was going on a ride-along. It would be my first ride in an unmarked car and it was surreal. I realized this was no movie, this was the real deal. As I quietly listened to them discussing the person of interest and what to do about me being in the mix, I knew there was no turning back. I was sitting in the front seat with Vic and his partner Sid, and there were also three men in the backseat. Quickly, Vic gave me a command, "Do exactly like I tell you." We increased our speed to get a bit closer and be able to read the license plate revealed by the taillights up ahead. I was now being given a lesson in stealth driving as all eyes were now on that truck; it could disappear with any quick turn. Dispatch was on the radio that was hidden deep under the dashboard, and things were now setting into motion as they were relaying the truck's license plate to dispatch. Vic said he hoped that Rod was not out of town and to have him notified they were coming into his jurisdiction. The conversation kicked into high gear as they talked about how to handle what would be waiting for them when the truck up ahead was finally stopped. The tension was accelerating knowing that this suspect was dangerous and there was nowhere to drop me off. I firmly said I would stay low and promised to do exactly as I was instructed. I knew lives could be at risk, including mine, and they didn't need to have the burden of worry nor distraction about my being with them. My heart started pounding because we were now entering the bridge to cross over into Portland. It was raining on this cold dark night and the car's headlights exposed very slippery pavement. The radio was playing Barry White's "Love's Theme" and the windshield wipers were keeping time with each cord of the guitar and rhythm of the drums. It was Vic's favorite song, and every time I hear it, I remember that dark night and what was to come. There was no turning back, we were all on this ride together and the energy inside the car changed to a more serious vibe…one you could cut with a knife! Keeping more distance between us, they watched the truck preparing to exit onto a road where there was no traffic in these wee hours of the morning. By the time we came to the exit, the truck was far off in the distance and appeared to be slowing down, then making a turn off the road. Its headlights were slowly pointing through the trees. It now became a driving test, because our headlights were turned off after we took the exit onto the lonely road. In perfect time, the rain had stopped. Pulling over to the side of the road, two of the guys got out of the car and quickly ran ahead to get a closer look at where the suspect was going. As they disappeared into the darkness, there was dead silence in the car. High anxiety filled me, worrying about what would happen next. Silently, I prayed they did not get caught and have no one to help them. The dead silence was interrupted with a reminder about another potential issue. There now was the hope that no one else would be driving on this road heading for that house. It would blow their cover and throw another dangerous situation into the mix. The car was filled with a somber vibe!

That night was like an action movie, only it was real life. The situation was very dangerous and I had become part of it and not able to leave the "theater". Sitting in this car with five Narcs, there certainly wasn't any popcorn. It seemed like an eternity before the guys returned and jumped into the back seat, giving them a status report about what was going on up that road waiting for them. There was one way in and out of that place and a couple of other cars were parked there with the truck. The radio was softly confirming that units were on their way and would arrive at any moment. The teams would all meet prior to approaching what was now described as a solitary houseboat hidden in the trees with the porch light illuminated. There were serious warrants out on the suspect and it was not his first rodeo. He had been eluding capture for quite a while, and with only one way in and out, the team had to prepare for a variety of events with the suspect and those inside with him. Desperate people, when cornered, do desperate things that can lead to loss of life. Inside the car, these officers were checking their firearms and getting ready for whatever was going to play out with this guy and whoever else was with him.

Parked on the side of the road, the backup started arriving, everyone hoping that no other traffic would be coming our way. It was all in the timing and the luck of the draw with this job and a game of Russian

Roulette was now in play with serious consequences. No rain and a night sky that was black were perfect conditions for a takedown. By now, all the other units were stealthily arriving. Vic told me again to keep a low profile as his team swiftly got out of the car to go talk with other officers. Time crawled and it seemed like forever before they returned to the car. As we were sitting there, one of the officers came up to the window to talk with Vic. My heart was pounding as he glanced over at me. Thankfully, there were no questions about who I was and it was as if I was part of the unit. Once their plan was put together, they slowly started driving down the road with their lights off. As we quietly turned into the side road, we could see in the distance a houseboat in the trees with the lights on, the truck, and another couple of cars parked outside. Sitting ever so still, the officers talked quietly about their alternatives and how to approach the houseboat. Cars blocked the exit, filling the driveway; and without a sound, there were men in the shadows who were quietly surrounding the place. They had to move fast in case someone came out of the house to leave. Prior to Vic leaving the car, there was a serious look on his face and his final words meant business. "Things are going to get very loud and there will be yelling, you will hear doors and windows kicked in, and you may hear gun fire." As he got out of the car, he pointed to the floor, telling me to lock the doors, quickly get down and place my head as close as I could under the dashboard. "No matter what is going on outside, you are not to get up, do you hear me?" Nodding my head, my heart was beating faster as the adrenaline was activated in both of us. Leaning back into the car, moving his face closer to mine, and looking in my eyes there was a final warning, "I repeat, under no circumstances are you to try to see what is happening, no matter what you hear. You are not to get out of this car unless you see it is me telling you to do so. You do not unlock this door for anyone but me!" In a matter of seconds, he shut the door and disappeared into the shadows. I was alone in the dark praying we all would be safe! Trying to get myself positioned, I could look up and see out the window the silhouette of the leaves on the trees from the faint glow of the porch light. My Extra Sensory Perception suddenly felt the energy shift…into a cold, deadly silence.

What happened next was a series of sounds, just like he had told me to be prepared for and to keep my head down. The place was surrounded and the team was ready to roll. First, there were numerous loud thuds as the door was being kicked in, then hearing them announce who they were, accompanied with lots of men's voices, some yelling commands. It sounded like your worst nightmare. Then, there came a "boom" and my heart sank to my feet. It seemed like forever until it stopped, hearing voices talking more calmly and people walking around outside. There was the urge to get up and peek out the window but I reminded myself of Vic's orders. It seemed like eternity until there was that knock on the window, Vic looking through the window telling me to unlock the door. "Is everyone okay?" was my first shaky question as he got inside the car for a minute. I could see people standing around on the porch and others going in and out of the house. He gave me a brief update about what had happened then told me I needed to go home. "We are going to be here for a long time, so I am going to have one of the guys take you back to get your car so you can go home." My heart was still racing and so was my mind and as the adrenaline ran through my veins, I had another lesson on how dangerous it was to be a police officer! At that moment, I thought I saw Rod outside the car door with that teasing smile saying…"Hello Elaina." Those two were in their element, loving the capture of a dangerous drug dealer who had at last just met his match with these two men! Looking at Vic, knowing he was still alive…they all were! I realized at that moment, that we ALL have one foot on Earth and one in Heaven. Those who do this type of work push the envelope even more so. I had a dangerous adventure with him that night so long ago, and I completely understood why he was pleased he had left Narcs without one of his men getting hurt on his watch.

So back to the present…as the conversation shifted, I knew that I would have to tell him what type of work I was doing and I expected a lecture. Upon hearing what profession I had chosen and bravely stating to him that I was committed to my work despite what he thought, he soon made me the recipient of that dark sarcastic humor he was known for, along with a most surprising challenge. "Well, if that is what you are going to do, then why don't you do something constructive with it?" That was the last thing I expected to hear so I said, "Just what do you mean by that remark, Victor?" His voice took a serious tone, turning my life once again in another direction. "Why don't you do something worthwhile with it like help the cops?" The thought sent butterflies into my tummy. "Cops? That is a very wild idea." I had been around enough cops to know their skepticism about this subject. Twenty years ago, I had to practically beg him and his guys to let me read their cards. He knew that and now was telling me to work with them? Shaking my head, I looked up at the ceiling, telling myself I would have to be out of my mind to even consider such a thing. It would be idiotic to try and introduce my world to a bunch of skeptics. "Oh my God, Victor, the pressure would be awful and such high stakes would be involved." Visions of detectives standing around laughing at me rushed through my head. In the past Vic and I always had a bantering relationship. He would tease me relentlessly. Now I was automatically on guard because it was hard to tell exactly where he was coming from with this subject. In the back of my mind, I did have to admit that the thought struck a chord for a variety reasons. Part of me wanted to accept the challenge just to show him I could do it. "I must be out of my mind." was the thought still running through my head as I heard myself ask him, "Just exactly how do you go about doing such a thing?" And feeling those prophetic chills running through my body. "That's easy, find a crazy detective like Englert," he replied with a little laugh. Englert was Rod Englert, the Multnomah County Homicide Investigator. That crazy detective was Victor's best friend. Rod loved cold cases and was relentless in solving those forgotten throughout the years. In the years to come, I would find detectives can be very intuitive also. It happened so fast my head was spinning. Vic insisted that I contact Rod who loved working cold cases and had used psychics on occasion. "If you are going to do that type of work, then use it to really help people," he said in that soft but gruff manner. Replying in a feeble voice, I did not know if I would be able to do that type of work and was very aware of the gravity of all that it entailed. Deep in my heart I knew this was a heavy responsibility Vic Calzaretta was passing on to me and destiny was arriving once more in my life. We three were coming full circle in life once more. Filled with a moment of panic and fear about all that his words entailed, I replied, "I don't know if I can do this, Vic. I don't want to waste their important time let alone know how to even do this type of work!" He then countered with a commanding yet teasing voice, "Rod loves working cold cases and has his hands full with some current situations. He has used psychics on occasion and I am sure he will guide you; so what's the problem?" Despite my protests, I knew deep down, that Vic was going to be in command with this subject. I could see his gleeful smile as we hung up the phone. As usual, Vic Calzaretta would not wait for me to pick up the phone. In a very short time the phone would ring and Rod Englert would be saying hello. "Hi Elaina, Vic just called and said you are working as a psychic and for me to give you a call. I think that's great! I would love to work with you!" Now there was no turning back no matter how I tried to escape, quickly explaining I did not know how to use these abilities in such a powerful way. Rod calmly replied, "Don't worry, Elaina, I will help you. I have worked with people like you and will teach you how to focus your abilities."

I was still very insecure about attempting this as it was such a heavy burden. Rod must have felt my apprehension because he added a last chip to the table. "Elaina, I have young girls' bodies being thrown on the side of the roads all over here and we have to catch the person that is doing these heinous crimes. We have to stop this!" I could feel the frustration and sadness in his voice reminding me once again what the public does not see nor feel about those in law enforcement who live in that dark, dangerous world every day of their career. At last, I agreed. My heart felt this man's frustration and the weight of the responsibly upon his shoulders each day of his life. "Okay, Rod. I will try to do this for you." It was mind blowing that in a matter of thirty minutes after hanging up the phone, another part of my destiny had arrived that day. Soon these two men, whom I always had trusted with my life, would open the door to the world of becoming a psychic detective. Again, we would walk together with one foot on Earth and one in Heaven.

In a week, I would find a plane ticket to Portland in my hand and a heart filled with overwhelming feelings. In a matter of time, I was renting a car and heading for my aunt and uncle's home where I would be staying for a couple of days. In the morning, as I prepared to leave for the Sherriff's Department, there was concern on Lavelle's face as she walked me to the door. Giving me a hug, there was a warning given. "Be careful!" Assuring her I would be, and reminding her that I was safe with Rod, I got into the car. It was raining as usual as I drove towards the Sheriff's Office with apprehension. A million thoughts were racing through my mind; Where do I start? What was the proper procedure to step into a murder case? How would my mind react when it started to consider the dark thoughts, feelings and actions of the people involved? Can I do this? As I drove through the rain, I reminded myself once again there were no books for me to read about the proper techniques and that I knew nothing about this subject. It was a totally new world that I was about to enter and only the detective waiting for me could open the door to that dark realm. The veiled look in my auntie's eyes came before me and I wondered what she knew about the path upon which I was about to embark.

As I drove into the parking lot, a large, dark cloud moved ominously towards the building I was about to enter. The dark shadow it cast upon the building and the windows brought an eerie feeling to me. My heart was pounding and the sound of thunder shook me as I prayed for guidance, now concerned if I should even get out of the car and enter the building. Was this a sign to drive away fast? Another strong boom from the heavens arrived and had me jumping out of the car. As I opened the car door, there was the awareness I had made my choice as to which way to go! Now running quickly into the building, shaking off the rain drops, I wondered if it was safer inside or out in the cold rain.

The Detective and the Psychic

Lots of little girls read the Nancy Drew mystery stories and wanted to become her. Little did I know just how that would happen in my life, and who I would become! Anyone who has spent time in a police station knows it is a very intimidating place. Whether you are there to ask for help or to consult on a case, the vibrations of pain, suffering, and suspicion fill every corner of the room. If you are a clairvoyant and a psychic medium, the energy is amplified even greater. Giving my name to the deputy at the front desk and showing him my driver's license, I then sat down and proceeded to center myself and my thoughts as best I could. Despite the overwhelming waves of feelings going through me, a comfortable, calm feeling swept over me with a knowing that I was supposed to be there. At some point, a detective checked in and sat down next to me. His words surprised me. Noticing my suit and a brief case, he assumed that I also was here on a case. "What agency are you from?" I decided to be quiet about the details surrounding my reason being there. "You can go up now," the deputy said pointing towards the stairs. As I approached the top of the stairs, Rod came through a door with a smile on his face. He was dressed in a light brown sports coat that matched the color of his hair. His neatly trimmed beard brought out his beautiful eyes that saw so deeply into the darkness. At first glance, it would be hard to know what he did for a living, and one might guess he was a professor. That he was! Just on a darker and more dangerous level. After a quick hug, he steered me to his office and we spoke briefly. Then he said, "Have a seat and I'll be back in a few minutes. Make yourself comfortable." As I sat down, my eyes surveyed my surroundings. A person's office speaks many things about who they are, and this one belonged to a man who had lived a most unusual life. Suddenly, I was bombarded with a sensory overload of what had transpired on so many pain-filled levels in his world. It felt like I was time traveling back to the office of Sherlock Holmes. This room was the entrance to another world filled with mysteries, death and unanswered questions. It was the office of a brilliant man who had gained recognition for being relentless finding the answers to very dark deeds committed by others and the blood trails that they left behind. No matter how long they had been unsolved, Cold Cases were part of his fascination. The room was decorated with a variety of unusual memorabilia on a shelf: a huge tennis shoe with a tag on it, and a human skull perched comfortably next to it that seemed to be staring at me. Seeing this odd display, I could not help wondering if they belonged together. To the left of this macabre décor was a black and white photo of a well-known actor. You never knew where Rod would show up especially if Vic was working a case with him. There were also a few technical books included amongst this mini forensic museum. Resting next to the skull was a hat with an emblem on it of men standing by tombstones with the words "Homicide: Our day begins when yours ends" It was a powerful message of what part of my life's work would become starting that day. In the years to come I would have a shirt that said the same thing! It took a while to adjust to the subtle bombardment of this display, asking myself quietly, "What has Victor got me into now?!"

At that moment, as if psychic, Rod quickly reentered the room startling me! In his hand was a file that he placed on the desk as he sat down.

Catching up on each other's lives for a bit, he laughed as I mentioned how Vic had gotten me here! The topic shifted and the room became filled with an intense energy and his manner became serious. Rod, the smiling friend, was gone and the detective took his place in this office. "Elaina, I am going to take you into another room to work; so please follow me," he said in a most serious tone. As we walked down the hall, my heart was pounding with uncertainty about beginning this journey. Walking through a doorway, he motioned for me to sit down in a brown leather chair. My eyes scanned the area. It was a well lit room and a more sterile environment, bringing me another new energy filled with flickers of faces and intense feelings. Rod went to a cubical across the room where he put some things into the folder then sat down on a stool before me. "How does that chair feel? Are you comfortable?" I told him it was comfortable physically, but I felt very strange things within that I could not explain. Smiling, then looking deeply into my eyes, he calmly stated it was the chair where a lot of bad people had been sitting to be interrogated. Shaking my head, I said to myself, "oh great! now why does that surprise me?" It was the perfect place for my first attempt at this type of reading. I thought of all the people who had been questioned while sitting in the chair I now occupied and said I had a question to ask him. "What if I start reading those that sat here?" We both had a laugh but mine was a nervous one, thinking of all those people he had questioned. Now it was my turn, and even though I had not done anything wrong, a feeling of high anxiety and fear filled me. Knowing how those suspects were feeling was unnerving. I had a brief moment of panic remembering the horror stories of well-meaning psychics who had given specific key pieces of information and then were considered suspects themselves. My rational mind immediately talked me out of that scenario because it would not work that way with Rod. Even so, the fear of the unknown remained. "I don't know what to do Rod. Where will I start?"

Pulling his stool up close to me, his eyes now looking even deeper more direct into mine, he assured me that he would help me step by step. "What I am going to do first is a little test. Are you comfortable? Can I get you anything?" Taking a deep breath and exhaling, I heard my voice reply calmly, "Just give me a minute to prepare myself." Closing my eyes, I asked spirit for guidance and protection. Not knowing what else to do, I asked to receive the White Light of protection and to be shown how to help regarding this situation. Soon the familiar feeling of peace filled my being. I could feel the bubble of light wrap gently around me and under my feet. In the years to come I would learn the importance of the ritual I intuitively invoking at that moment. Opening my eyes, Rod proceeded to hand me a photo. I found myself looking into the eyes of a young girl with dark hair. After a few minutes I heard his soft voice asking, "What can you tell me about this person?" With my left hand holding the photo, I began sliding my right over her face. At first I felt nothing and was unclear as to where I should start, but I continued to try to find a signal of something. Time seemed to pause in that quiet room, and after a long period of silence and strange new sensations hitting me, Rod moved closer. Hearing his voice again, he asked me more firmly, "What can you tell me about her?" It was as if I was frozen and had no compass. Feeling like a fool I asked, "What do you want to know?" In a most patient voice he said, "Give me anything that you feel. Where is she? What is she doing? Who is she with?" At some point I felt him very near my face then saying in a very strong voice, "WHAT'S HER NAME?" In that moment, I heard a name from a voice that sounded as if someone was telephoning me from across the ocean. There was distortion on the line. As I tried to focus, the name appeared before me C-A-R-O-L-E. Quickly responding I said, "Her name is Carole spelled with an E at the end of it!"

I opened my eyes and looked at Rod for a response but the detective was not giving up anything. He quickly asked me, "Is she dead or alive?"

The "ocean" voice within me abruptly stated, "DEAD." It felt as if I was in a hallway watching Rod and myself engaging in this conversation hearing my response to that statement. "God forgive me if I am wrong," I thought. The energy I then felt would be the signal that always brought verification of the pain-filled accuracy of those words. At that moment, as I looked deeper into this girl's eyes, my body began to become aware of a new sensation taking hold of me. As my hand ran rapidly over the photo with my fingers touching all of her face, I felt myself leaving my body. A fuzzy feeling or numbness arrived and I was now feeling myself "In someplace." A deep sharp pain ran through my head…hearing my voice crying out then quickly disappearing back into the shadows. I could hear Rod's voice in the distance but I could not see where he was. I could only hear his voice asking a question: "What's going on?" Waves of pain were assaulting me, bringing confusion. Why would something be hitting me when he only asked me a question? Could he not see me? Not help me? His voice once again brought me back to the connection with him, despite the ever-so-deep pain filling me with fear. "I feel heavy sharp pains," I said pointing to the side of my head near to my temple. "Oh! It hurts so bad! Please help me!" The pain was overwhelming with each blow. I was feeling sick from what I was observing and experiencing at the same time! I felt frozen…not knowing who or what was lurking in the shadows of my mind and body. My hands felt like lead as they slowly touched other parts of my body that were being harmed. I tried to pull myself away from this place, at some point my eyes opened to gather strength, but I found myself looking down at the photo of this beautiful young girl again. I could not turn away from her and the more I stared at her, it was as if I was falling into those eyes that were calling me to help her. This was not just a piece of photo paper, it was a human being, a soul screaming for the agony to stop. Suddenly, the pain was overwhelming, bringing a powerful and most violent blow. It was accompanied with a visual flash of an object above me coming down towards me again. I was lying there helpless in the shadows not able to move out of the way. My body jerked as a sharp edge struck my head. I called out, "Something is hitting me in my head." Rod turned me in the direction of what was creating all this pain. "What is hitting you? Can you see it?" His voice guiding me to shift my sight. The object above me moved so quickly that it was impossible to get a good look at it. It felt like the end of a hammer used for framing, perhaps something that was used in construction work? All I knew was that I wanted so desperately to get away from it and the pain it created. It was as if I was lost, never to be found, not knowing how to get out of that place.

Rod's voice called out numerous times, "Where are you? Tell me what you see?" I tried to step out of the panic and fear; to get clarity took effort. As my eyes tried to focus, to observe, they traveled slowly up above, to the left, to the right, forwards and backwards. From where I was lying, it felt like a box, metal on the floor. Was it a van? A truck? There were no windows but there was a bit of light towards the front. Was I in a remote area? All I knew was that I wanted to get away from this place but did not know how to do so. I had no guidelines and was struggling for what seemed to be eternity to find a way out. I called out from within me asking for angels to help me. At some point, I heard a whisper, "Ask for the Light, Elaina." Immediately, visualizing the way, the Light slowly arrived surrounding me with that soothing feeling as it wrapped me in a blanket of comfort. After a time I began to relax, feeling my heart now beating slowly once more. There was a peaceful rhythm activated. I do not know how long it took. When I enter an altered state, there is no time. Opening my eyes, I found myself back in the chair, and Rod was sitting at a desk across the room. It appeared he had been taking notes about the horrific drama we had just experienced together. Moving my legs and arms, feeling my body once more, it took time to remove the heavy numbness and to find myself once again. The sound of the stool moving towards me brought me back to where I had been at the beginning when I entered the room.

Rod was sitting up close to me. "How are you feeling, Elaina?" Then asking if I would like some water, he left the room and returned with a cold bottle of water. The taste was so good, grounding me once more, bringing me slowly back into the present. Somehow, I had been in two separate realities, observing and reenacting a murder; how I got there baffled me. Even now, the victim and her killer were still within me, sending waves of intense feelings and pain into many areas of my body. Sensory overload had taken hold of me in a most horrific manner and I prayed it would go away completely. At some point, there was a quiet moment and Rod scooted his chair up close to me. Staring deeply into my eyes, he said softly, "Elaina do you know what you are doing? You are becoming a forensic tool by letting me use your mind to help me understand more about what has happened to this young girl."

Quietly, I asked, "Did I do okay?" Part of me felt as if I was still someplace else, drained and exhausted from fighting for my life. There was also a dull throb of pain by the side of my head that remained. The flash of an object coming down towards me in the shadow created a shiver that ran through my bones.

"Boy, oh Boy you did good!" he exclaimed. His words, then revealed the other side of the mirror. "Do you think that you could look at some other pictures? They are not pleasant, but I think you need to see them." He scooted his stool back over to his desk, grabbed a folder and moved back in front of me. "The young lady in that photo is dead," Rod said softly. "Her name is Carole and it is spelled with an 'E'. The pain that you were feeling is because of the wounds that were inflicted upon her in that exact area." He handed me a photo of the body. "This is a photo of her body during autopsy. As you can see," he said pointing to the photo, "she suffered blows to that same area of the head and body where you were experiencing excruciating pain."

The girl in the school photo was the same one as the autopsy picture I was holding but she wore no lipstick, had no nicely combined hair and no beautiful smile. In this new photo, she was lying peacefully upon the coroner's metal table with a sheet covering her naked, cold, lifeless body. Her head had been shaved to expose the deep wounds that were inflicted and on other areas of her body. As my eyes gently scanned her, the count was the same and I was comforted knowing, this young girl would never feel pain again. As the flashes of the object appeared above me once more, there was also the experience of her last breath, freeing her from the monster…saying goodbye, leaving her parents and loved ones who were looking for answers. "Why- how- did this horror happen?" and "Who did this to her?" Her family could not even start to heal the pain until all questions were answered. The coroner searched for the secrets in his examination of her flesh. The detectives left no stone unturned to find the answers and hunt down the one responsible for such a heinous act.

Finding the answers was the responsibility of Rod Englert, along with so many others throughout his career. This young victim would walk with him until the mystery of her death was resolved. Rod's world was filled with not only her pain, but her family's pain as well. He carried her face before him constantly hearing the nagging voice that asked, "Who-what-where-when and why did this vicious act happen?" The mystery of her death followed him through the night and into his dream world. This case haunted him even in his moments of relaxation and private times. The young girl's pain was gone but her death became a part of others' lives. I realized that day that this feeling would walk with me too, each time I stepped into the world of homicide. As I entered the inner sanctum of a homicide division and joined those who tirelessly worked there, I too became privy to the world of their secrets, pain, death and danger. This was my initiation, bringing me the rare experience of working in the shadows alongside them. I discovered that day for myself, that there were steps to walk through when doing this type of work: stepping out of my body, entering the shadow of death, reenacting the event, becoming victim and perpetrator…then finding myself coming back into my own world to activate the next level, and receiving clarity from the detective who verified my experience. This work was very real and not a morbid fantasy.

I was being trained by one of the best, who was now showing me the way to a part of my own future. Soon, I developed a methodology to profile and work as a crime scene analyst, using the unusual gifts passed down to me. For the first time, I was beginning to understand the sadness that you can see in a police officer's eyes. It seemed the burden had now been passed on to me as well, recognizing that my "gifts" had now become a curse at times.

Psalms echoed within my soul *"Yea though I walk through the valley of the shadow of death I shall fear no evil for thou art with me"*

I had entered the shadow and wondered if there would ever be light again.

Before I could acclimate to this first powerful experience, Rod added another level to this new path. He asked me to return to Multnomah County Sheriff's Department on October 4, 1984 to deliver a seminar on being a psychic. The seminar was attended by over a hundred investigators waiting for me. Before he opened the door, he said with a smile, "Don't mess this up, I have put myself on the line for you." My heart dropped to my feet hearing his words! Quickly regaining my composure, the big door opened revealing an auditorium filled with rows of chairs of law enforcement personnel from various surrounding agencies…quietly waiting for me.

Rod escorted me to a chair in the first row then motioned for me to sit down. As he walked up to the podium to join the others, I tried to dismiss the vibe of all eyes upon me. Silently praying that these men and women would be open to what I had to share with them, I focused my inner energy. In a matter of minutes, I was introduced. I stepped up to the podium to share with these men and women how I had entered their world of murder. Time slowed and the room was filled with intense silence. There would come the question and answer time with many hands being raised in the air. They had a test for me too. The Captain of the division had three sealed envelopes that were given to me. The envelopes contained information on open missing person cases. I was handed each envelope separately and asked if the person was missing or dead. As I held each one, I called out: "Missing, Missing, Dead." I had them in perfect order! The first two were missing and the last one was dead. The latter had been found in the mountains around Vancouver, Washington where she had been kidnapped and killed.

At the end of my talk, everyone exited the conference room, and Rod escorted me to the door. Little did I know that Rod had another surprise in store for me. As I walked out the door, I was bombarded by local television cameras, lights and microphones pointed at us and reporters asking questions. Once again Rod brought another layer of my destiny to me, revealing that there was more training to do and he expected me to follow through properly. Doors opened swiftly from that day forward.

I also knew that Victor Calzaretta was getting a kick out of this whole situation because it was happening at warp speed without giving me time to say "No!" I met Vic for dinner one night prior to my leaving to return to California. I was prepared for his banter a final time.

I soon learned the reason why investigators did not trust psychics. There were many psychics who sought out the press to get publicity. These "psychics" would contact the police and then announce that they were working on a case, stating that they (the "psychics") were called to help the investigators. Other "psychics" would contact victims' families expressing their desire to help the families, then proclaiming they were working on a case. Many "psychics" have websites that look like a commercial for their involvement in cases. Others give inaccurate information to the newspapers and television which causes nothing but confusion and ends up being a waste of precious time. It is no wonder that "psychics" are a turn off for investigators and this dichotomy makes it more uncomfortable for credible psychics and mediums who have genuine abilities. Few psychics have a documented background in this type of work and that continues unfortunately to this day. Documented means references by law enforcement, not from someone outside of an investigation. It was the opposite for me because I never contacted the police. They contacted me. I had an immediate understanding that it was wise and appropriate to keep a confidential and low profile when working with the investigators for three very important reasons: first, secrecy was key to not compromising a case; second, this work was, and is not about being famous; and last but certainly not least, this type of investigative work is very dangerous. Who would want killers knowing that you were working with detectives to find them? Especially a psychic investigator that was unknown! That day at his office in 1984, Rod Englert passed on to me the very serious nature of this work and all the responsibility it entails. I heard his words of guidance every time I did a lecture or worked on a case. Life had swiftly taken a major turn in the road and I knew it was destined to be. The Psychic Detective had been activated in me...then and for the rest of this life!

Law Enforcement Associations and Seminars

University of Nevada Reno July 21 1984
Department of Criminal Justice

Multnomah County Sheriff's Office October 4 1984
"Psychics as Investigative Resources"

University of Nevada Reno Criminal Justice Department
"Psychic Awareness an Investigative tool" 1984

Truckee Meadows C.C. Criminal Justice Dept.
Principals of Investigation 1986
"Parapsychology and Criminal Investigation"

American Polygraph Association Reno NV 1984
24th Annual Seminar Advanced Polygraph Instrumentation & Techniques
Lectured: *"Unconventional Investigations"*

National American Polygraph Association August 1989
California Association of Polygraph Examiners
Character Profiling and Analysis

C. A.P.E.
California Association of Polygraph Examiners Feb.1991
Newport Beach California
National Training Seminar Lecture 10 HRS:
"Character Profiling Methodology Application in Investigative Setting"

American Society of Law Enforcement Trainers
Milwaukie Wisconsin January 7-11th 1992
California Homicide Investigators Association 1992-1993
California Homicide Investigators Associate 1993-94
CHIA Conference Reno Nevada March 3-5-1993

The Valley of the Shadow of Death

Life as I had previously known it was rapidly changing. My husband was also revealing his conflicted feelings about my abilities. It takes a certain kind of person to be in the life of someone like me. His new attitude about my work was breaking my heart. I longed for him to be happy about my blossoming career and the prosperity to come but his growing anger escalated. After a trip to the bay area, we got into an argument. Our verbal altercation quickly escalated into a physical confrontation. He hit me and slammed my head against the wall. It was at that point that I knew our relationship was over. Domestic violence had reared its ugly head in my life! He tried to be kind and smooth the situation over, but my heart and my head were hurting from his actions. Deep inside I knew I must get out of this situation and promised myself that I would not forget this moment. My head ached and the next day I called my doctor and told her what happened and that he had said he was very sorry for hitting me. What she said to me became a prophesy, "You need to think seriously about this relationship, Elaina. Once domestic violence starts, it never stops nor does it have a happy ending!" She continued on firmly, "If this pain continues or you have problems with your vision, then you need to come in and see me immediately." I was witnessing the materialization of a different side of my husband. A stranger was emerging bringing more darkness which was splitting us apart.

The signals continued in the weeks and months after the assault but I ignored them. There was the night lying in bed talking about a friend who was going through a divorce. Suddenly, my husband said if it were him, he would get a female attorney because women always wanted to be with him and they would work hard for him. In a calm voice he said, "No woman will ever take my money," stating he had ways to just disappear. Listening to his words filled me with an uncomfortable feeling. He even went so far as to tell me he would change his identity and use his brother's first name for his own last name. I thought it was an odd thing to say especially when he was a very attractive man who turned heads and was so ego-driven to be in front of the camera. My silent thoughts whispered there are things you can change about your appearance, but you cannot change the look of your hands or your teeth unless you cap them.

I heard another whisper as I drifted off, a knowing that I must be very careful and get out of this situation! I promised myself to not forget this moment. I prayed for my helpers to arrive. There was an energy of foreboding in the room that night as I closed my eyes to sleep. Angels were revealing painful things to me that I did not want to see. His behavior continued to be extreme in bizarre ways. Looking back, maybe his behavior had always been there. Maybe I had just not observed it or wanted to see it. It seems there is truth in the saying "Love is blind."

My Guardian Angels whispered things to me that were often hard to accept since they were about someone I loved. I also had an uneasy feeling that lingered in my bones. I knew it was time for me to move out of our house and make temporary quarters in a rental property owned by my sister. Shortly thereafter, our separation papers were drawn up, and I decided that once the papers were complete that I would move to Reno, Nevada. I was strongly compelled to be far away from this man. And even though my heart was sad, I could see my life was rapidly unfolding in a new place and the people were welcoming. As I continued to visit Reno for the radio show and client appointments, it became apparent to me that I was to move to this wonderful "Biggest Little City"; I felt a lot of love and support for me there. With the beautiful mountains and the wonderful people, Reno had everything! It was not big, like Las Vegas and was a tight-knit community that had its own interesting history. There were very nice casinos that not only had fine dining, they had well-known artists performing on a regular basis!

"Destiny is saying yes to the calling we were born with, while fate is what happens when we fight or ignore our calling" -Alberto Villoldo

One Friday afternoon I was packing for my move when the phone rang. My soon-to-be-ex-husband told me he was coming by to bring me separation papers to sign. I asked him if we could review the documents on Monday because my attorney was not available until then. But he was very edgy, insisting that I review and sign the papers immediately! "I will be there after 5p.m.," he staunchly said. An ominous feeling came over me that I tried to dismiss. As the late afternoon sunlight started to fade into grey skies on this November day of 1985, a chill pervaded the air and so did fate. Turning up the heat, I tried to shake off that nagging feeling but it would not go away. For some reason, I did not recognize the signal I received that night (as I usually had throughout my life)…the one that whispered danger was near. Overwhelming feelings clouded my intuition as I got ready, praying that this meeting would go smoothly. As early darkness approached, there was a knock at the door. I opened the door, and my husband entered with papers in his hand along with the bitter cold and damp night. His over six-foot height towered above me. With barely a hello, he sat down quickly. He insisted that I sign our separation papers right then and there. Looking at the clock, I said to him nicely that it was too late because my attorney was gone until Monday. His persistent demands escalated and the voice of reason had departed. He grew very agitated when I told him again that I did not want to sign any documents until my attorney could simply review them. What was supposed to be just a few pages had turned into a very large document. There was also the question as to the why there would be a separation not a divorce running through my mind. Was he thinking about a possible reconciliation? Or a tax break for himself?

Carefully, I stated a final time that I would be unable to sign any papers until my attorney could review them the following Monday. Then taking a breath I firmly asked, "You taught me to be a good business woman so why are you not agreeing with the reason I want to wait?" The energy in the room shifted once more and I could see and feel anger filling his entire being. His voice was escalating, demanding that I sign the papers immediately! Suddenly, I had a strong feeling that I needed to get him out of my place as soon as possible. Very cautiously I managed to coerce him to leave. We walked out into the dark, cold November night. Instead of heading towards his car that was parked by the curb, he walked down the sidewalk in the direction towards my car that was parked in the driveway. His anger and voice escalated as he told me that he was taking my car away and was going to leave me without transportation. Shocked by his threat, I pleaded with him to reconsider and let me keep the car as we had previously agreed. My pleas were accompanied by tears but to no avail. There was pleasure written all over his face as he proceeded to unlock the car door.

In a last-ditch effort to help myself, I turned around and headed back towards the house, telling him that I was going to call his brother. I said perhaps his brother could talk some sense into him. A few feet before I reached the front door step, he came up behind me, leaned down, and grabbed me around the chest. He then swung me up through the air and threw me to the ground. The corner of the concrete front step penetrated deep into to the left side of my upper abdomen. I must have passed out for a few seconds. Then at some point my dazed eyes opened and all that I could see was the grass next to the sidewalk. There was a sickening sensation inside of me from a very deep pain. I laid there trying to catch my breath. Without offering me any type of assistance or expressing any level of concern or remorse, my Jekyll and Hyde husband calmly walked away, got into the car (that he had promised me for my move to Nevada), and drove away. The gentleman I had known and loved had transformed into a cold, cruel, greedy, jealous monster capable of inflicting serious and deliberate injury. At that moment, I knew something was horribly wrong inside me. I continued lying on the ground at my front door step, unable to move for what seemed like an eternity. At last, I slowly picked myself up and managed to get myself back inside the house. My hand was shaking as I reached for the phone to call my brother-in-law. I left a message telling him what had happened. As I hung up the phone, there was a knock on the door. My heart was beating fast and I was filled with fear. I looked through the peep hole in the door and I saw my son standing there. He was going into the Navy and had been visiting the neighbors across the street. He saw that there was dirt and leaves upon my clothing. With a worried look in his eyes he asked, "What's wrong, Mom?" I reluctantly told him what had happened and said I was going to call the police. He then said to me in a very concerned voice, "Be careful Mom! That will make him even angrier and I will not be here to protect you. Just get out of here! You only have a few weeks until you are moved!" Then he asked me if I needed him to stay. I quickly responded, "You will be right across the street, honey if I need you. So, go enjoy your night with your friends."

After my son left, I thought about what he said and decided to call the police to ask for a drive-by watch. I wanted to let them know that my husband had taken my car and also wanted to give them a description of his other car that was still parked out front of my place. The recording on the end of the line said that due to a high volume of calls to leave a detailed message. After numerous tries, I finally left a message. I decided that I needed I go to the hospital emergency room and that I would call the police again after I returned home. Angels work in strange ways. I called a friend to take me to a nearby hospital emergency room. I spent a few hours there. The physicians and nurses kept me under observation, documented my husband's assault on me, gave me some medication, and then sent me home. I still felt severely weakened when I left. I told myself that the trauma was internal bruising that would take a while to heal. Surely these injuries could not be life-threatening. The hospital had released me and there was only a red swollen mark on my left side from being thrown against the step. Only later did I learn that the hospital had not performed all the necessary and proper internal medical scans. They had taken down my statement, pumped me full of drugs, monitored me for a few hours then sent me out the door with a life-threatening injury. When we got back to my place, my husband's other car was gone. It was cold and dark, and I was yearning for the security and warmth of my cozy bed. Shaken, and in physical and emotional pain, I said goodbye to my friend and locked the door. After a final check of all the doors and windows, I crawled into my bed. I was shocked that this incident had actually happened! I was in the middle of moving to Reno and starting a new life, hopefully filled with peace. It was supposed to be a happier new beginning of my life. While it was a new beginning, it certainly was not a happy one. I was now enduring emotional pain caused by a heinous act committed by someone I had loved, which would bring a physical pain that would be like no other in my life. So much had happened the past few months. I could not understand the reasons why my life was taking such powerful twists and turns. Closing my eyes, shaking, I prayed for better days to come. Fate and destiny seemed to join in mysterious ways that night. I learned more in the days to come. It was very apparent that nothing was by accident and neither were the people who were arriving in my life! So many people…in very powerful and unusual ways. I was about to walk through the Valley of the Shadow of Death, not only regarding my own life but the lives and deaths of others as well. The impending experience would bring many loving strangers and many mystical experiences into my life. The beautiful gypsy in the tea room, and her whispers to me that were so long ago forgotten, had now circled around and back into my life.

Pain, Danger and Death

After that most painful event, more intense moves and changes started manifesting in my life. Soon, because of my separation, I proceeded with my plans to move to Reno. In the weeks prior to my permanent move, I took a trip to Reno for a few days to participate in the talk show, see some clients, and start looking for a place to live. I had rented a small office above a shopping complex, and it looked like step by step my move was commencing. On this trip, there was an unexpected change in my schedule. There were police cars parked next to the restaurant below my office. On previous visits to Reno, I would occasionally eat lunch or dinner there. I got to know the owner by spending time in the restaurant after closing hours. On one morning of my latest trip, I was talking to my answering service, writing down the names and numbers of callers who wanted appointments when suddenly my new friend, Mabs Martin, was standing in my doorway. Mabs had the office next to mine. She was a beautiful and vivacious woman with a lot of style and class. On this particular morning she was wearing a Chanel navy blue and cream woven wool plaid jacket, accessorized perfectly right down to her toes. She entered my office like she was on a fashion runway. Mabs was the owner of a very successful modeling agency named Showcase Modeling. From our first introduction, I found her introducing me to many people in the community. Mabs also found a place for me to stay with a good friend of hers until my move to Reno was completed. Everything was falling into place…smoothly as always when Angels are working. Mabs was one of my "Angels" and soon she brought a powerful event into my life. She excitedly told me in her Southern Lady drawl that a burglary had occurred. "Honey, I thought maybe the police may want to talk with you also." In a matter of minutes, she strolled out of the office.

I walked down stairs and headed next door to the restaurant. An officer was interviewing people regarding a break-in, and soon enough I was talking with him. With pen in hand, he took down my information, then asked what type of work I did and if I had noticed anything suspicious. He wrote down my name on the report and when he heard I was a psychic, he suddenly asked, "Would you be interested in talking with Detective Eubanks regarding the case of a woman who has been murdered recently?" He told me that the victim, Mary Holliday, was a popular school teacher and had been found murdered in her home. He mentioned that the detective handling this case also had a personal connection with this lady. She had been his eighth grade homeroom teacher. I told the officer that the detective could call me. I also gave him the name of the first investigator I had worked with (Rod Englert) as a reference. I had not even completed my move to this town, and once again, Destiny was arriving with me! It would be another part of my soon-to-be new career. Shortly thereafter, I found myself walking into the Reno Police Department and heading for the Robbery Homicide Division to meet Detective Eubanks and discuss the associated case. While talking with him I discovered that our birthdays were the same month and day which brought amazing teamwork when we worked together.

We took a drive to the house where the murder occurred but we were unable to go inside because the scene was still being processed. So I attempted to see what I could pick up from just standing outside by the windows. I could not see inside the house at all. At some point, I intuitively saw where they found her body. I then reenacted how her death had occurred. A powerful revelation came to me regarding the relationship between this woman and her killer. Her attacker was no stranger. It was a most evil act. In my vision, I described the type of weapon used, the number of blows, the specific body parts affected and the body position between killer and victim at the time of the assault. As if watching a movie, I described the killer's clothing at the time of murder and what the suspect did with his bloody clothes. This was a "Hide in Plain Sight" case. We continued our dialogue upon returning to the police station where I described the suspect's house right down to the paintings hung on his bedroom wall. There was a creek running to the rear of the residence, a specific area upon the property used as a sanctuary by the suspect for its emotional importance to him. For some reason this heinous crime seemed to spill out of me as I described what I saw and felt from the clairvoyant level. It was so powerful and more information continued to come through me. I was then taken downstairs to a room with stacks of boxes. I was given a "Test" when Detective Eubanks and Dave Keller handed me a sealed evidence box. They asked me if I could pick up anything from holding it in my hands. As my hands held the sealed box again, I saw flashes of a house and described many details that I would have had no access to. I had not even moved to the area yet. I also stated that there were some sort of gloves on the killer's hands. As one detective recalled, "She began rubbing her hands and told us that the killer's hands had been inside these items in the box and in a manner such as wearing a glove." The box held "Trace evidence bags" which had been placed over the killer's hands at the crime scene.

Detective Gary Eubanks wrote a three-page letter of documentation regarding my involvement in this case. The letter contained his observations including the detail I provided to him regarding every confidential key of the case that he had been tightly guarding. How this situation had unfolded, I knew not. Very powerful things were happening to me at that time, especially when it came to revealing extremely heinous acts committed by others! At that time, I did not know that I too had one foot on Earth and one in Heaven on a very personal level. As far as the case file, I had no idea if I had failed or passed the test but the look on all the detectives' faces verified something which would be disclosed years down the road. This case was also my first time of working up an unknowingly accurate profile and insight into a killer…a person who was most cautious in revealing as little as possible about himself while maintaining a posture of "cooperation."

I did not know until many years later just how close Detective Eubanks had been to Mary Holliday. During the time of her murder, his calm professional manner was all that he revealed. There are times, when an investigator sees a murder victim that he has known personally in some way. For Detective Eubanks, it was so. Upon his visit to the coroner's office, he found himself looking down at the brutally bludgeoned body of a woman that had been unrecognizable that first time at the crime scene until the blood was washed away from her face. It was almost the same now but there was a flash of deep recognition in this moment of silent observation and who she had been in his life so many years ago. Looking at her in this condition, it hit him like a ton of bricks! It was all brought back to him as he looked down at her battered body. They both had come full circle now. In the quiet morgue, his past had walked into the present!

Mary Holliday had been his teacher many years ago, and now the kid who had moved to Reno from Florida was also standing in that room. Memories came flooding back to him, as he remembered her in those happier times. It was hard for his mind to recognize and accept that this was his beloved teacher. She always had enjoyed taking time to talk with him after school and sharing stories together. He shared with her about living in Florida, Ernest Hemmingway and all the different areas in the State of Florida. Ms. Holliday would tell him about Nevada and its history and share her desire to retire to her ranch in Fallon and write a book about her beloved Nevada; the wild mustangs, and all the beauty that she had discovered throughout the years.

Before her death, she had been planning to move out to her family ranch to (at last) write that book about Nevada. She was also an amateur botanist and painter.

The adult, who was now a homicide detective looking at her resting upon the table, quickly took charge of his personal feelings. There was no time to be distracted. He would have to grieve at some point later. Exactly how or when that time would come was not known at that moment. It's how a police officer must handle these types of situations. It's a never ending, revolving door of death that keeps turning and turning. Then, there are countless other victims that need to be focused upon and families waiting for justice and answers. Each death or horrific act the detectives investigate becomes a blur of pain that must be put "somewhere" until they can take the time to look at all their feelings resting deep within themselves. In the meantime, for many, a couple of shots of whiskey or a few beers will bring some comfort, numb their feelings and hopefully help them sleep. Anything is welcome that can help block all the empty eyes of death that are staring back at them each night in their dream world. Mary Holliday died in a most brutal manner and was now another tragedy. Detective Eubanks would carry this traumatic experience with him for the rest of his life.

A trial occurred eleven months later. Sadly, the verdict would be a repeat of the O.J. Simpson case. Only this perpetrator would kill his mother and walk out of the courtroom not convicted. When Mary's son discovered that she was changing her will and leaving her inheritance ($350,000) to her

---

grandchildren, he took steps to ensure that would not happen. His two sons filed a civil action against him in July of 1986 stating that he did kill their grandmother and that their father was the last known person to see her alive. In the end, no one won the prize and the inheritance was all used for probate. While the money is gone, the stain and the shame still walked out the door…no matter how loud their innocent cries.

From that day forward, the phone would ring and I'd hear Detective Eubanks' or another investigator's voice asking, "do you want to take a drive? Do you want to play who-dun-it?" And I headed yet again down to Robbery Homicide, or to another crime scene with a new set of eyes…hoping to find clarity…searching for pieces of the puzzle…to find the who-where-what and why…leaving no stone unturned. I believe each case was given by a Divine Source that whispered to me. I stepped into the shadow of death and walked with them for a while.

My life changed again that day at the restaurant below my office and in the years to come I'd make many more visits to Investigative Divisions. In many ways, it became a work place and almost home. And with every visit, I didn't know if it would be an hour or 4-5 hours before I left. The people that were now arriving in my life brought powerful life-changing events filled with pain, danger and death. Not only for my own life, but for theirs too.

Confession of the Secret

Prior to my move, one sunny morning I again headed for Reno to participate in a Criminal Justice class at the University of Nevada, Reno. As I entered Reno on this beautiful and sunny late fall day, I was filled with anticipation. Still shaken from what had happened to me that fateful Friday night, I kept telling myself that soon I would feel better, that it was just that my body bruised inside, and it was taking longer to heal. It was a comfort knowing I would be moving to this town very soon. I checked into the hotel and called Detective Bob Bogison to let him know I had arrived and confirm when he would pick me up for the Criminal Justice Class. As I was unpacking, I suddenly felt a deep, sharp pain on my left side below the rib cage. The pain was so intense that I was forced to lie down on the bed. The detective soon arrived and was waiting outside. Slowly getting up off the bed, I looked at myself in the mirror before walking out the door. I saw a nicely dressed woman whose face was very pale and her eyes were filled with pain. I also sensed something else more foreboding and dire. Saying a prayer, I walked out the door and climbed into his car with a smile on my face. As we drove through the town heading for the college, he commented, "You look like you are not feeling good. Do you need to go to the hospital?" I saw a deep sense of worry in his eyes. "Are you sure that you feel good enough to do this?" With my head down, I softly replied that I would be alright and thanked him for his concern. I dreaded the next question that I knew was coming from him because I had all the symptoms of a victim of domestic violence including shame, the fear that no one would believe me, and feelings of isolation. While many stay in such relationships, I had the strength to leave but still carried a variety of heavy emotions inside. Once we have the strength to speak out, that is when we find we are not alone anymore. Taking a deep breath, I knew it was time to be brave and answer the question that was going to arrive next.

His extensive years of investigative experience gave him the scent that something dark had occurred. "Do you mind me asking, what happened to you?" he said softly as we headed slowly up the street. Despite wanting to keep silent about that night, suddenly, fighting back the tears, the incident spilled out of me. I could feel this man's energy as he fought to keep his composure, sensing that he was shocked, then feeling his quiet anger when uttering a few strong words under his breath regarding my husband. As he parked the car, he pulled a small notepad out of his suit jacket. He assured me that if I needed anything, he would be there for me. "You won't have to be afraid when living here," he said firmly. "We will keep an eye on you when you get settled." He then asked for my husband's name and birth date and the address of the house in Sacramento. While he was making notes of this and the location where I was currently living in Sacramento, he looked up and said I was to keep in contact with him until I moved to Reno. "Under no circumstances are you to be alone with this guy again. If you must make contact, do it in a public place and if you can, take someone with you." Shaking his head, he said, "If there is a problem, you pick up the phone, call the police there and call me!" He looked, into my eyes again and firmly asked, "am I making myself clear?" As his words entered my being, I nodded my head in agreement. It was the first safe feeling that I had since that fateful night. It was the first time someone showed concern about me regarding the traumatic situation with my husband, and I suddenly realized how alone I had been since it happened. My heart was saddened for this man who professed his love for me, asked me to marry him then revealed a very dark, dangerous Jekyll and Hyde persona. From that day forward, he showed not the slightest concern or care about me, doing everything in his power to deny and distance himself. I would not want his karma.

After opening up to this kind detective, I felt relieved. I prayed for strength as we entered the Criminal Justice classroom. My strong mind proved to be a gift to me at that moment. Somehow, I managed to control my pain to a great degree and my lecture was very successful. Happy that my presentation was well received, we left the college and climbed back into the detective's car. He shared with me his impression of my work and he asked further questions, "Elaina, how are you able to see and feel these things related to a murder?" I replied, "I don't totally understand that myself, guess we will learn the answer to that one together." Those words brought us both a good laugh and would come to be a prophetic statement occurring many times in the coming years as we worked on cases together. In December of 1985, I warned this investigator about being in the line of fire around the day of January 18th, 1986. I envisioned him in the early morning hours, outside in the dark. There would be a flash accompanied by a loud noise to his immediate left. I told him that he would survive the ordeal. At the time, Detective Bogison did not know he would be going back out on the streets in a patrol car on January 18th, 1986, and that he would find himself in this danger that I described. A shootout would occur and the perpetrator would be killed.

At that moment in the car, I did not know that the deep pain getting stronger inside me, warning of danger, would walk with me as I moved closer to the month of May! Destiny or Death kept occurring one way or the other each month for this detective and I. All I knew was that I felt blessed that this man had lived. When we got back to the hotel, the kind detective placed his business card in my hand and said, "Call me if you need anything while you are here or when you are home." Thanking him and saying goodbye, I went back to my hotel room feeling the resurfacing of that deep pain on my left side…the flash recurring in my head of my husband throwing me down on that step. The thought of food was not appealing as I placed my purse on the table and walked towards the bed. Closing my eyes, I prayed that God would help me in the days to come, give me the strength to complete my move, and take my pain away. I had to return to Sacramento in the next couple of days to finish packing. Despite the fear that remained, I was comforted now that this detective knew what had happened and had information should anything happen to me again. The Angels were bringing my protectors near to me. To this day, I still do not have a clue how I made it through the coming months: getting settled in my new home, staying alive, but living in denial of the reasons for all the nonstop pain. Angels had to be walking each step with me because I should not have been able to do all that I did. The nagging pain on my left side was increasing and I was experiencing a hypersensitivity of impending violence for others. My world changed more each day as my feet now stepped upon the path, called the Valley of the Shadow of Death.

Ultimately Great Responsibility

"The world is a dangerous place, not because of those who do evil, but because of those who look on and do nothing." ~ Albert Einstein

Even the month of May had life-changing consequences not only for me but for a few of those I loved. Little did I know that one year later my life would almost end again and a dear friend's life would end in the month of May. On an early Sunday morning May 17, 1987 I was awakened from a deep sleep by the ringing of my phone. My dear friend, Mabs Martin's son, Jim Whiting, was calling me. Dread and panic filled me as I heard the police radios in the background. I heard fear in Jim's voice. He pleaded with me to come quickly to Mabs' house! "Elaina, its Jimmy! Mom's missing. She did not come home last night…none of them did! I need you to come over fast! Please help us find them!" Heading for her house that quiet, early morning, I had a sick feeling in my bones that would become a familiar signal too many times in the years to come. At the four way stop sign on Longley Lane, there were no cars in sight. Looking up at Mt. Rose, with my eyes scanning left and right, I asked out loud, "Mabs, where are you? Show me girl!" As I crossed the road, I suddenly looked in the rearview mirror. I saw her smiling face and heard her voice, "I'm dead honey but please hurry, the girls are still alive!" With a flood of emotions filling me, I drove faster towards her home talking out loud to her. "Oh my God! Please Mabs show me where you are!"

Although it was only a couple of miles away it seemed like eternity! It was the beginning of a horrible nightmare. Time slowed to a crawl and I felt a dark foreboding aura surrounding her place as I pulled into the driveway. I parked my car amidst patrol cars and unmarked cars belonging to detectives and the FBI. My heart was pounding as I sat there silently praying for protection and Archangel St. Michael to bless and helps us all to find my dear friend and those with her. Taking a deep breath, I walked to the door where Jimmy was waiting with tears in his eyes. He guided me into the house. Upon entering the home, I saw it was filled with police, detectives, FBI agents and those radios that I had heard in the background when I answered the call. Standing in the kitchen with Mabs' son and seeing the desperation in his eyes was heartbreaking. The feelings were like nothing I had ever experienced in my life. I am called to the house of a dear friend who was kidnapped and murdered and now forced to put those feelings aside and become the psychic detective. My empathic abilities were being activated along with every vibration of that home in the past and present. That day I was introduced to FBI Agent Dave Spencer from the Reno office. Little did we know that morning destiny would arrive again in the future for us. There would come another time in our lives we would find ourselves working together once again. As I was leaving Mabs' house, I was invited to go down to the police department to see if I could assist the task force that was in the process of being formed. As the investigator closed my car door with a "Thank you for coming," his words changed my life once again. "We will call you once we are ready." I heard a strong whisper that there was no time for becoming emotional! I could hear Mabs' words whispered to me in the car "Please hurry, honey! The girls are still alive!" The days and hours to come seemed surreal. It is called "time is of the essence." After checking in at the front desk of the Reno Police Station, I headed down the hall towards Robbery Homicide whispering to myself, "You can't break down now Elaina no time for that! You must be brave now and help find these girls alive! It's too late for Mabs and her friend Dorothy Walsh." It felt like Mabs was walking behind me keeping me moving forward despite my dread of what awaited me at the end of that hallway. Feeling my persona shift into warrior mode, I took a deep breath and prepared myself to enter the nightmare that was waiting for me behind the door at the end of the hall. With each step, I asked for strength to prepare me for the moment I would enter that room. There were also uniformed officers in the hall coming and going from their shift. Many knew who I was and what room I was heading for. I saw the look in some of their eyes, the silent nod of their heads. Hearing one familiar face saying, "Thanks for coming, Proffitt," they knew Mabs had been a close friend of mine.

In a matter of seconds, I found myself in front of a door that would take me into an evil world of pain and horrific acts. Taking in a deep breath to center myself, I then exhaled my personal feelings and entered the task force room. As I took a seat at a large table with the FBI agents and detectives, my whole being was bombarded by all that was happening in that room. The maps on the large conference table and a board on the wall filled with notes gave the room an intense energy. You could cut the air with a knife! This was no movie or TV show…this was the real deal, live and up close, what the public does not see! The energy in the room was electrifying. A thought quickly crossed my mind as my eyes scanned each investigator in the room. I knew that this killer was going to having a powerful force to reckon with because they were all coming for him!

There was an FBI agent sitting across from me with a very serious look on his face. His piercing eyes gazed into mine, and he had a quiet but powerful presence. I was wondering how he would perceive me and the strange message I received from my dear friend in the car that I needed to pass onto him. His words soon put me at ease. "Thank you for coming, Ms. Proffitt. I have been briefed on you and what you do and know that Mabs was a close friend of yours." Looking directly into my eyes with kindness in his voice he said, "I know this must be very hard on you and we appreciate anything that you can tell us to help resolve this case swiftly."

It was in that room that I felt one of the heaviest burdens in my life. When you have the ability to feel and experience another person's agony and pain while being murdered, it is indescribable. When it is someone you know personally and care about deeply, it is a nightmare! When you know that innocent young girls are being harmed and could also die at any moment, the pressure becomes overwhelming. It took all my strength, calling on Archangel Saint Michael to help me step aside from all my personal feelings; become detached from the pain, and step into the calm center of the cyclone to bring me clarity and focus. My whole being was raw and the blood in my veins felt ice cold. I had to stay centered and allow my mind and abilities to become a forensic tool. My empathic abilities kicked in as I sat across from the agent. I knew he was a force to be reckoned with, a seasoned hunter of predators. I felt safe with this man knowing he was open to listen to me no matter how crazy I may sound. I was also grateful that the investigators who knew me had assured him that I was not one to send them out on a wild goose chase. Taking a deep breath, I then shared with him a strange event that happened the day before Mabs went missing. She had called and invited me to go with her the next day up to Lake Tahoe. I can still hear her voice with that happy Southern Lady drawl now reflected in my own. "Oh, come on now honey, go with us it will be a nice day at the lake Elaina. We should be back by 12:30." She then told me how she had met a nice young man and he had picked them for the anti-drug commercial. She hated drug abuse and was a member of **M.A.D.D.** (Mothers Against Drunk Driving.) I had considered going but thankfully listened to my inner guidance. I needed to stay home and rest. Despite her repeated invitations, I reminded her that I was still recovering from my own medical drama in May the prior year…still with one foot on Earth and one in Heaven. "Sorry, Mabs. I am not feeling up to a day trip. I will see you next week." Suddenly, I felt something. I could not quite pinpoint exactly what it was but I had that heavy feeling in my bones. "Mabs, do you feel okay? Girl! I am worried about you! I want you to slow down and to rest more or you are going to end up in the hospital also." I then proceeded to give her a lecture about how she was always on the go and I did not want her to have a heart attack or an accident. Mabs promised me she would not work so hard after they all got back from Lake Tahoe, with the nice young man, the photographer. Then there was her cheerful "Love you honey" and "See you on Monday" which would be the last words I would ever hear her speak to me when she was alive.

Mabs Martin would end up being a real angel in a matter of hours and now I was sitting in the task force room trying to help find her and those who were with her. Suddenly, I felt my eyes become full, taking on what is described to me by investigators as a glassy or vacant look. That is when I am out of my body, in another place and observing my surroundings or becoming the victim or perpetrator. (Remote Viewing) I was now in what I call "level". It is then that dialogues begin between the investigators and myself. I retain very little of the conversations unless I am in a work mode; then I have total recall. I also have flashes of standing up with my back next to that white board with all the writing on it and I was looking down at the large map on the table. My fingers touching certain areas and describing the surroundings. I saw what appeared to be a bedroom with what seemed to be shag carpet. "That's where Mabs is…on the floor!" Flashes of terror ran through me and my throat hurt and I felt like I was wrapped in something. I saw green. There were flashes of another room that seemed to have no windows. "That's where the girls are!" I felt the water was not far away.

Time stood still in that room and when I walked out of there, I was weary from the all the varieties of energies that I had spent. In my heart, I knew that I had done all that I could and prayed that it would help the investigators capture this psycho and find the girls alive! My heart was still filled with a deep pain knowing I would not rest until this nightmare was over. Most often it is a longtime after the experience that I receive total confirmation by an investigator who worked with me. I will not speak of all the things that this evil person did to them all. My dear friend and her elderly friend suffered greatly and did not deserve to die the way they did. God blessed us with the girls surviving their ordeal and they were rescued just in time! I know Mabs was smiling when the task force found them.

This time for me, it would not be a stranger murdered but someone close to me that I loved. Maybelle "Mabs" Martin, 69 years old, and her friend Dorothy Walsh, 73, along with two young girls from her modeling agency. Alecia Thoma, 14 and Monica Berge 12 had been lured and kidnapped, and Mabs with her friend Dorothy had been murdered by a 28-year-old serial killer named Herbert Coddington, posing as a professional photographer doing a shoot for an anti-drug campaign. He drove to Reno in a BMW with the unusual license plate TVETEEN to scout local modeling agencies for victims. None of the girls fit his fantasy until he arrived at Showcase Finishing and Modeling Agency owned by Maybelle "Mabs" Martin. Within 24 hours her car, a white Chrysler New Yorker, was found at Lampson's Plaza, a South Lake shopping center. It was near the "Y" where highway 50 and Stateline 99 meet. It was also close to Coddington's residence at the Tahoe Verdi Trailer Park where they would find his car with the license plate they were looking for. Inside the mobile home, they found the bodies of Mabs Martin and her friend Dottie Clark Walsh wrapped tightly in garbage bags. They were in the rear bedroom. They had been strangled with Flex-Cuf. 2 ligatures that could not be released once cinched up. He would not get the insanity plea with all the writings/notes he had made regarding the deliberate steps he had taken to create this heinous nightmare…turning a dark fantasy into reality. There was other evidence that showed his intent, including the two survivors. He was sloppy and had left his finger prints on a model portfolio at another agency, and a trail of bread crumbs to his location. The jury would find him guilty of two counts of first degree murder with multiple charges. He was sentenced to death on January 20, 1989 and now resides at San Quentin Prison's Death Row.

His mission had been to control the two young girls who were with Mabs' modeling agency Showcase Models. In her final moments, Mabs Martin's last words to her killer would be, "Don't take the girls! Take Us!" Until the end, her concern was for the girls even offering her own life…which he assured her…he would be doing just that.

After the girls were found and the funerals took place, it was bittersweet. I could not attend my dear friend's "goodbye." I was so weak and open empathically that I would have collapsed from all the grieving and pain in the room, that of her son Jimmy as well as my own. I also was still fragile and trying to restore my own health from my close call in May of 1986. Sharing my inner conflict with an investigator about going to the service, I was told it had been a concern of a few of them. Some had been worried about what would happen to me after all that I had been involved in and what would happen when walking into that room. Those days became a blur for me, and unless someone shares with me what I was doing, I still cannot remember. When I look at the photo in the newspaper of people at the service there are flickers of feelings but no recall. It took a long time for me to clear out all of what I had seen, felt and experienced on so many levels. I have no regrets. I would do it all over again.

Life is fragile and choices can be dangerous or they can save our lives. It is for all of us, one foot on Earth and the other in Heaven. I had a choice that Friday afternoon on the phone with Mabs; should I stay home or go with her? I could have been in her White Chrysler New Yorker that day heading up to the lake but something told me not to go. Years later, I was speaking on the phone with Retired FBI Agent Dave Spencer. I told him that I wondered what would have happened if I had been with them that day. Spencer told me, "We talked about that Elaina and we strongly felt he would not have pursued it." He then said, "Your presence would have unnerved him." At times, I wonder…if his words were true.

Twenty-eight years after that horrific crime, I heard another validation of what came through me in those dark days. At last, my pain-filled heart found some comfort, knowing that my participation in the search was not in vain. Retired police officer Pam Engle and I attended the Reno Police and Detective Association Ball in the winter of 2015. That night I was able to spend time with several investigators that I had worked with on various cases throughout the years. Retired Detective Dave Larsen reminded me of the time we worked together on a multimillion dollar diamond ring theft and the trip up to Lake Tahoe. "Elaina, you had no idea where we were going and somehow, you became a GPS and guided me to the front door of the suspect!" We had a good laugh, and then the mood shifted. Retired Detective Randy Houston shared a very powerful part of the search for Mabs Martin, her friend Dorothy and the girls. "Elaina, I have never forgotten what you told me sitting in the break room at the PD when you told me about the chaperones, the girls and the three trees. I remember being amazed when I saw the circumstances surrounding the case when they were rescued…your telling me prior to going up to Lake Tahoe that they would be found near a store in a specific location…that when I got out of the car to look up; there would be an unusual tree that had what appeared to be three limbs...you said to me, 'Mabs and those with her were very near.' If I then looked up a bit further, that was the location that they would be found with the killer. There was a window that you could see the lake from." Tears filled my eyes. This was a most humbling gift from spirit, hearing his confirmation. Often when doing investigative work many times I have no further communication regarding an incident and never know the outcome of my work. Also, it was rare that there were victims that were alive on the cases I worked on. My heart filled with joy that the girls were found alive...and are living good lives to this day. Despite the personal pain I experienced, I feel blessed to have been a small part of this tragic case and to have worked with so many talented investigators throughout the years. It is a most humbling experience to this day. Working on the murder case of a dear friend and almost being in that car are amazing odds. My life has never been the norm. It seems one foot on Earth and one in Heaven follows me in a myriad of ways. So many have been filled with danger but always with angels intervening.

"Let me tell you something, there are a lot of kooks out there. You have to be careful."

Those were Mabs Martin's final words to her son as they worked in the flower garden the day before she died. Her last words to me alive were, "See you on Monday, honey! I Love you."

Her last words to me from the Other Side, "I'm Dead. Please hurry honey! The girls are still alive!" are words that will walk with me to my grave!

Prophecy

During the years of my investigative work, I developed a most powerful and unusual sixth sense that activated anytime a police officer's life was in impending danger. Since suffering my domestic violence injury and the perpetual nagging pain associated with it, something mysterious began happening to me. Detective Eubanks was the first one to experience this most unusual and dangerous prediction phenomenon. One day I looked at Detective Eubanks and envisioned him being involved in a shootout. I immediately shared my vision with him and warned him about being in the line of fire within a matter of days. With a surprised look on his face, he asked me to be more specific. As if turning on a faucet, words suddenly began spilling out of me describing the event in accurate detail including the location, time of day, and the background of the aggressor that was specifically involved. As I looked at Detective Eubanks, I saw and felt a very strong death vibration around him. Forty-eight hours after our conversation, Detective Eubanks was involved in a bank robbery stakeout and encountered the armed robbery suspect who deliberately attempted to shoot him. The suspect was shot to death by Detective Eubanks' partner, Detective Bob Penagore, from an angle of advantage. Detective Eubanks took a lot of teasing in the days prior when he wore his body armor, a bullet-resistant vest, each time he went out on a call in very hot weather. Within this same timeframe, very intense and powerful things were happening to me. I had one foot on Earth and one in Heaven regarding my own physical condition. My health issues were becoming more serious as each week and month passed. My gift of sight was also becoming stronger on many levels. The premonition about Detective Eubanks was not the only one that I had. I had additional visions and premonitions about other officers which helped them avoid serious harm and even death.

During one of my visits to the Reno Robbery Homicide Division, I soon met other investigators and was invited to speak at a Criminal Justice class at the local University. My life was quickly turning in a variety of strange and serious directions as I was preparing for my move.

Pain and prophecy intertwined in my life. Along with the intense pain-filled work I was performing, I was also experiencing my own intermittent and increasing physical discomfort. I also had a sensation that a portal was opening for me, and I felt like I was being pulled into another dimension. I started feeling as light as a feather…lighter and lighter with each passing day. My spirit hovered between the real and ethereal, and I saw and felt visions and sensations about the lives or deaths of others. With each passing week and month my pain threshold continued to increase. I heard constant whispers telling me that something was horribly wrong inside my body. Everywhere I went I felt that chronic nagging reminder on my left side…followed with my whisper, "It will go away soon."

The Forgetful Man

Predictions for these investigators continued through the years. I would hear, see and feel violence and death around them describing the scene as if I was watching a movie. I also had visions of other life-changing events for those I worked with. One night I began working with Detective/Sergeant Steve Pitts of Robbery Homicide on a very bizarre high-profile case that would soon be called "Amnesia Man." Michael Ritter vanished the night of September 16th, 1988 after telling his wife on the telephone that a man was at the office door saying his car had broken down and he needed to use the telephone. The next morning his business partner found their office ransacked and bloodstained…alluding to foul play. There was also over $5,000 missing along with the man's car. Twelve days later, some very strange and most bizarre anonymous letters were sent to the Los Angeles Times newspaper and the Reno Gazette Journal. It would also be a long three weeks of continuing drama.

Soon, I got a phone call from his poor distraught wife asking if I would help find her husband. My heart went out to her and I said I would do so if the police department contacted me. I tried to comfort her. I explained that if the police did contact me I would have to cease all communication with her, and I would be working exclusively with law enforcement so as not to compromise the case. I told her that she must agree and try to understand that I worked in this field in a very different way than other psychics. I said goodbye to her and prayed that this crisis would be resolved fast and with a good ending.

Chaos quickly ensued when a psychic from California contacted the man's wife and the Department stating that the alleged victim was out in the desert with his hands behind his back lying face down. The town was in a frenzy with what this woman was saying to the press. Soon, helicopters, the fire department and others began fervently looking for this man. The case appeared to be getting out of control, and needed to shift into a more organized direction and back into the hands of the police. It was then, I received a phone call from Sergeant Steve Pitts asking if I would be able to meet him that evening at an address given to me. The determination in his voice said it all; he was going to get to the bottom of this mess now and get some clarity fast! I learned that night that when Steve was involved, it would be "step up to the plate and hit a home run" because no one would rest until it happened. The thought also crossed my mind that the California psychic would be scared to death of Steve which I must confess brought a smile to my face; she was wasting critical time and resources with her alleged predictions. Before we hung up the phone, Steve also asked if it would be okay for award-winning Senior Reporter Ed Pearce from KOLO TV to shoot a Secret Witness segment that included showing me working that night. They agreed to watch from an outside window to avoid distracting me and since my work is usually kept out of the public eye.

In a matter of hours, I was at the crime scene and introduced to Ed Pearce. I felt comfortable in his presence and after we talked for a few minutes, he went to prepare his cameraman for getting the shots he wanted when I entered the office. I then started working. First, I was shown all the areas in the office building. My sensory perception started to activate. I was left alone in the victim's office while Detective Pitts and Ed Pearce were just outside, close to the window. The cameras were also rolling. After I scanned the room for a few minutes, I felt that something was not right with this crime scene. I kept returning to an area of the carpet despite having no clues as to why. I had none of the strange symptoms that usually filled my body such as smacking my lips or tasting blood (mirroring what usually happened to victims at other crime scenes and confirmed on other extremely violent cases involving lots of blood).

After a while, I walked outside into the dark night, looking in all directions. I asked silently to receive the answers as to why I was getting such a strange vibe in that office. It felt empty, not like other scenes where a crime had occurred. Still, I kept trying to receive the signals that are usually given to me in these types of situations…but got nothing once more. Suddenly, Detective Pitts approached me in the dark, his voice bringing me back from my inner focus. "So, what do you feel about that office?" I shared my confusion and other strange feelings. "Something is just not right in that office." In his commanding voice, he said, "I want to know one thing. Are we or are we not dealing with a possible kidnapping-homicide here and is this man out in the desert as the other alleged psychic states?" His eyes held mine with that powerful demeanor, commanding answers from me. And I blurted out, "No! He is not in the desert and he is alive! Detective Pitts, something is really off here!" As I looked behind Detective Pitts at the mountains and shadows in the night sky, my eyes again scanned in all directions. I felt a flicker of the missing man's energy in my intuitive radar. "It feels like he is going south. I see sunshine, California!" He said, "That's what I needed. And now we can go with what I felt also. This is staged and no kidnapping-murder!"

The accuracy of my statement was reinforced in the days to come as I continued working Detective Pitts; what I was feeling and seeing was spot-on on many levels. He also clarified why I kept returning to that certain spot in the office. "I don't know how you did it but you kept returning to the exact area where a pair of broken glasses with a speck of blood were found!" He also told me that he and Ed Pearce were watching me through the window, waiting for me to show some of the usual symptoms that I have when reenacting a murder. He said that I didn't, for example, touch my throat (which felt mushy if it was death by strangulation), smack my lips (if there was a stabbing or lots of blood) or the other signals that would happen to me.

Side note: Recently I was speaking with Ed Pearce and we were reminiscing about that dark night of the "Amnesia Man" investigation. I asked Ed Pearce what he was doing when I started working inside the scene that night. Ed responded, "I was an observant, sneaky reporter that night. Staying where I could watch you work and putting myself within earshot so I could hear what you said to Steve Pitts when you emerged. As I recall you said something like 'This is weird. It's not a crime scene.' You were right!"

I discovered that each high-profile case on which I consulted had a complex inner world within the investigation that the public was not aware of. It's like being in the center of a cyclone, assessing the chaos, potential danger, and pain that I had to enter with the investigators. This is the reality of what it feels like to have such a heavy burden. There is an understanding that the reason for the focus, commitment and desire to leave no stone unturned, sometimes goes on for years. Spending time in a Robbery Homicide Division tells many stories. An office desk reveals many things about the person who sits at it, and it whispers of their inner drive and what makes them tick. This is especially true when it is the desk of a detective. And it was with Steve Pitts' cubical where, along with the photo of a murder victim and a mug shot or two, there were two powerful visuals posted to the wall. One was the photo of a 357 Magnum with the barrel facing you and the other was a powerful quote tying it all together:

"There is no hunting like the hunting of man and those who have hunted armed men long enough and liked it, never care for anything else thereafter"- Ernest Hemmingway

Through the years, I also learned that it is an addiction in some ways. Like a chess game, this work tests the mind and capabilities against a dangerous perpetrator, and one is literally under the gun to stop the nightmare from happening again and to bring justice for the families of the victims. As the focus of the investigation started to quickly come together, the Reno Police Department held a press conference to clear up the media reports that were given by the California psychic who was claiming that the missing man was out in the desert with hands tied behind his back. The investigators stated that the California psychic's information was not accurate and they had not asked for her assistance. The department also clarified that there was only one psychic that they consulted with on occasion…Elaina Proffitt, who had been quite helpful regarding this case, and had provided very accurate information on numerous cases prior to this one. "Amnesia man" would become a high-profile case in a matter of days. This "victim" also became a writer of that persona, "Amnesia Man." Through his bizarre writings to the L. A. Times and the Reno Gazette Journal during his travels, a 50-page diary was created. When I am working on a case that is in the media a lot, I try not to watch the news or read the newspaper. I want my own interpretations to arrive without seeds being planted by outside sources. During the next three weeks, upon a visit to the task force room, I felt he had moved to another location. I saw what appeared to be southern Nevada. At some point, I also kept picking up something very confusing about the trunk of a car. In one of the bizarre ramblings in the diary sent to the newspapers, Amnesia Man had awakened to find himself locked in the trunk of a car. The complete "Amnesia Man" journey can be found online. It was quite the adventure not only for him but for his family and all the agencies trying to find him! On October 8, 1988, he returned to Reno in an alleged "state of confusion and amnesia." I never could understand if that was true, how could he find the church that he belonged to? Which was not close to town? He then said, "I don't know who I am. I want you to help me find my family." The good part of this drama is that no one was dead out in the desert.

I must make something clear. Psychics do not come in and solve a crime. Good detective work does. And sometimes they get assisted by new pieces of key information which can help them escape their tunnel vision; they use the information shared by a real psychic that can tie it all together for a powerful resolution.

Note: In May, 2015 while having lunch with soon-to-be-retired Police Chief, Steve Pitts and his wife Tamera, Steve and I were reminiscing about the work we had done together. I reminded him of the prediction I had made about him one day at the police department. I felt and saw a position of great responsibility and power coming into his life many years down the road. A heavier burden would be placed upon his shoulders. It would be a path that he never thought he would step foot on because he had other goals in mind. He was not pleased when I told him that I did not see him leaving the building. And sure enough, later in life he would become Chief of the Reno Police Department having an amazing career.

Consulting on cases also brought me the understanding that I was not the only one who had extra sensory perception or felt impending danger. Those individuals who work in law enforcement also have "hunches" from time to time when working up a case at a murder scene or when patrolling the streets in daily life-threatening situations.

Near-death experiences (NDEs) occur in many ways and they leave a deep awareness and many unanswered questions about what is beyond this physical realm. Those in law enforcement are also affected (underneath that strong demeanor they carry) in each case they encounter. Often to the public, officers seem distant and cold when speaking with the grieving families of victims or at the crime scene. They do not have the luxury of baring their emotions. Their work requires that they push their feelings aside in order to continue searching for a perpetrator or when they are standing at a horrific scene for hours with the dead.

Reno Police Officer, Pam Engle was at the scene Thanksgiving Day in 1980 when Pricilla Ford began her driving rampage down the sidewalk of Virginia Street in downtown Reno. Ford drove so close to Officer Engle that she had to jump back to avoid being hit as Ford continued to drive down the sidewalk! Officer Engle watched in horror as Ford struck down a total of twenty-six people; five people were killed immediately while others died from their injuries later. A living nightmare, the gutters and sidewalk were covered with debris, clothing, body parts, the injured, and the dead. People cried out in agony as Pricilla Ford accelerated to 40 mph and continued to drive her Lincoln Continental 100 feet down the sidewalk on Virginia Street trying to hit more people...all this with a body lying on her car. The sound of ambulances and police sirens added to the heinous site as Officer Engle watched the drama unfold as if in slow motion. It was like being in the center of a cyclone. Officer Engle tried to remain calm as she called into dispatch to get emergency responders on their way. As her eyes continued to see death and destruction all around her, she triaged the situation and informed emergency responders so they could assist the injured versus the dead.

On foot, she ran after the car that was preceding Northbound on Virginia street. Everything seemed to happen in slow motion as she tried to keep a field visual to notify other officers which way Ford was heading. At last, at the 6th and Virginia intersection, Pricilla Ford's car stalled due to the amount of damage caused by the bodies and obstacles that she had struck. Officer Engle remained at the scene until 7:00 p.m. that night until released from duty. She had no time to breakdown or process what she had just been through. All the suffering victims were more important at that moment. When she was released from the scene, Officer Engle returned to the station for debriefing...reliving the carnage again. The next morning she was required to be at briefing, acting as if nothing had happened. After the briefing, she got into her patrol car and drove to 2nd and Virginia. While stopped at the traffic light, Officer Engle was suddenly struck with a case of PTSD causing her to experience powerful flashbacks of what she had witnessed the previous day. She returned to the station immediately! Shocked and upset, she told the watch commander what had happened and was sent home using her own sick time. No counseling of any kind was provided, and the officers on the scene had to deal with their personal traumas on their own. To this day, Officer Engle can still see Pricilla Ford in that car and the results of her dark deeds...and so do many others who were working that day.

The public does not see what I have seen when leaving the house of a family whose children have disappeared or been murdered. They do not see the tears in the investigators eyes and the dead silence in the car as we start heading for another location, or the deep sadness in their hearts. I have. And as a strong empath, I have also felt their deep pain. The officers are the forgotten victims at these times. The public does not know or care what they are feeling when they arrive at a murder scene or how it impacts their daily home life. No one knows what the officers experience as they sit for hours with a psychopath trying to find answers while not reacting to the story of the horrific things that were done to a victim. Sadly, there is indifference from citizens because with our busy lives, we don't care or want to know. We just want them to solve the crime and do it fast…in about two hours like a Clint Eastwood movie.

I formed bonds with investigators, their families and others that remain unbroken to this day. I could not see the reasons that these warriors came into my life so quickly, until many years later. We all choose a path to walk in life. Some of us travel a more powerful, pain-filled and dangerous road. However, doors also open to help so many who have had a loved one fall victim to a heinous crime. In the years to come, many souls would show up on my doorstep seeking comfort and understanding.

New Beginnings

At last, my move to Reno was completed in December of 1985. January, 1986 arrived with my new roots established. I loved my new, cozy apartment and it felt safe. I continued doing talk shows, seeing clients and living a generally busy life. Reno was good to me and I met many loving people who welcomed me into the community. However, the dark reminder from my physical injuries would not go away. I continued trying to dismiss it, denying its existence, how long it had been there, and the reason why! My mind was strong and it was as if I could separate myself from it for periods of time. The nagging, chronic pain was something that I wanted to forget as well as the how it was caused in the first place. I heard the whisper, "It will go away," each time the pain occurred.

With each passing month, denial was my constant companion as I kept telling myself it was just a bruise. Using my ability to go into an altered state of mind, I put myself into a deep, meditative state and tried to remain there as long as possible because it caused the pain to go away. My ability to project a lot of my pain "somewhere" outside of my body allowed me to work for periods of time. At times, when I got dressed and looked in the mirror, I could see that my weight kept dropping and the trauma victim I saw in the mirror started to be revealed. My eyes were changing from the pain. Even my skin was becoming sallow. On my left side, there was a deep, sickening pain below my ribcage that was wrapping around my side. Pain was whispering louder with every passing day, week, and month that something was wrong! Terribly wrong! Then it stopped for a while. It is fascinating to me how we can go into denial when a life-threatening illness or emotional trauma touches our lives. In light of my current dilemma, it seemed that I was getting educated not only about the body, but also the mind, heart, and soul as well. I could not have ever imagined where this would take me along life's journey.

Looking back, I am amazed that I had five months of emergency room visits, and when a doctor finally arrived for me, he was never in town. I was a walking time bomb that would, in a short while, go through a door on a journey from which I may not return.

Aloha

The New Year 1986 arrived and in the month of February I felt the need to go to Maui. It kept calling to me with the hope that I would find rest from the pain that I was trying to escape and praying the ocean would heal me. A new Reno client, Johanna, owned a condo there and invited me to visit her in Maui when I was still living in Sacramento. Her husband had died and I had been walking her through this painful event each time I went to Reno prior to my move. Johanna was a beautiful and kind woman and there was an immediate friendship from the first time we met. We had a lovely time and I felt an immediate connection to this beautiful island. Johanna introduced me to other residents that also had beautiful island homes in the Kihei area and I quickly found myself with a few new clients. Now at last living in Reno, one day she suggested that I go to Maui to rest and get some sunshine and that I was welcome to stay in her condo. "I have some dates open in the weeks to come, why don't you go? See some of your new clients, relax and maybe the sun and the beautiful ocean will make you feel better and heal," she said cheerfully. In a short time, I was on an airplane heading for the islands. For some reason, I wanted to be with my dear friend Janet who had moved to the island. When I told her that I was coming over, she said she wanted to take me to a few places to recharge my battery and have me experience the beauty of the tropical surroundings. Janet always took good care of me when we both lived in Sedona and her knowledge of healing, nutrition, herbs and energy brought me comfort. We were the first metaphysical people allowed in Sedona, Arizona in the early '70s. We were flower children, "hippies," and while they usually ran those types of people out of town, we found helpers in that beautiful place and opened up a shop in a large house at the end of town. We had a wonderful Natural Foods Restaurant and Herb Shop which included a variety of metaphysical books in my section of the store. All my life, children were always drawn to me and soon there was a young Hopi boy who came into the store with a group of Native Americans. For months, none of them would speak but finally this young boy did. He followed me around asking questions about the books and spirits. He slowly opened up to me about his life. One sunny afternoon he told me about his grandfather (who was the Medicine Man) and how he used herbs to heal...not the white man's medicine. "My grandfather can see spirits and has big medicine. He uses these things when sick people come to see him." Moving closer to me he quietly asked, "Do you have more of these?" pointing to the shelves filled with a variety of herbs in big glass jars. Janet was filling a plastic bag from one of the herb jars. Smiling at him I replied, "Yes, we do. See that lady standing there? She knows a lot about how to use them; so tell your grandfather that if he wants some just let us know." Out the door he went with a wave and in a matter of time we got an important message...the medicine man wanted to buy our herbs! That conversation had opened the door to our providing the Hopi Nation with all the herbs that they needed. We prepared for days and nights to receive the Chief, his wife and First Council at our place for dinner in order to discuss the business of purchasing herbs from us. For us, it was like having the President and First Lady of the United States come to the house!

Knowing I was going to see Janet in Maui made my heart joyful and brought back the good memories of our years together.

At last! The airplane was over the ocean and looking down at the water filled me with peace. Soon the Hawaiian Air flight attendants were pushing the cart up the aisle offering a free Mai Tai drink that was wearing an umbrella and small orchid. The flight attendant placed the drink upon my tray along with some packets of macadamia nuts. It was the perfect way to start my trip. Sipping on the rum drink, I prayed my tummy would not start hurting because it was just too good to turn down and the wonderful relaxing feeling it brought me was exactly what I needed. Looking out across the water was so soothing and soon I drifted off to sleep. At some point, I woke up to the sound of the captain over the speaker telling us that a movie would be playing soon and the headphones would be handed out. The flight was enjoyable and it seemed time stood still. The plane touched down and I entered the airport feeling immediate peace. I picked up my rental car, the map to the condo, and headed onto the road with a sigh of relief; I was on the island at last! Driving with the window down, breathing in the soothing island breeze, I soon arrived at the condo. Carefully lifting my suitcase out of the trunk, I stood there for a moment taking it all in…the sun, the crystal blue water so close, the trade winds, and the sweet scent of flowers filling me with life force. The sensation was intoxicating. With key in hand, I opened the door and entered the living room. Outside the sliding glass door was a beautiful ocean view calling to me. Stepping out onto the lanai, the sound of the ocean was welcoming me. I was tired and happy but felt that I must rest also. I took my suitcase into the bedroom, unpacked, and headed for the shower. A nice shower was perfect and soothed my body. I decided to go down to the pool, get some sun and get in the water. I relaxed for a while and then went down to the grocery store that Johanna had taken me to the first trip. It was a perfect afternoon and I felt blessed as I drifted in and out to the sound of the waves nearby. I talked myself into getting some groceries before sunset. Putting on my island cover up and sandals I jumped into the car and drove to the store. I filled my cart with pineapples, mangos, papayas, bananas, avocados, sprouts, tomatoes, cheese, and a loaf of fresh bread to make some sandwiches. Turning the corner, the Hana Bay rum on the shelf caught my eye and then I headed for the juice section for the carton of Pog (a blend of Papaya, Orange, and Guava) island fruits that went perfect with the rum. Once again, I prayed that it would not bring me pain in my stomach. On the way to the checkout, I grabbed a can of macadamia nuts including some with chocolate. I was ready to get back and watch the sun go down over the water, which is always the highlight of every day in the islands. After I got back to the condo and unpacked the grocery bags, I called a client that I had seen during my first trip and let her know I had returned and to pass the word that I was available for readings. Before the sun went down, I planted the seeds for a variety of activities. Finally, I watched the sun slowly set on the horizon. A lovely first day in paradise was about to end, and after watching the local news and some TV, I headed for bed.

The very early dawn arrived and the wakeup calls of the birds chirping outside the window started before I knew it. I made some Kona coffee, took it out to the lanai, and enjoyed watching the sunrise. Around midmorning the phone rang with a client wanting to book a session and some friends wanting to do the same. My routine became spending few of my days attending to client appointments and the remainder of my time going to the beach or just resting by the pool. While I felt my energy was higher and light-activated, I also had a strange feeling at times that my feet were on the sand but also…in another place.

The Hallway

One early afternoon while I was reading for a man who was a chiropractor, I closed my eyes and soon was drifting to the sound of the ocean. I suddenly felt my energy shift but not in the usual manner. I started the reading in one direction and was abruptly outside of my body with messages spilling out from what seemed like another dimension, one of foreboding. It seemed like I had gone through a doorway into someplace very far away. I felt what appeared to be people in a dark, cold hallway. In the years to come I would start to recognize this scene many times over and its meaning for me. It is a place where we never want to be, and one that I would find few can go that far into. Most are not allowed in this dark place, and at that moment I discovered there were other powerful abilities being activated inside me like never before. This was not like working on a murder case…traveling to a location and reenacting the crime. Somehow, I found myself in a very dark and strange place! Even I did not understand where I was or what would happen. I felt a blanket of protection wrap around me and I quietly observed my surroundings. My eyes were drawn towards the end of a long corridor to what felt like a beautiful place. It was filled with a light, far away in the distance. I knew I was supposed to be there but for some reason, I remained in the darkness. As I prayed for protection and understanding, a tall, young man appeared before me with his head bowed. A feeling of overwhelming sadness projected towards me. "Hello, who are you?" I called out. Despite my apprehension, I was then guided to ask, "What are you doing here? Are you lost?" There was no response, only waves of emotional pain. I had no feeling inside me telling me to turn and walk away. I moved closer to him without even consciously thinking about doing so. Standing close to him, I heard myself speak, "Can you look at me and tell me why you are in so much pain? I will try to help you, so don't be afraid." His skin looked pale and his cotton plaid shirt was wrinkled and dirty with stains that appeared to be mud or blood. I could only see his profile;. his head was turned to the left, as if hiding from me. I heard my voice echo through the hallway, "Are you hurt? What happened to you?" Moving closer, I felt him try to turn away even more from me. "Don't do that!" I commanded him. "It's alright! Please let me see you so I can help you." Suddenly electricity shot through me and the light flickered around my body as if it was a shield. In the distance and to the side of him, I saw two beings that were waiting for him with peaceful but intense looks upon their faces. I then spoke again, "Do you see those two that are waiting for you? Why don't you go with them? It's alright, you will be safe!" I felt energy spilling from my hands and fingers towards the young man. As he moved slightly, I noticed that my hand was touching his arm, although I didn't remember touching him. "Please let me see you now, I am not afraid. You can't stay here like this. Your family is so worried about you! Don't you know that they still love you?" At that moment, the young man turned towards me. The sight was horrific and one I would see many more times in the years to come…as well as on the Other Side. The whole left side of his face was gone, only blood, torn flesh and gun powder on the areas where the appearance of skin remained. His shirt became alive with wet blood and my heart pounded when his one remaining eye looked directly into mine. The temperature in the hallway became even colder and the hallway was shrinking. Praying for helpers as I looked at this disfigured young man, I heard his request, "My name is Stephen. Can you tell them that I am sorry?" The voice was not coming out of what was left of his mouth. Overwhelming anguish spilled towards me, as with head bowed, once again he whispered, "I just couldn't take anymore." In an instant I knew how he felt; every emotion, conversation, his deep depression and the loss of his girlfriend. I could feel everything that had brought him to that final moment and destructive action. It was as if I was watching a movie filled with sorrow and danger and I could do nothing to stop what was going to happen!

Somehow knowing what I was to do in this awful place, trying hard not to react to the horrific sight of this tortured soul, I then heard myself whisper in a firm but motherly fashion, "Honey, we must clean you up now, and you need to help me." As the words came out of me, healing light ran through me, ready to be activated. It was as if my whole being took on a life of its own in an unfamiliar way. In the years to come I would recognize what this feeling was and how to use it. There was an inner whisper running through me on all levels as if fine tuning my whole being. Instinctively, I knew not to link with the young man's pain. The healing energy as a medical intuitive was inside me, only this time it was on the Other Side, not upon Earth. A form of psychic surgery was activated within me just as I had witnessed when living in Mexico. I had watched those healers from all over the world work on people at paranormal conventions. I even sat next to them when they were visiting my home there, but I did not realize that they may have been working on me also! In the dark cold hallway, a voice (not male or female) whispered to me that I was now working on a young man that was disfigured by a gunshot wound to his head that he had inflicted upon himself. This was a victim of suicide who needed his soul light activated so he could turn around and go with the others who were waiting by the creek. His torn flesh did not even exist in that condition anymore. I was to assist in pulling out the roots of violent pain from his emotional and mental body that was filled with agony. It was as if I went deep inside his world and was standing from afar once again watching and feeling the events that had brought him to that horrible act of violence. For some reason, I understood, and saw the wounded areas on levels that cannot even be spoken in words. Praying for guidance, I felt a presence with us and what felt like warm air wrapping around me. Opening my eyes, I saw the two men who had been waiting at a distance. Their appearance and clothing looked like anyone you would pass on the street on Earth. One was wearing jeans and a plaid shirt. His hair was shoulder length. For some reason, I knew who they were. There was a light shimmering around each one of them, and I called out to them: "You are the guides! You have come to get him but he does not see you!" A blue light shimmered around them with a magenta glow at the top of their heads. Their smiles and the nodding of their heads brought me a sigh of relief. Help had finally arrived just as an ambulance would pull up and medics would take over on the Earth plane. I started to step back from the young man, but my feet would not move. The panicked feeling that I might be stuck there filled every part of me, then quickly turned into a calm and peaceful feeling. I somehow knew that I was safe and I was drawn to look at the two helpers once again. There was what appeared to be a small gold stream trickling by that separated us. I knew that the young man must turn and see the helpers in order to connect with them and move out of the dark cold hallway. Somehow, I became the bridge for his soul to continue the journey into the light. Within my stillness, I heard their whispers, "For some reason you are here on the Other Side and you two have found each other. You have the unusual ability it seems to be here in this way with us. Somehow, you must convince him to turn around and leave the past of that last fatal act that was inflicted. Please be still, know we will assist you."

Silently, I asked what would happen to this tortured young man when he did what was asked of him. "We will take him to the healing chambers where he will rest and heal deep within his being. He will be counseled and prepared to enter the next step of his journey into the portal what you call Heaven. We will assist you. Just have faith, Elaina, as you are never alone with this." For a moment, I felt light-headed and did not recall telling them my name. Suddenly, I felt energy entering the top of my head and flowing through my body all the way down to the bottom of my feet, which I now noticed were not wearing any shoes. This essence filled every part of my being. My body was shimmering with a light that wrapped around me like a cloak of protection. Moving even closer to him, I asked him to speak his name and tell me exactly what happened. "I don't remember right now," he said in anguish. "My head is hurting so badly now, where am I?" It became cold for a second and then I heard the voice saying to remember the guides that were standing close by. I then felt my body become warm again. Words came through me, hearing myself describing to this young man where we were, and what had happened a long time ago. "Your name is Stephen and you took your life. Your heart was in deep pain; you did not love yourself or feel you were worthy to live anymore. You shot yourself in the head, and committed suicide, but you need to know that does not exist anymore. That is illusion just like those wounds on your face and the blood on your shirt and all that pain filling you in so many ways. You can make that go away! We can make it go away!" It was so still in that hallway; so cold and dark and my urge to leave that place was overwhelming. "Somehow, I came here. You must have been calling for help, so we need to get busy so you can leave this place and we both can get out of here." Moving even closer to him, I asked him, "can you see the light?" "No!" was his agonizing reply. "I can't see anything! I am so alone! Please don't leave me!" With overwhelming agony and fear spilling from him, I found my energy moving closer to him as if I had my arm around him, comforting him and then I heard my voice firmly saying, "I will help you. It's really cool looking! If you just turn around, you will feel so much better!"

Knowing he was overwhelmed, I was guided to go step by step with this soul. "Let's just take a breath now, Stephen, and then let it out gently. Just one second at a time here, focus just on you and me…nothing else." Energy was pouring out of me as I whispered to him, "There is a beautiful light behind you. It will make you feel so good, I promise you." The calm, soothing sound of my voice was almost hypnotic as it described over and over again what I was seeing for what seemed like eternity. "You are loved; you must heal now. All you must do is turn around to the light now. You do not have these wounds anymore for you are on the Other Side now." I pointed my finger behind his shoulder towards the two silently waiting men, and with excitement in my voice, I exclaimed, "Just look at them!" Suddenly, he turned and his appearance started to change. Flickering shimmers of light got brighter and brighter. Quickly, and before he could shift again into the grey darkness, I heard myself saying firmly to him, "You need to go with those two angels standing behind you. They will help you heal. They understand what happened to you. Trust that you will also see your friends and family there. Don't you want to see them?" At that moment his appearance shimmered and the deep wounds on so many levels finally dissolved before my very eyes. My heart was filled with peace as I felt an unseen presence moving closer. I said, "You are all nice and clean now and will feel so much better when you go to them." Knowing I could not stay in that hallway much longer I whispered softly, "Everything will be just fine. No need to be afraid. You are safe now. You will be healed and understand all of this soon." I saw that the two men across the golden babbling stream had gotten closer to us. Looking down at my feet, I could see we were not far from the banks of the light-filled brook. The two waiting on the Other Side had gentle smiles of welcome as they looked at this young soul. Suddenly, I heard their silent whispers to me. "You cannot come any further now, Elaina. It is not quite yet your time to cross." And in the twinkling of an eye, the young man was walking through the little stream and onto the Other Side looking at me. "Tell them I am so sorry I hurt them. I was so stupid to do what I did! I hope they will forgive me," he said in a voice that sounded like he was standing right next to me. The two angelic beings smiled before they all turned around facing what seemed to be a huge round window of swirling light. The young man was between the two as they moved further away from me. For some reason, I had the urge to run after them and as my foot moved forward, it was stopped once again. Looking down at that golden water in the stream, I was curious what exactly was keeping me from the Other Side. How did I get to this place? Why did that all happen with the young soul who was in so much pain? Why did I endure all these feelings that I could not put into words? With a heavy sigh, I looked back across the stream and saw a final glimpse of the three entering a light-filled circle that was swirling as if it was a heavenly star gate. It took all my strength to force myself to turn away. I felt the hypnotic pull to go with them.

Slowly slipping out of the dark hallway, I returned to my body hearing those words spoken to me: "It is not quite yet your time to cross." There was a soft echo with each fleeting breath, bringing me back to Earth with the sound of the ocean not far away. Back in my body, the man sitting at the table was looking at me with amazement and tears in his eyes as he exclaimed, "Wow, that was pretty wild! It felt like we had traveled to another place! The hair on the back of my neck was standing up! I did not mention him to you." By the look on his face I knew that something powerful had happened. "That was my brother!" His voice filled with sadness. He then shared the story about the young man and how they had found him. "This has brought me some peace to know that he made it and is healing." At last, there was a new understanding of what had happened. "I wish I had been there for my brother before this happened. Maybe it would have turned out a different way." As the session was ending, a sudden message was given to him. Looking at me with concern in his eyes, my client quietly stated that he had an intuitive impression that there was something seriously wrong with me internally on the left side. "I sometimes get those impressions and have learned to trust them." Then he said, "If you can lie down on the carpet, I can check this." Slowly stretching out on the floor, surprise and fear ran through me. I had been having a good day and the pain was quiet. Watching his attention focus on the left side below my rib cage area, I felt my body becoming guarded. The moment he gently touched the area there was a deep, searing pain. With a worried look in his eyes he told me that he felt some type of internal mass in that area. "Go to the doctor immediately when you get home," he said with a concerned tone in his voice. My thoughts were reeling! This was the first time someone had recognized there was something serious going on inside me! His not knowing what had happened to me alarmed me and I promised him that I would do as he asked. Helping me up from the floor, he then said with a kind but firm voice, "Be careful what you are doing while you are here! Take it easy." While I was saying goodbye, my whole being was swirling around the room as he walked out the door. It seemed that angels were continuously caring for me.

Needing some fresh air, I walked out the sliding glass door. Standing out on the lanai for some sweet island air, I heard the phone suddenly ring. It was my friend Janet. She was coming by my condo later for a visit. It had been several years since we had seen one another and she wanted to make some day and night plans for us to have some fun and catch up. We agreed upon a time for her to stop by later. Hanging up the phone, I thought it would do me good to go lay out by the pool for a while and feel the ocean breeze upon my skin. I was still trying to process what had happened to me in the reading and the place I somehow had visited. The warm, tropical sun felt good upon my skin and soothed me as my soul drifted in and out of my body. I wanted to stay by the pool forever but my dear friend would be arriving soon. With perfect timing, there was the knock at the door and my dear friend's smiling face was in front of me. Immediately, it was like we were back in the '70s living in Sedona. A lot of experiences had transpired in both of our lives since those days. And her own spiritual journey had taken her all over the world.

Taking a drive to a local fruit stand, we stopped and picked up some fresh fruit, including pineapples, mangos and papayas. While we were there, we had a delicious mango smoothie. Taking a sip of the delicious drink, I felt my feet back on the island. Breathing in the trade winds and having healthy nutrition gave me hope that I would regain my health once again. Even my skin was turning golden, giving me a healthier appearance. Gazing out at the ocean, I prayed that I would feel strong and healthy once more in my life. "Tomorrow, dear, I am taking you to a special place to overnight. So be ready for me to pick you up around 10:00 a.m. You are going to love this place!" Janet said with smile and with smoothie in hand. Climbing into the car, we headed to West Maui to the old historical whaling town Lahaina. She needed to stop at a health food store to sell them some wheat grass she had grown. Things had not changed. It was like being back in Sedona where we were always hopping in the VW Bus and heading somewhere to sell our honey or other natural products or to buy some for ourselves. We were always the gypsies off on an adventure and it did my spirit good to be with her once again. After we dropped off the wheat grass, we went to get some lunch. "You need to have something healthy to eat, Elaina," she said with a smile. "I know the perfect place for us to go." Driving a few blocks, we pulled up in front of a small little place with a brightly colored sign. Upon entering, it was like going back in time to the '70s with the people wearing tiedyed clothing and smelling like sandalwood and patchouli! We found a table and ordered an iced chai tea as we looked at the menu. I felt like I could eat something more solid so I ordered an avocado, tomato and sprout sandwich on fresh homemade wheat bread. "Just like old times!" I said laughing. "You always take good care of me girl." Janet then took it upon herself to give me a mini class on the benefits of cleansing colonics and how healing they were. "Maybe that will help make you feel better dear," she said softly. "I can do one on you if you would like." I fought back the urge to choke on my iced tea as the mere thought of the procedure of cleansing my colon! It was NOT on my list of healing in Maui. And then of course, listening to her talking about my colon, I got the whisper from within, "No, do not do this!" The pain in my abdomen area had not been diagnosed by a medical doctor yet and I felt this could be dangerous to do at this time. Finishing our lunch, we headed back to the condo in Kihei enjoying the ride. While I felt good for a change, I was tired and felt very full from the lunch. I could not remember the last time I had eaten so much food. I prayed that the sickening pain would not return. Looking out at the ocean, I breathed in the island air and wished that I lived there.

We got back at the condo, and as we said goodbye Janet called out, "See you tomorrow for our adventure!" I could see the blue water as I walked down the path. Soon the sunset came and with it the longing for that special soul love in my life to share the sun's dance on the water as it sank slowly into the ocean. I turned on the overhead fan and the gentle breeze of the trade winds from the lanai refreshed the living room. Pouring a tiny bit of Hana Bay rum into a glass filled with ice, I added some of the local "Pog" juice to create my own island drink. The taste of the banana, mango, pineapple and other delicious fruits was the perfect way to watch the sun go down and to just let my mind drift to beautiful places. The sun goes down early in the islands and the locals go to bed early because they live for the surfing, fishing and other activities in the morning. As I sipped my drink, my eyes focused on the ball of fire getting closer to the horizon. Such a breathtaking sight, combined with the rum soothing me, I knew I was in paradise! Drifting in and out of my quiet reverie, I heard the whisper from within, "You cannot come any further now, Elaina. It is not quite yet your time to cross." Suddenly, I felt fearful, and although it was a warm tropical sunset, a chill went through me. "Something" was happening to me and I did not have the courage to face whatever it was. Looking out at the beautiful ocean and sun dipping down, I felt so alone and filled with sadness. I knew I was on a lonely journey that was beginning to accelerate. I went back inside, showered, and put on a light cotton nightgown. Looking in the mirror, I saw myself with a golden tan starting to appear. This was comforting because lately I had been looking very pale. And while I was pleased with how I looked, inside me I felt only sadness, confusion and fear. I crawled into bed and wrapped the covers around me because I felt chilled. I tried to ignore that ache on the left side of my abdomen, no longer conscious of how long it had been there.

As I closed my eyes to the sound of the ocean outside the window, I heard the words the client had said to me that morning, "See a doctor immediately when you get home." I then drifted off saying my prayers to the angels, "Now I lay me down to sleep. I pray the Lord my soul to keep." And soon was carried off into a deep sleep.

Adventure to Hana

"If I take the wings of the morning, and dwell in the uttermost parts of the sea"
– CAL (Grave Stone of Charles A. Lindbergh)

Waking to the sound of the birds chirping and seeing a beautiful new sky filled me with peace. As I got ready for the day with my dear friend, I was glad that I made this journey, could see her and receive new energy. The sun, trade winds, ocean and sky brought new strength to me each day. Soon there was a knock on the door and Janet's smiling face greeting me. "Are you ready for a little journey?" she asked as we walked out the door. With laughter and anticipation, we got into the car and headed up the road. "We are going to take a back road to go see a friend of mine on the other side of the island in Kipahulu. It is about 10 miles beyond Hana and few know this way to go. It cuts a lot of time off the journey because the main highway takes a long time to travel," she said. The brass zills (finger cymbals for dancing) hanging from her rearview mirror chimed as we turned the corner and went off the pavement. "Hana has a powerful energy to it and many strange things can happen there. It is hard to get to for many reasons," she explained as the car slowly crawled up the hill and over the rocks. Once again, we were two hippies on a road trip and for a time I felt free of pain. Just looking at us was taking me back in time! Our hair was blowing in the island breeze and we were wearing colorful coverups, bracelets and sandals. Time stood still as my eyes took in the scenery of the ocean down below.

Slowly, the landscape started to change and I saw a winding road through the lush trees and green landscape. Janet said cheerfully, "We are going to Charles Lindbergh's Maui home and we'll spend the night. My friend Robert is a caretaker there and I thought you would like to spend time at this special peaceful place." In no time at all we were arriving at this amazing property and her friend Robert was greeting us with a smile and an "Aloha." I could feel this was going to be a special time on this quiet and isolated large property. It was on a hill filled with banana trees and lush green grass and had an amazing view. Down below was the ocean surf and black lava headlands and their powerful energy. It was like going back in time. My senses were flooded with so much beauty and the sound of silence as I breathed in the trade winds. It captured me, as it did Lindbergh. I was told that in 1971 the aviator had purchased five acres from his good friend Sam Pryor, a Pan American executive. Lindbergh built a rustic-looking lava-walled A-frame home near the edge of the 100-foot-high cliffs. The house did not have electricity, which made life even simpler. We were taken to a small stone cottage with a little screened-in porch and lots of overgrown vegetation around it. There was such a stillness in the air. We entered the cottage and explored this cozy little place. Robert showed us the kitchen area and pointed his finger upward and said that we would be sleeping up in the little loft area. There was a small white ladder attached to the wall that we would climb up to reach it. We walked back to the porch, sat down at a small table and relaxed from the bumpy ride. After a bit of listening to the two of them catching up the news with each other, I decided to go outside and sit down on the green grass for a while as my left side and tummy felt sore from the jostling drive on the bumpy road. Rain clouds were arriving with a sprinkle of warm rain. Returning to the cottage, Janet suggested we take a rain bath to cleanse our bodies and auras. She slipped off her cover up and headed for the grass. "Come on, let's hurry! The rain will not last too long." I pulled off my beach cover-up and followed her out, lying down on the soft grass, feeling the warm raindrops touching my skin. Silently, I hoped I would not get sick out in this isolated place; it felt good to just to stretch out on the grass for a while. "Maybe this rain and the Earth will heal my naked body," I thought, pulling each drop into my body as I breathed in and out. Starting to drift out of my body, I dozed. Time passed and the sun was now warm upon my body as I dozed lightly. Feeling the ocean breeze against my skin, it felt as if there was no time at all. I was taking in all the energy from the rich island earth and recharging my life force with each breath of ocean air.

At some point, I heard Janet saying softly, "Just checking on you. I did not want to wake you up."As I drifted back into my body I murmured, "Yes, I feel much better now. Such an amazing energy here from all directions." Time had flown by and the midafternoon light was changing in the sky. "You need to hydrate so let's get some water in you," she said as she helped me get up from my green resting place. We went back to the porch and I had some much needed water and felt refreshed. We walked back into the little kitchen area and Janet started getting things organized. "Go take a little stroll around the property while I make us some food and get us settled a bit here," she said as she started taking things out of the bags. I stepped back outside and there was only the silence, the massive lawns of green grass, the banana grove, and the sound of the ocean as I slowly wandered through this peace-filled place. I felt tired again so I sat for a while, closed my eyes and asked for healing from the sun and tropical breeze. Even in the midst of this very special place I had a nagging feeling that something was going to happen to me. I needed to find a doctor when I got back home because the chiropractor had stressed the importance of doing so. No matter how I tried to explain it away or pretend I was healthy, that whisper from within would not go away, even here in one of my

155

favorite places to visit and recharge. Lying down on the lawn again, I went into a meditation feeling the connection with this earth, water and sky. Drifting for a while in this soothing tropical energy took all my anxiety away. Only the sound of the sea, the birds, and the ocean breeze blowing on my skin gave me peace that I soaked up. I hoped that I would have access to its calmness when I returned home.

After a while, I opened my eyes, sat up and looked around me. I must have slept for quite a while because in a very short time the sun would soon be on the horizon. The sky was starting to change colors and soon there would be another gorgeous sunset in paradise. Purple, indigo, pink, orange and red would cast another new painting in the sky. I stood up slowly and started to head back towards the cottage but suddenly found myself looking in the other direction. Just a few yards from where I stood was the A-framed house built with thick lava rock. I found myself slowly walking in that direction filled with curiosity. It seemed empty, and as I got nearer I felt hesitant because I did not want the occupants, if there were any, to think I was snooping. As the late afternoon sun was dropping further towards the sea, its prisms of light shined through the trees catching my eyes. I turned my head and saw that I was not the only one looking at the beautiful sky. There was a man standing closer to the house looking out to the ocean. He was a nice looking older man with light colored short hair and his slender body was dressed different than what you would expect on the island. He was wearing a long-sleeved shirt, a pair of light casual work pants, and had no shoes on. As I was staring at him and wondering where he came from, he turned around slowly and much to my surprise looked straight at me. Startled, I hoped he would not ask me what I was doing here and ask me to leave. That was not the case; it was as if telepathically we both understood that we were appreciating the sunset approaching the horizon, sharing the love and serenity of its beauty in this special place. Then, almost in the blink of an eye, I felt a deep melancholy as I watched him start to walk around the corner, dissolve into the light and disappear.

Feeling light headed, I started walking towards the cottage and heard Janet in the distance calling out, "Let's have a bite to eat," bringing me out of my reverie and dropping me back into real time again. "Yes, that sounds good!" I replied walking up to the porch and sitting down at the picnic table. A plate of fresh papayas, bananas, nuts and avocado, tomato and cheese sandwiches on homemade wheat bread with glasses of wheatgrass juice was waiting on the little table for us to enjoy. "Perfect way to recharge our energy!" she said with a smile as the sunlight touched her dark hair with a splash of red, creating an aura through each strand. Taking a bite of the sandwich, I nodded my head in agreement. It tasted so good and I was hungry for a change. "Thank you for bringing me here, Janet. It truly is paradise and we are getting to have another adventure together like all those we did in Sedona." I was so happy to see her, and felt blessed that we finally found one another again. We were both gypsies, having lived in many interesting places and traveled together. It seemed we had come full circle once again. We two in the same place always brought an adventure or two. "The last time I was going to catch up with you was when you told me to meet you at the Bombay airport when you were living at the ashram in India," I said laughing. "I wanted to do that one but just could not get the money together at that time. We must keep that one on our list!"

As we relaxed watching the sun starting to dance over the water at last, it was not long before her friend Robert came through the door carrying some groceries and a six pack of beer. "Looks like we are going to get some more rain this evening," he said as he went into the kitchen area. Coming back out to the porch, he placed a lantern on the table. "I put a lantern up in your girls' sleeping area also." Sitting down at the table, he took a bite of his sandwich as the sun dipped down below the horizon. I listened to them talk about the local news and enjoyed each bite of avocado, tomato, and cheese. Darkness was arriving and soon he was lighting the lantern. Then with a wink he asked, "Now, how about some beer ladies? I bought some for tomorrow too." He went back to the small kitchen returning with the cold bottles. I toasted, "Here's to another day in paradise and thank you for bringing me to this beautiful place."

There was no watch or timeclock on the island, only the sun, the moon and the big sky. In ways time slows down, and is referred to as being on "Maui time." As the night arrived, so did the rain. Sitting out on the screened porch with the light of a lantern, the three of us sipped beer and talked about the island and the local buzz about one of the members of the Beach Boys band wanting to buy this property. Everyone was concerned that he might try to build on this historical place.

As it got darker, the rain started pouring harder, as if the sky opened and poured a gigantic bucket of warm water on top of us! It was a surrealistic moment because the wind started up in the darkness. Breathing in the rich, wet earth was intoxicating. Since most locals go to bed early in the islands so they may get up with the sun, we decided to call it a night! We said goodnight to our friend, headed to the back of this tiny cottage and climbed the ladder up to the tiny loft. With each rung of the ladder, I felt a pull deep inside me bringing a prayer that I would not fall. There was a grass matt on the floor and a light sheet to cover each of us. The pillows we brought were inviting as the sound of thunder arrived. Preparing our sleeping areas across from each other, we stretched out and got comfortable. The light of the lantern sitting between us cast shadows on the little ceiling. "I hope you will not be in pain, Elaina," Janet said softly pulling her sheet around her. Suddenly, the raindrops were so powerful against the little roof that it startled me. Lifting myself up slowly, I peeked out the tiny window screen between us. The sky lit up revealing leaves swaying in the trees and the sound of huge raindrops echoing against leaves. It was my first storm on the island and it reminded me of just how this magical place stayed so green and filled with flowers and fruit. Lying back down I wrapped my cover around me trying to warm up. I had been losing weight and silently questioning why this was happening. Maybe it was because I wasn't as hungry anymore and I was just too frequently uncomfortable after eating. I dismissed these thoughts as my dear friend and I quietly talked for a while about all our journeys together and those when we were apart, for so many years of our lives. We took delight in the fact that once again, time had brought us together after such a long stretch of not seeing one another and had brought us to this magical place together again. As our eyes got sleepy, Janet turned the lamp out with a "Goodnight." Closing my eyes and listening to the sounds of the rain and wind, I had a wonderful last thought. I was in Maui with Janet who was "family" to me and I was sleeping in this amazing little cottage that had been visited by a man who was a part of history forever, Charles Lindbergh. This was his property and cottage where he had spent time.

My mind traveled to that larger house close by and the man I saw standing there waiting for the sunset. Wondering again how strange it had been I said to Janet, "I thought you said there was no one on this property but us?" "We are," she said. "Why do you ask?" Rolling on my side, looking towards her in the dark I quietly said, "We are? Well, I saw a man down by that A-frame house before the sunset started; so I don't think we are the only people here. I hope we don't get in trouble for being here."After a quiet moment, Janet's voice replied in the dark, "There is no one allowed on this property now, only my friend who is caretaking. No one stays in that house now," she said firmly then adding, "That is 'Argonauta', Lindbergh's home. He is buried on this property and we will take you to his grave site tomorrow. It is close by on the grounds of the Palapala Ho'omau Church." For a minute my mind was trying to sort all this out, and still confused I said, "I swear there was a nice looking older man with short light colored hair standing by that A-frame, he even looked around at me," adding, "he was there by the house looking at the beautiful sky just like me! He was wearing a long-sleeved shirt and what looked like work clothes which I thought was strange and I felt a deep melancholy come over me when looking at him." For a moment I was afraid I was sounding a bit crazy, but the story continued to spill out of me. "I don't know where he went so fast, it was like he disappeared, dissolved right in front of me!" Feeling unsettled, wondering if my feeling sick was playing tricks on me, in the shadows Janet turned on her side and towards me, "Are you okay?" She asked with concern in her voice. "This guy dissolved in front of you? What do you mean?" The sound of the rain became louder as the wind kicked up outside and thunder rolled startling both of us. "Oh my God, you are scaring me Elaina! Do you mean he was a ghost or something?" she said in a serious voice. Pulling my sheet up tighter around me I mumbled, "I don't know what he was or is, but I saw him! That's all I know and it is not just us who are on this property. Let's just go to sleep girl," I said softly feeling exhausted.

"Now, how am I supposed to sleep if there is a strange ghost or something walking around here?" Janet asked in the dark. Suddenly it was very quiet and then we both started to giggle. "I forgot about that part of you!" she said laughing. "Oh, my God, Elaina. I hope I can sleep tonight after this one and he doesn't try to evict us tonight!" Laughter broke the tension in this powerful storm and soon we both drifted off peacefully.

"After my death, the molecules of my being will return to the earth and the sky. They came from the stars. I am of the stars." Charles Lindbergh

In the morning, we woke up to a cloudy and peaceful sky and coffee which was the morning high point. Janet had a way of making the best coffee I have ever tasted no matter where we were. Even though my tummy hurt at times when I would eat, I took the chance for a sip of her magical brew. Even here she weaved her magic and we took our cups out to the screened-in porch and the morning with the sun trying to peek through the clouds. "We will still have some rain today," Robert told us as he came up the porch steps. Going to the tiny kitchen he returned with a cup in his hand and joined us at the table. "We will take a tour around here in a bit while the sun is still shining," he said sipping the delicious Kona coffee. "That was a pretty heavy storm we had last night. Hope you were not afraid up there with all that rain hitting the roof above you." Janet and I looked at each other. I was going to keep my mouth shut about what was discussed in the dark but Janet had other plans. "Yes, it was a pretty intense night up there and Elaina added more to that with her talking about her walk down by the A-frame and seeing an older man in a long-sleeved shirt there also. Seems they were watching the coming sunset together." Taking a sip of her coffee she added, "She told me he just disappeared right in front of her." She tried not to laugh. "You told us there was no one else on the property, but she is insisting we are not alone. Crazy, huh?" Instead of the expected laugh and teasing, there was surprise in her Hawaiian friend's eyes as he looked at me. "Tell me more Elaina, what did you see there?" I found myself sharing what I had seen and felt when I was close to the A-frame house. He listened quietly as his eyes met mine. "Again, what did you say he looked like?" he asked with a serious look on his face. I looked over at the house then described the nice looking older man with light colored hair cut short. "He was barefoot, wearing what looked like khaki work clothes and wearing a long-sleeved shirt which I found odd for the islands." We walked outside and looked towards the house, looking in that direction there was complete silence. "Come on! I want to show you something," he suddenly said. In a matter of minutes, we were at an isolated cemetery on the slopes of Haleakala. In this peaceful place, next to the Palapala Ho'omau Congregational Church, the eyes see just a few grave sites in traditional Hawaiian style surrounded with smooth lava stones. Walking through the quiet grounds as we were approaching a grave under a tree separated from the others, Robert told us that Lindbergh did not like being in the public eye. It is said to be the reason it is so hard for many to find his grave site under the shade of a particular Java plum tree. Looking down at the simple marker there was inscribed, *"If I take the wings of the morning and dwell in the uttermost parts of the sea…"C. A.L*

"Elaina, did you know anything about this man before coming here?" he asked quietly, as his brown eyes looked into mine. I said I did not, only that he was the famous aviator and I was surprised that he was here. Then he said, "He came back to Hana to die. He had become sick with cancer and was hospitalized for about a month. He knew he would not live so requested to secretly return here to Hana. The locals kept very quiet about the situation and were very protective of this man and his wife."As I was looking at the inscription on the marker, he continued the story of how Lindbergh himself sketched out the simple design for his grave and coffin. He even asked his Hawaiian neighbors to dig his grave and to build his coffin. He wanted it all to be plain and simple. The grave I was now standing before was 12 feet deep, approximately 10 feet wide and lined with lava rock. Robert said "under those lava rocks the coffin was a plain, eucalyptus wood box built by the local Hawaiian cowboys." He died in the early morning hours on August 26, 1974 and was 72 years old. I was surprised when Robert said, "This man was buried later that afternoon without being embalmed. His casket taken to the grave site in the back of a pickup truck." Looking down at the grave shaking his head he said, "You can't get much more real than that!"

"Elaina, what you described about the man who was by the house and the clothes he was wearing was what Mr. Lindbergh asked to be buried in upon his death. Those were the clothes he wore back at his house, a khaki work shirt and cotton work pants. He also asked to be buried barefoot." I felt chills moving up my body as I remembered the man and his melancholy and how he looked at me then disappeared before my eyes. Looking at the grave, it seemed surreal as our friend then spoke of Lindbergh's funeral. "He also asked that people come to his funeral in work clothes, and he wanted to be buried as soon after his death as possible without the services of morticians."

It was a reminder…standing there by the grave and listening to the story of such a famous wealthy man leaving this earth in such a simple way from his last days and breaths on earth and even with his burial…no fancy tomb or pomp and ceremony. Looking at the grave it was a silent reminder no matter how much money or fame a person has it all ends the same for us all. On dying, the aviator said, "It's not terrible, it's very easy and natural." I felt his words deep inside me and I could not help but wonder, was he talking to me about what was to come?

"We will head back in a bit," Janet said to me, "We have the ride back to Kihei and we need to do so before dark, so see you in a few." Nodding my head, I felt as if I was in a dream. I wondered if it was not by accident that there were no other tourists on the grounds at this moment. Looking out to the sea in the distance and the beautiful grounds, I then looked at the grave and said a prayer. I quietly thanked this man for allowing me to see him by the house and for letting us stay on his property. Who would believe that I had watched a Maui sunset with the greatest aviator in the world, Charles Lindbergh? Whispering "Mahalo" (Thank You), I knew it didn't matter what others believed. I would carry this experience with me the rest of my life.

Soon we said goodbye to Robert and this peaceful historical place. Driving towards Kihei, with each mile I knew I would soon be packing my bags to return home. I had a sense of foreboding and felt waves of fear about the unknown that would be waiting for me when I went home.

Despite my denial, I would soon have to confront the fact that each pain was getting stronger, its movement wrapping around my side and to my back was warning me! With each mile that we drove towards Kihei, I knew that it was not a bruise and I would have to find a doctor to help me.

We got back to the condo in the late afternoon just as another beautiful sunset arrived. "I will come in for a while," Janet said, turning the car off and opening the door. Inside, we poured ourselves a large glass of water and went out onto the lanai. It felt good to be back and a shower and my nightgown sounded inviting. "I hope you can come back and see me next year, Elaina," Janet said with a smile on her face reminding me of all the things we could do on the island during my next visit. As I listened to her and nodded in agreement, for some reason I had a feeling that I may not see this place or her again. Trying to shake off that whisper inside me, I looked out at the sea and saw some whales in the distance. "I would love to get closer to them out on the water," I said softly, trying to change that feeling inside. We sat in peace watching the waves kissing the shore and enjoying the trade winds. Then it would be time to say goodbye to my dear friend as the sun was starting to head for the horizon. "Make sure you go to the doctor the minute you get home," Janet said, giving me a last hug goodbye. "I promise and I'll let you know what is going on." There were tears in my eyes as I watched her get into the car. Deep sadness came over me once again because I did not know if I would ever see my dear friend again. I headed for the shower. The warm water and the perfume of the island flower-scented soap was soothing and felt so good on my skin. Stepping carefully out of the tub, I wrapped a towel around my head and another around my body. After my shower, I went into the kitchen to get something to eat because I was feeling weak. I grabbed a large fruit smoothie from the refrigerator and a straw from the counter that Janet bought me at the fruit stand before dropping me off at the condo. I went out to the lanai and sat and sipped on the delightful nourishing drink. There were a few whales out in the distance with the sprays of water shooting up over the surface of the water. "Thank You for this gift," I whispered as I watched the waves rolling in to the shore. The trade winds against my skin felt divine as I thought about all the wonderful experiences that I had on this beautiful island. This would be the last Maui sunset because in the morning I was catching a flight back home. Savoring every last minute of the sun dropping down to the horizon with its amazing colors in the sky, I felt peace and happiness and I resolved to remember this feeling and beautiful place…no matter what happened in my life.

SIDE NOTE: While editing this part of the book a final time, I went back to Maui on January 25, 2013 with Shawna Larsen to sprinkle her mother's ashes. Pat Larsen was a close friend, like family to me since the late '80s. At that time, her daughter Shawna was seriously ill with lupus. She had done healing work with me on a regular basis. While doing so, she became lupus free and is to this day. I became what the three of us called "Shawna's Other Mother." Pat, Shawna and I traveled to Maui years ago and spent a lot of time there together throughout the years. Pat had been battling cancer the past years and on July 14th, 2012 I helped my dear friend cross over. It was a long day and night, helping her slip out of that pain-filled body, but we three did it together. The next year, Shawna and her sister Lisa, gifted me a trip to Maui for our birthdays and as a gift from the family for helping Pat move more quickly into the Light. It also would be a most sacred journey because we sprinkled Pat's ashes into the sea. While I was there, Janet was visiting from Bali, so we came full circle once again on this beloved island. I had not seen her since my trip in 1986. My dream in 1986 of us seeing the whales together came true. We three went on a whale watch trip together and it was amazing!

Once again destiny has arrived in my life. I found myself in many ways, coming full circle with death, healing and closure at last in so many ways.

The Viking

Returning home, although I was so thin, I still had a bit of a golden tan and at least I thought looked healthier. Denial continued to be my constant companion as I tried to regain my health, but each week I had attacks of pain becoming increasingly severe. It was a constant cycle that kept repeating itself, draining me more each time. I went to the emergency room where they gave me pain medication, kept me for a while, and then sent me home. I told the staff that I had a ride home because otherwise they would not have given me the injection. Still, they couldn't tell me what was wrong. Since I was unfamiliar with this new town, it was a challenge. At that time, I had no family support to help me think more clearly. I also had the underlying trauma of what had happened to me, bombarding me at times with flashes of that porch step. The road I took to the hospital was not filled with a lot of traffic, and it was just a short drive, so I always prayed I'd get home safely each time. After many repeated visits to the ER, I still was not getting any answers. I was never admitted to the hospital for any further testing, which I believe in retrospect would have revealed a serious life-threatening problem. I would only get the answers I so desperately needed at a future date on another visit to the ER when I was finally admitted to the hospital.

One day an angel-in-disguise appeared while I was at a tanning salon. As I was signing in at the desk, I met a man named Michael Alukas. "Are you the psychic, Elaina Proffitt?" he asked with a smile that lit up the room. His Nordic appearance spoke of strength and his eyes sparkled with Light. I said yes, and he told me that he had listened to me on the radio many times and walked the spiritual path. Soon, we became friends and he would come over to visit and ask to take me to lunch. Usually, I would try to avoid these sorts of invitations because eating hurt my tummy, and when I did eat, it had to be in very small portions. "You need to eat, Elaina, to keep your strength," he would say to me gently. It was very apparent something was not right with me and he became concerned for my wellbeing. One sunny day he came by to take me outside into the sunshine. "Let's get you more grounded and back into your body," he said helping me slowly into his car. Michael said he was going to take me for a walk in the beautiful meadows at the base of Mt. Rose near Lake Tahoe. A moment of panic came over me as I looked up at that beautiful mountain in the distance. "I don't know if I can do this, Michael. I am not strong enough." With a big smile, he patted my hand. "Don't worry, I will take care of you!" I would find through the years those words were always true when spoken by this Viking. Winding up the mountain highway, we soon arrived at an area where there was a beautiful meadow and cars parked along the side of the highway. A cool mountain breeze touched my face as I looked at the sunshine above, taking it all in.

What should have been an easy walk was labored and so slow. As my feet touched Mother Earth, walking in the trees I found myself wondering if I was going to float away. My fragile body whispered she was tired from all the pain. I had to admit that I was only getting weaker not stronger. It did feel good to breathe in the mountain air and see the rocks and trees along the hiking path. Michael was vigilant, monitoring my every step. He would tell me a year later that he had given a great deal of thought about taking me on that walk. "I decided if something did happen what better place to leave your body then at the base of this beautiful mountain named Mt. Rose." In a short while, it was time to slowly start heading back to the car. Carefully tucking me into the front seat, Michael praised me for how far I could walk. "Now I am going to take you for something to eat and then back to your apartment for some rest," he said with a big smile. I knew I needed nourishment for strength but was not looking forward to this event. We stopped at a sushi bar and had some lunch. I was praying the rice and seafood would be tolerable. Sipping the tea, I felt more energy and was so appreciative of the wonderful day that Michael had given me. As the waitress placed the bill on the table, Michael said, "I think it is time to take you home now; you look like you might need a nap."

When we got home, we relaxed in the living room sitting on pillows around the coffee table. We talked about spiritual books, Vikings and Tibet which I discovered he knew a lot about. While I was listening to his stories, I began to feel weak and had a pain so severe it dropped me to the floor! Michael immediately carried me to my bed. "Do you want to go to the hospital? You don't look good, Elaina." The pain was slowly fading and I insisted that I just rest. If I did feel worse I promised I would go to the hospital. With a concerned look in his eyes he said, "I am going to stay right here and keep an eye on you for a while until I feel you are better." Not taking "no" for an answer, he sat with me until I insisted he go home; he worked nights and had to sleep. Looking back, I see that this kind stranger was sent to me by angels because I had no close friends in my new area. He became a guardian who would watch over me in the months to come. Carefully walking him to the door, I said goodbye and promised I would go to the hospital if I felt the need. Slowly, I returned to my bedroom and got under the covers. Lying there, I drifted in and out, exhaling the pain and breathing in gently, feeling more soothed. As my eyes drifted towards my doorway into the hall, a beautiful woman with short red hair appeared, wearing a black velvet hooded cape. She was just standing there, looking at me lying on the bed. I had seen spirit energy since I was a child and they would come and go throughout my life. My first impression of this spirit was that she was "Lady Death." I immediately dismissed the thought but I knew that she would not be leaving. I saw this spirit multiple times in the months to come. As I drifted off, I heard myself whispering to her, "What do you want?" She just stared at me and a feeling came over me that she was silently waiting for something…it felt like it was me!

Time would tell who and what this was all about. I knew I would not be able to ignore what was happening to my body much longer. It was more than just a bruise from the corner of the step where I was thrown down. Silently praying for protection and the right doctor to swiftly arrive in my life, I fell into a long, deep sleep.

The Power of Words

In the months to come, I continued to drive myself to the emergency room at the hospital that was close to my place. This turned out to be another blessing. It seemed to be no accident that I was guided to rent an apartment nearby. I still do not know how I was able to continue making these trips to the ER. Soon my constant visits created another problem. I started getting the feeling that the staff thought that I was a drug addict despite my records from the emergency room in Sacramento. Still, they did not do more in-depth testing. No one was really seeing the changes in me each time I walked through the doors because many of the new nurses on shift had never seen me before. At last, an ER nurse told me, "You need to get a physician to check you and order necessary testing." I told her that I was new to the area and did not even know what type of doctor to see since no one ever had given me a name. At last, I was referred to a physician. Finally, I felt hope! His office was in a complex next to the hospital. I called and got an appointment which was a relief but I then ran into another issue. From the first day I met him, I did not like his energy. He always seemed distracted and not fully present when I met with him; his lack of attention and caring concerned me. He would give me prescriptions for pain medication and tell me he would be away at a conference. It seemed like eternity until, at last, weeks later he ordered some tests. Soon after that, I walked into his office where I saw him looking at some x-ray images on a light box on the wall. When I sat down, he told me the results of the tests. He pointed with his ball point pen to a large mass on the tail of my pancreas. Heart pounding, I summoned the courage to ask, "What is it, Doctor?" He replied abruptly. "I don't know." It seemed like a horrible dream. My eyes kept looking at the images and I felt fear moving through my whole being! My eyes scanned every inch of the images as I asked for inner guidance about what was inside my body. Then he said quietly, "This does not look good." Sitting next to him looking at the images, the reality checks finally arrived and my intuition whispered to me that this was a bad vibe! My heart was pounding; I felt weak, alone and in shock. In my twenties I had worked for a doctor and discovered I had a lot of natural understanding about the body. I found myself reading his medical journal magazines and discussing various things with him. "Elaina, I feel you would be a wonderful doctor," he said to me from his office. "I would advise you to think about medical school because you have a natural understanding about medicine and are a quick learner when I teach you something." While life took me in another direction, and I had a child, years later I did end up working with medical professionals, and with those who were dying using my medical intuitive gifts. Those experiences were very helpful to me at this most critical time! Sitting in this new doctor's office looking at the images of my organs, I was finally looking at the reason for my excruciating pain. It was also the beginning of a great learning journey about serious medical issues and communicating with doctors who literally have your life in their hands! At that moment, my "classroom-in-medicine" had arrived and I would be getting a degree in a most powerful way! I felt a survival energy activated inside me, which put me on alert from that day forward. I knew that if I did not stay strong, have clarity and speak up about my treatment that I would die! I learned the power of the word and how a doctor's words cannot only contribute to a patient's ability to heal but can also contribute to their dying. I learned that their listening time is short, and you must be organized regarding what you need most including asking questions (which is hard to do when you are seriously ill). That realization brought a panic running through my veins because I knew I needed even more angels to guide me. I also had another exhausting burden on my shoulders. I was alone even though a family member was an hour's drive away. There was no one that called to check on me, no one to be with me in the doctor's office to ask questions and take notes so I would not forget important instructions or information!

Also, I realized that consulting on murder cases was bringing me an even stronger awareness of death and just how fragile the body and life can be when assaulted. Reenacting the assault and death of another person for investigators was one thing, but now I had this "death" energy in another form inside of me! Again, the flash of that concrete step as I was being thrown down onto it, that sickening feeling, the impact of it slamming deep into my left side, and the deep sadness and fear that filled me as I looked at this strange image on the x-ray. I felt disoriented from the memory of that incident, the words of this doctor, and those images that were on the light table. I felt so alone with no one to lean on. It is one of the saddest things that can happen during a life-threatening event. The appointment ended and the nightmare began with this doctor saying that he was going to be out of town at a conference, and we would investigate further after he returned. His distracted demeanor made me feel like he had already left, even though he was still in the same room with me. He handed me some prescriptions to have filled immediately, and with a serious tone said, "this should take care of the pain in the meantime." My mind was reeling with questions and I knew I would have more after I left the office. Before getting up from the chair, looking him straight in the face, I bravely asked, "What should I do until you get back from your conference?" It took a moment for his reply, bringing me yet another nightmare. I tried to look him in the eyes and heard him say abruptly and without much compassion, "Well, this might be a good time for you to put all of your affairs in order. That will be one less worry for you." Confused and filled with fear, I then dared to ask exactly what meant by that. Immediately feeling his energy shift, I knew that he did not want to discuss that with me. Numbness overcame me and I was ushered out of the office with a "goodbye." I heard him say, "if the pain increases go to the ER. where another doctor will be on call." Prescriptions in hand, I walked back out to the car in a daze, praying I would make it home safely. Knowing I did not have enough energy to stop and wait at the pharmacy, I used all my energy to get safely home and onto my couch.

When I got back to my cozy apartment, I felt a comfort and peace wrapping around me. Placing my purse and the prescription orders onto the kitchen counter, I took my shoes off and sat down on the couch. I turned on the television for company and to take my mind off what had just happened. I felt overwhelmed. When a doctor suggests you put your affairs in order, it is a heavy feeling like no other. I would not wish it on anyone. Stretching out on the couch I tried to focus on the news segment to take me away from what had just happened. A short while later, the phone rang. It was my dear client, Johanna. I told her about my visit to the doctor and she immediately offered to take me to the drugstore to pick up the prescriptions. Soon she was knocking at my door putting me into her car and heading for the pharmacy. I felt so exhausted from my doctor's appointment earlier that I waited in the car, loving the sunshine warming my body because it seemed lately I was always cold. Johanna returned to the car with a worried look in her eyes. "The pharmacist told me that this prescription is enough to drop an elephant to its knees, so you need to be watched closely and not drive." Then she told me about how I was to take them: one for the pain and the other for nausea. She tried to smile, and then pointed to a shopping bag. "I also got you some 7-Up to help settle your tummy, a couple of magazines and a few other things to have in the refrigerator." I thanked her. Looking at the pills, I became a bit panicked as I visualized a big elephant dropping to its knees. "Would they do that to me, too?" I thought as we headed down the road towards my apartment.

My worried friend helped me up the stairs and into my place making sure that I was set up in my bedroom. "Please don't drive anywhere and call me if you need me. I don't think you should be alone, Elaina. Just try to rest and call me if you need me. Don't worry, we will figure this all out in the next day or two," she said, giving me a hug, "I am going to bring some things in here so you do not have to get up," She said lovingly. I was still in shock from the doctor appointment, seeing that image showing that shadow inside my body. Watching this beautiful woman go into my kitchen, I thought of how Johanna had come to me for counseling when her husband had died, and now she was caring for me. It all seemed surreal. I had to accept that even caregivers need care at times.

I got into my nightgown, pulled back the bed covers, and opened the blinds to let the beautiful sunshine spill into the room. Johanna returned from the kitchen with a large glass of water and put it and the pill bottles on the nightstand. Taking one of each out of the bottles, she placed them on a napkin resting on the nightstand, brought me some saltine crackers, a glass of 7-Up, and a couple of magazines. "The pharmacist said you might get nauseated from the pills, so the crackers will help with that. Let's not take these until you let me out, lock your front door, and eat a bit of food. Also, we need to get an extra key made for me so I can get in if needed," she said in a comforting voice. Agreeing, I handed her my extra key as we started towards the door. "Call me if there is a problem with the medicine or anything! I will check on you in about an hour or two." I thanked her again and closed the door with a sigh. Walking into my kitchen, I could see she had left the light on above the stove for me. In the refrigerator door were some grapes and variety of cheeses, milk and some rice pudding. I made a small plate of cheese and some crackers and went into the living room to lookout the patio window at the beautiful mountains with the late afternoon blue sky above. I loved being on the second floor with such a wonderful view of Mt. Rose. Since leaving the pain-filled memories of Sacramento, I had found a wonderful place to call home that was bringing me many opportunities and many loving people. I closed the blind on the patio door, went into the living room and turned on the television. I sat down on the couch, nibbled on my food, and watched the end of the evening news to unwind from the stress and give me a bit of a distraction from all the drama of the day. Soon it was dark and still not wanting to take those pills quite yet, I flipped through the channels until I found a favorite show "Miami Vice." It reminded me of the young detectives I had worked with and how we all loved the show. A concern crossed my mind. Would I be able to continue consulting on cases? It took a lot of energy to do so and to handle the dark, pain-filled energy of investigative work. I felt tired and knew that I would not be able to watch the show much longer. Eating the final piece of cheese and crackers, a slight pain started to remind me I'd have to take the medication soon. I called my answering service to see if I had any messages. The lady on shift that evening gave me a few names and numbers of those asking about an appointment. Knowing I would have to see how I felt in the morning before returning their calls, I put the notepad and pen back down on the table. My day had been overwhelming and I knew I needed to sleep soon. Those pills were waiting for me. I went back to the kitchen with the empty plate, and I felt exhausted. I looked into the bathroom mirror while brushing my teeth and saw my sad, worried eyes looking back at me. I could see and feel inside that things were starting to all unravel, becoming something quite foreboding. Despite the constant whispers to myself, "You'll be okay" and "Maybe sleep will make you feel better," my tendency all those months to dismiss the pain had placed me in an even more precarious situation.

Crawling into bed with the doctor's words echoing in my head, I took the medication hoping it would make me forget them. The phone on the night stand rang and it was Joanna checking on me. I told her I was in bed and had just taken the pills and thanked her again for all her help. She said she would call in the morning. Soon enough, the pain started going far away as powerful drugs ran through my body. At last, I could relax and drift off into a deep sleep. Saying my prayers, I asked that my son be protected and gave thanks for my new friends and all their kindness. I asked for my healers and the Angels of Healing to be with me in the days to come.

The next morning I realized that I had finally gotten some much needed, uninterrupted sleep and I felt a bit better. I would learn that you cannot heal if you do not get proper rest. The medication seemed to let me recharge my battery and I had some good days. But as I approached the coming month, I was becoming more unable to see clients because my energy was changing and I worried about how I could pay my bills. I prayed so hard that God would help me. I had no one in my personal life and my son was out to sea in the Navy. Each night, taking my medication, I would start to worry and feel helpless and alone as I pulled the covers over my frail body. Saying my prayers, I asked for helpers to arrive and for healing. A soothing feeling would come over me and the whisper, "All will be well. Just be in the present at this time." Soon the medication would take hold and I would drift off to sleep, once again wondering if I would wake up in the morning.

There's no Place like Home

Another month arrived and it seemed like forever before Archangel Raphael would enter my life. He is the Angel of Healing, Physicians, Nurses, sick people and healing powers. Now, I was sick and needed him to arrive! As I became weaker, suddenly strange events started occurring. When I was able to go out shopping, things would appear in my hand and I had no clue how they got there: books on healing, bath therapy salts, people that had knowledge and "sight" passed on information to me. This would be a common occurrence in my life and I learned I needed to trust, use and not question. Looking back now it was obvious that they all were sent to me by Archangel Raphael. Although it felt like it at times, I was never alone and the angelic helpers remain with me to this day.

Soon, the first of a couple of times being admitted to the hospital arrived. It was now becoming more than just a simple ER visit where I would be able to go back home after a few hours of monitoring. Those days were over now and the big reality check was that something very serious was happening to me. Lying in the hospital bed on heavy pain medication, an IV stuck in my arm, and hooked up to a monitor took this medical drama to a whole different level. To this day, I recall certain events that are flashes and emotions, words and images. I would wake up one morning finding myself again in the hospital. A nurse was changing the IV that was next to my bed. I said that I did not remember how I got there. The nurse said I had arrived the night before in a lot of pain and had been admitted. I became filled with fear because I had no recall as to what had happened or who had brought me to the hospital!

As she gave me an injection, she said, "This will make you sleepy so take a nap. Giving you a heads up, you are going to be having a crowd of doctors standing around you in a couple of hours," adding with a smile as she put the syringe down on the tray, "you are going to start a fan club because it is rare that a young person like yourself has this type of health issue. They are usually elderly," giving me a wink and a slight giggle, "not to mention that you are beautiful!" She started out of the room. "The nurses' station is going to be buzzing today!" Watching her heading for the nurses' station outside my room's big glass window I could not imagine in any way that I looked beautiful!

I woke up to see a crowd of doctors in their white coats entering my room, standing in a semicircle at the foot of my bed with smiles upon their faces. As they were talking and examining me, one doctor in particular stood out. He was tall and slender and had eyes like a hawk, not missing anything as he quietly scanned his chart and then me. Something was different about him, I said to myself, as they quietly talked at the end of my bed. I knew that something was happening but I didn't know if it was good or bad. They told me they would be ordering a few more labs and tests. After a few more days, I was released with new prescriptions waiting for me at my pharmacy. It all was becoming such a blur as if I had one foot on Earth and the other someplace else. I don't remember how I got home but the phone rang as I walked in the door. The hospital must have contacted my parents while I was there because I heard my mother's voice on the phone. I told my parents what was found on the x-rays, and that a sudden pain attack hospitalized me. It was apparent that the hospital had contacted my parents because my father said he was flying me up to Portland to see his doctor. Dad's doctor had removed a large cyst from his pancreas and he was one of the best in the area. In a matter of days, I found myself on my way to Portland. As the plane took off climbing high into the sky, I said a silent prayer that I would have good news from this new doctor when it touched down a couple of hours later. Looking down at the scenery turning from the gold color of the desert into the lush greenery of Oregon, I knew I was returning home. Memories traveled through my mind with each mile as I remembered all the times with my grandparents; I closed my eyes with the thought of them. Time must have passed quickly because the captain was saying we would be landing soon.

I could see the guarded surprise upon my dad's face when he saw his daughter at the gate. Walking to baggage claim was exhausting but I did my best to keep a smile on my face. Soon we were in his car and heading towards home. I thanked him again for the ticket and for taking me to his doctor for an opinion. I leaned back in the seat and looked out the window at the green trees and hills. We made small talk as we crossed the bridge over the Columbia River and past the city. In no time, we were heading up the familiar country road and into the driveway. The dogs barked their greeting, replacing my now deceased grandparents. This had been their place, always a source of comfort to me growing up. The yard was starting to bloom: azaleas by the front windows and porch, daffodils, crocus, the breezeway where the silver dollars and poppies grew and then there were those lilac bushes, white and purple just starting to bloom. I still did not remember my words about them so long ago but felt comfort seeing them again. I did not realize I had come full circle, a final time at my grandparents' house. That place where the little girl watched her grandmother as she placed the lilacs in the beautiful vase and the words she spoke. Forgotten also was the woman in the tea room which had been just a few miles down the road and her whispers to me so long ago that I would enter into the Valley of the Shadow of Death. I got out of the car and headed slowly towards the house. I saw my mother standing in the doorway with a dish cloth in her hand and a smile upon her face. I caught her brief "look" at my father behind me and the concern in her eyes. I was carefully guided up the steps and she gave me a hug. Coming into the house, I remembered when I was a young girl and those happy times when my grandparents were alive. My father took my suitcase into my old bedroom, while my mother guided me to the couch as I hear her familiar, cheerful words as she headed towards the kitchen, "I am making us some tea, just relax. You are home now." Dad entered the room and headed straight for that old blue recliner that seemed like it had been there forever. Sitting down he turned on the television and reached for the pack of unfiltered Camels on the table next to the chair. It was piled with his crossword puzzle books, pencils and small notepad, as usual, all neatly organized. As the smoke swirled from my dad's cigarette, my mother came in with the old TV trays and placed one in front of me and the other on her side of the couch. She asked my father if he would like a cup of coffee and he nodded without saying a word. She came back from the kitchen and quickly brought it to his end table. Watching her head back for our tea and return in a moment with the china cups, teapot and those familiar Keebler fudge stripes cookies made me smile. She always had a stash of those and a few other brands usually hidden in her secret places, just like Dad would hide the Black Velvet whiskey bottle from her.

It was a sunny afternoon; the front door was open and I could see out to the large yard with lush green grass. With Mother sitting next to me, we sipped our tea and enjoyed keeping the conversation light and away from the real reason I had returned home. For just awhile it was a peaceful time away from the seriousness of what was going on. The tea tasted good and I was praying it would not make me sick as food and drink were starting to increasingly cause me pain and nausea. But the dreaded pain started up anyway. I felt myself getting weak and I looked at the clock, noting that I was past time for my medication. I apologized and said it was time for me to lie down for a bit. My mother stood up quickly. "Of course, dear, it has been a long flight and I am sure you want to rest," she said with concern in her eyes. Offering me her hand, I stood up and saw my face in the large mirror over the fireplace. My skin was pale; my body had become frail, and I was slightly hunched over from the pain. For a brief moment, I had been enjoying myself and had forgotten the reality looking back at me in the mirror. A feeling of dread now replaced the happiness of my arrival. "Sorry, but I have to lie down," I said looking at my dad, whose eyes were filled with concern. "I will feel better after I rest," I repeated once again hoping to sound cheerful. My mom guided me to the bathroom and I ran cold water on a wash cloth and put it to my face. The cold, crisp water felt good and gave me a bit of clarity to walk to the bedroom. I headed for the room I had shared with my sister so many years ago, and put on the pajamas my mother had laid on the bed for me. Getting into the bed was a comfort, I felt safe, as I always had in that room. The thought of snuggling up in the blankets was soothing, the sheets smelled so clean and fresh which was one of the things I always admired about my mother. On nice days she would hang the wash outside and let the sunshine and wind cleanse and dry things. To this day, I have never smelled bed sheets or towels so fresh as hers always were. I was exhausted from the journey and needed to rest. With a cheerful smile on her face, she put a glass of water next to my medications on the nightstand. "Drink some of our good water, honey. You know that will make you feel better." We always had great tasting water there, and every time Michael and I visited I would drink glass after glass and take a few plastic jugs home with me. I took a sip with the medication then drifted off into a deep sleep with the image of my mother out at the clothes line hanging up the wash on a sunny, windy day. Suddenly, I heard my name being called and my grandmother's face appeared before me with her eyes filled with worry. "Grandma," I whispered seeing her so close to my face. Without words, she was letting me know she was there and in the next moment my Fader (grandfather) with his kind smile appeared also, so close, both looking at me and then dissolving right in front of my eyes. Time stood still in that faraway place I had traveled to, hoping to escape from the fear and pain that was haunting me more each day. In what seemed like a matter of minutes, I woke up to my mother standing over me, telling me to get up because it was time for supper. The strong medication was still working and I felt better. The thought of having to eat something was not appealing. My mother made another attempt to get me up, this time her voice was a bit more insistent. It seemed once again I was in the role of the child whose parents are telling them, even insisting, that they obey. It is the realization of the cycle of life, and even at some point in old age or illness, parents are told the same by their children. It was my turn to be in this challenging role and it was apparent that I was starting to do things that were not for the best interest of my body. I had little desire for food and it became a challenge that had painful consequences.

I walked into the dining room, taking in the beauty outside the window. The beautiful azalea bushes were right in front of the window and were peeking at me once again reminding me they had been there since I was a young girl staying with my grandparents. Over to the right by the chain link fence was the old chestnut tree I use to sit under on a sunny day. And those large lilac bushes were still resting by the fence. Despite the stormy life we had all had together, it was a comfort sitting at the table with my mother and father. Our conversation was kept light and after I picked at my food, I headed for the couch where my mother had sheets, pillow and blankets waiting for me. We all got comfortable in the living room, silently knowing the dreaded conversation would begin soon. A reminder of the reason I was back home. With my father's head nodding the go-ahead signal, my mother made her best presentation of what tomorrow would bring. "Now, tomorrow your dad is taking you to Kaiser Hospital to see his doctor," She said proudly. "He did the surgery on Daddy when he had the cyst on his pancreas. So, he wants him to look at your records and give his opinion on what is wrong with you." My father then took control of the wheel, and said in a serious commanding tone, "We will leave around 10:00 a.m. to get across town to Kaiser." That name was always said with importance, changing the whole mood in our home when it was spoken. It was the medical insurance coverage we had thanks to my dad's long hours working on the shipping docks all those years. After his announcement, we spoke no more on the subject. Kaiser Permanente, my dad, and his doctor would be running the show now. My mother, with a proud confident look upon her face, headed back to the kitchen to finish the dishes. Watching television with my father, I drifted off once more. Soon a deep pain woke me up and my mother brought me my medications and helped me take them saying, "It's almost 9 p.m., honey, and you can sleep here on the couch or go into your bed later when we get ready to go to bed." After fighting the pain for a while until the drugs took hold of me, I then drifted in and out of sleep. There was the sound of quiet sobbing and a gentle hand touching my shoulder. It was my father leaning over me, softly covering me back up, his hand lingering gently upon my shoulder. He had tears in his eyes. In my whole life, I had never felt such love and tenderness from my father. With his alcohol addiction to numb his own emotional pain, his hands were always filled with anger and would at times hit me with powerful force when I was growing up. It took all these years and this event to finally, for this one moment in my life, experience those hands that hurt turn into a father's protective, loving touch. Now it seemed he was becoming one of my healers on my journey. I don't know how long he was there because I kept floating away, light as a feather, on my pain medication. At some point, he said something to me and then left as I closed my eyes again, going into a deep sleep. He was also born with the gifts, and I feel he knew at that moment that something was horribly wrong and must be found soon…before it was too late. (There would soon come a time when I was hospitalized once again. Drifting in and out of body, opening my eyes to his presence once again, in the hospital room sitting in a chair...his head bowed in his hands and he was crying softly.)

At some point during the night, my mother guided me to my bed, and when I closed my eyes I was carried away deeper into another world. It seemed like I was spending more time sleeping, and not just because of the medications. The desire to leave my body increased because I found refuge in a place I cannot describe in words. My days of clarity about time and space were fading. And the next day, the healers would start to arrive at last!

The Name I Would Not Forget

In the morning, Mother helped me into the bathtub as if I was a child again, her telling me the schedule for the day. "Today, Daddy's doctor will take a look at you and don't you worry, things will be okay honey!" The warm soap and scented water felt good on my skin and bones, and I felt light as a feather in that warm water and it felt so good. She reappeared and grabbed a fresh towel and leaned down to let the water out. "Time to get you out of here, dried off and dressed. Then you need to eat something," she said trying to smile, even though she saw a frown on my face at the mention of food. Drying my back and legs, she handed me the towel and helped me to the toilet seat to sit on the lid. "You just sit here and keep drying and I will bring your clothes," she said. In a minute, she was back and helped me get dressed. "Now let's have just a little to eat, you need to be strong."After breakfast and brushing my teeth, I walked out to my father's car. The engine was on and he was ready to roll. His blue car was always immaculate and he was proud that he had bought it years ago, when it had only 6,000 miles on it. With Mom standing on the porch waving goodbye, as we backed down the driveway, my eyes caught those lilac bushes that were blooming next to the chestnut tree. Breathing in, I could smell their sweet perfume. We drove to the hospital to meet with Dad's young doctor to get a second opinion. Dad tried to assure me that it would be good news. As we crossed the bridge over the Willamette River, I could see the wharf down below where he used to work as a longshoreman, also known as a "stevedore" a Portuguese word meaning a man who stuffs or loads ships. They start out as a casual worker which means they get picked last to work until they become a longshoreman. It took time for him to become a member of the union. It was a rough and tough life and they had to pay their dues to get their foot in the door. At first it was not a fixed job, and he would have to turn up at the docks in the early morning hoping to find someone willing to employ him and the others for the day. When he was at last admitted into the labor union it meant seniority, high pay, an extensive benefit package, and flexible schedule. My father made a lot of money and good medical insurance was one of the benefits.

Portland has unforgiving weather, and as we crossed the Columbia River, I reminded him of the days when he lifted heavy sacks onto a ship in icy cold weather. "I don't know how you did it, Dad." As he nodded his head in silent agreement, I knew he was traveling back in time to those years. I wanted to keep talking to forget what was awaiting me at the hospital a few miles away. "Remember when you took us down to the ships from faraway places and showed us around and said hello to the guys you worked with?" Reminding him of that time and him taking us to a ship from India for a tour, he smiled. I used to enjoy hearing about his work and the people he met from faraway lands. He was in the Navy during Pearl Harbor on a minesweeper, the USS "Bobolink". I grew up learning the history of that war from him. It must have been a past-life connection; I felt an affinity for those life and times on and by the sea. I always thought he had been a pirate in another lifetime because he worked on the water, in the world of ships carrying precious cargo, the sound of many languages being spoken, and rough, tough men. After a few drinks of whiskey, his words would be a universal mixture of many of them combined. It was called "pidgin", a trade language used by numerous language communities around the world to communicate with others whose language they did not speak. It was a rough and rowdy group of men, and while I never said anything, I remembered the times he came home with whiskey on his breath or what was becoming a black eye with the story of being in a fight on the slippery wet docks. These were big strong men who worked hard and drank hard and sometimes fights occurred. He never missed work and was out the door at 4:00 a.m. no matter how he felt. Just as with pirates when in port, there were times when someone from another land would come to our house and the liquor would flow as they talked about cargos and ship captains and our guest would tell stories of their land. Then there were those cans of crab meat and other exotic foods and items that showed up in our cupboards, gifts from the men on the ships. Sometimes there would be a gift for my sister and me from the Orient or Nordic lands. It was a hard life; it was part of the game. And when at last you got a full time position, the money was good and the medical insurance kicked in, which was then, just as now, like gold. That hard work made retirement very comfortable.

Soon the walk down memory lane disappeared as we got to the familiar streets near the hospital. When I was in high school I had been to this same hospital for a knee injury from a school skiing trip. Now, so many years later, here I was again. Dad went up to the desk and handed them my medical records and told them I was here. After we filled out the paperwork, we were taken to the doctor's office where I saw a young man in a white coat sitting behind a desk reading. As he looked up, I found myself looking into some very intelligent and kind eyes. There was a wonderful energy around him as he greeted us, walking around his desk, shaking my father's hand then reaching for mine. His hand touching mine felt very warm and comforting. I watched nervously as he talked with my father asking how he was doing. I listened quietly as my father told him the reason why he brought me to see him. "Doc, she's not getting answers in Reno, except that there is something on her pancreas and I knew you could help straighten this out for us. She is getting too skinny and she's in a lot of pain and she eats like a bird." The doctor looked again briefly at my medical reports from Reno. "Yes, I have been going over these," he said in a serious voice, looking at me. He then asked me some questions. I saw concern in his eyes as he spoke about the seriousness of the area that was injured, and about the need for surgery. In a delicate manner, he said the outcome was very fragile and could not be totally diagnosed until there was further testing. "I can say, you will be looking at surgery and until they operate they will not know the complete situation." Then he added, "there is a long recovery time; so now, we three need to decide how to proceed. I really can only see two options that need to be decided at this point."

I became frightened as he softly spoke about recovery time and that a decision would have to be made about where to do this surgery. Looking at my father, then at me he said to me in a serious tone, "Best if you and your parents talk about where you should have this surgery. I must tell you that this is a very serious operation and the outcome is unknown. You must know that you will be unable to fly after surgery for a very long time. Recovery will take time and depend upon how the surgery goes and what we find." His eyes met mine. "You might be more comfortable in your own surroundings to heal." He glanced over at my father. "Bob, that is something you, your wife and your daughter all need to discuss and then we will take the next step. I can do the surgery and we can work with her medical insurance, so that is not an issue." Sitting there watching both of them discussing me, I listened to his words and had a feeling that there was more he did not speak about. Smiling at me he replied, "I am flattered that your father has brought you all the way from Reno to see me, but do you not know that you have one of the top pancreatic surgeons in the country where you are living? It is one of his areas of expertise and this doctor is known for his skills because no one wants to operate on the pancreas. The

190

survival rate is not always good." There was great respect in his voice for this doctor in Reno, along with a shift of the energy in the room that was more ominous. "Elaina, if it was me in your shoes, I would see Lindsay Smith in Reno and from reading your records, I suggest that you make an appointment with him immediately upon returning." Writing the doctor's name on a piece of paper, he gave it to my dad. "Bob, if she has any trouble while she's still here, call me and we will get her in; don't worry about that." I felt comfort when I looked into this young doctor's eyes a final time, and I knew that God had whispered to my father to have me meet with his doctor. If we had not done so, more precious time would have been wasted and my life would have slipped away with the wrong doctors. We said goodbye, and I put his final words into my heart as he gave me a hug, "I wish you the best Elaina and know you will be in good hands with Dr. Smith."

Leaving the hospital, we were both in a lighter mood. On the drive back we had a ray of hope riding with us. The sun was dancing on the river below as we crossed the bridge once more. I promised myself repeatedly I would not, must not, forget this doctor's name, no matter what was happening to me!

At last we drove up to the house into the big yard with the beautiful apple, cherry and plum trees and the flowers that were getting more colorful every day. With dogs barking a loud hello, my mother, wearing her apron, was waiting at the door with a smile and anticipation of the news. I saw her eyes looking at my dad who was behind me as I carefully walked up the steps. Since the moment I arrived, there had been none of the constant horrible fighting that I had grown up with; my parents were a team on a serious mission together. Mom was looking to my father to be the strength and leader in this crisis for us all and he had stepped up to the plate. When we got into the house, she cheerfully said, "Auntie Lavelle called and wants to see you tomorrow, Grandma and Lauretta will be there also." As she continued talking about visiting them, there was an undertone of anxiousness in her voice waiting to hear what the end result was with the doctor. "Why don't you lie down for a while and rest? You look very tired. We can talk later about what the doctor told you," she said as I headed for the bedroom. Sitting down on the bed, I was worn out. Soon she appeared with a glass of water, a plate of saltine crackers with a slice of cheese to take with my medications. She was also keeping an eye on me while I was putting my pajamas on. It seemed like it took forever. I was so tired and exhausted but it had been a good day and gave us something to hang onto…hope. I felt like a child again as she helped me pull up my pajama bottoms because my left side hurt whenever I bent down. It was very frustrating because my mind was always so strong and I could work nonstop for hours. Those days were over and it was very hard to accept my body's current condition. Sitting on the bed I reached for the crackers and cheese took a nibble. Water glass in hand, I took my pills. Once I was ready for bed, Mom headed for the door adding, "I am going to leave the door open so I can hear if you need me. Dinner will be in a couple of hours." The thought of trying to eat made me shudder. Lying down on my bed, I tried to get comfortable and heard the voices of my parents in the living room; I knew what they were talking about. I pulled the blankets up around me and closed my eyes as the medications brought their soothing relief. Suddenly, the lady with the short red hair and the black velvet cape appeared once again, looking at me. For a moment, I felt frightened. She was not just in my apartment in Nevada; she had followed me to Oregon. Trying to compose myself, I asked for angels to protect me from her. As the medication started running through my body, I relaxed once more. Floating off into a deep sleep, the scent of those beautiful flowers outside the bedroom window comforted me.

It seemed like just a short time before my mother was standing over me waking me up with a "dinner's ready." With my energy recharged, I got up, washed my face, combed my hair and headed for the living room. Daddy was sitting in his chair as usual watching the news and smoking his unfiltered Camel. It was like going back in time, hearing the pots and pans banging in the kitchen and the nightly news ritual. Soon we headed for the table and I found myself eating mashed potatoes and a small portion of the pot roast that had been prepared. When we finished, mom placed a dish of tapioca pudding in front of me. "This should make your tummy feel better. I know how you loved this pudding when you were a little girl." Then she added, "why, I can also make you an eggnog!" which was another remedy we got when we were sick. After dinner, we went into the living room and soon were talking about the decision that needed to be made about where I should be for the surgery. My dad repeated what his doctor had told us and soon all three of us were on the same page. Not wanting to add more stress to my parents, I would return to Reno and have the surgery there, since we now knew there was a famous surgeon living in that area. I could recoup in my own bed with the care details to be worked out later. Dad spoke the doctor's name with a serious tone. "There is a Lindsay Smith that is considered the best in the country regarding critical surgery on the pancreas. Doc said he could help her, but felt this doctor in Reno would be her best shot." Suddenly, there was a flicker of hope in the room and it all revolved around a doctor that we had not even met yet. Looking at my parents, I spoke this stranger's name again, "Lindsay Smith." Then, expressing my fear I added, "I hope I am not so sick that I forget his name and don't even know where to find him." I was so overwhelmed, things that used to be simple were now confusing. Fear and panic were moving through me and my hands started shaking. My pain-filled body took my power away and I felt like a child again. In a flash, my mother went into the bedroom and came back with a pen and paper. Sitting down beside me with a smile she said, "don't worry honey, I will write it down for you right now and put it in your billfold." I watched her writing the name on the paper. She then went back in the bedroom and brought my purse. "Let's put it in there right now, sweetheart, so you can see that it is there and then you won't worry so much." She held up the piece of paper to show me, then folded it and placed it in my billfold. I was comforted at that moment watching her do this simple thing. Knowing that doctor's name was in there, I took a deep breath and laid down on the couch again. It was exhausting carrying the fear of forgetting his name when I got back to Reno.

Just watching television with my parents and having them near me was comforting; having people around you is a great part of healing. The essence of love and companionship can heal, nurture and activate compassion for all involved. It feeds and soothes the body, mind, soul and heart especially for someone who is ill; it also brings good karma to those who reach out when a loved one is seriously ill. It is a horrible feeling to be alone and facing the unknown. It is the reason I am here for others, when it is the dark night of their soul and they are alone.

It was a peaceful evening and soon I was off to bed, my mother reminding me that the next day we were going to Auntie Lavelle's and that Grandma would be there too. The next day would be the "first-born gathering."

Matriarch Blessings
Coming Out of the Closet

At noon, the next day my mother and I drove into Portland to my Auntie Lavelle's house. We had such a good time. I found myself being fussed over by Auntie Lavelle. My Auntie Lauretta was also there and it was good to see all three together in the same room and listen to them as they talked openly about the work I was doing. They shared a few stories of Lavelle and her two sisters and how they sat at the bus stop when they were young and "read" people. Observing them, I was reminded that it had taken a television show to bring us to this lovely conversation. The secret was now out of the closet and they saw that I was not dragged off and burned at a stake. Mother also finally understood some of my behaviors when I was a child, such as not being able to sit close to some strangers because I could feel them so deeply without them saying a word. As I talked with these beloved women, they listened intently. I explained that I always asked angels to protect me and bring to my door those I could help. Nodding their heads, it seems I passed the test on that one! I wanted them to know that I felt those who came to me were not there by accident. The work was uplifting and empowering for people and was at times very serious. These unusual abilities were being used very frequently with those who were suffering on a variety of levels: deep emotional wounds, a lack of self-worth, grief and loss, serious health issues, or those who were dying. But even in this serious work, there were the gifts of smiles and lots of love exchanged with each person I worked with. The rewards were many. And knowing that I was a part of someone making a positive life change, finding hope and belief in themselves, cannot have a price tag. The Matriarchs, with their beaming smiles, nodded their heads in approval and I felt a sense of relief.

Growing up, no one told me about the "gifts" that were passed down to me. The only glimmer I had of them was the time my sister and I had stayed a weekend with Grandma Proffitt. She was a strong woman that made sure her hair was always in place and she dressed nicely. She loved going out and there was a time that she played the piano at the silent movies. Men were attracted to her and she married a couple of times. She had a classic car, a dark green Model T that she would drive around town.

It seemed strange the day when she told us that she "knew things" before they happened. She shared the story with us about the time when my father was in the Navy at Pearl Harbor. Grandma Hoo-Hoo (as we called her) looked at us and said she had a feeling that something very bad had happened and she could not shake it from her bones! Soon there was a knock at the door and a telegram delivered that said he had been injured out at sea. I remember looking up at her hand moving and that opal ring she always wore glowing as she said, "I can tell when someone is going to call me on the telephone and who it is also! I see their face before it rings." I did not know at that time these were things that I too would be able to do all my life.

Those were the only things my grandmother said to me when I was a child. And when I was an adult, there was the time when everyone was gathered around the television at my parents' house to watch the tape of the Noon News show I had been on a few hours earlier. This was a first! They had never all gathered at my parents' home at the same time for an event. It was a big deal and I was more nervous about them than the skeptics. The past year Auntie Lavelle had been fussing about me blasting the gifts out into the world. She had finally sat me down and confessed the family secret revealing there were a variety of spiritual gifts that were passed down from our ancestors. At last, I knew that I was not crazy all those years. She explained to me that I had quite a few of those gifts and in very strong ways. She had been silently waiting all these years to see who would be born with them. It was an adjustment for her when she heard that I was doing interviews for newspapers and talk shows. "We only do this in private! People will harm us!" Very quickly, she took me under her wing when she found out that the media was courting me to do a show the day after my first law enforcement speaking engagement for Multnomah County Sheriff's Department. I invited her to come with me to the television station for a show and my Uncle Lloyd helped me get her there! I wanted her to have the experience so she would not be so fearful about my wellbeing. She did not know that this was just the start of being on the front lines and that I would be seen by millions of people all over the country. Oh, yes! It was a big, scary thing for her to do, as it was the big "coming out party" for the family, you might say. I sat on the stage and watched her in the audience. She was very nervous and watched me like a hawk. It was also a big scary time for me because I would be talking about my work as a psychic detective for the first time.

The next day Auntie Lavelle was at the television station with me when I walked on set. I sat down a few chairs away from the co-anchor, an anorexic woman. She took one look at me and knew she would not be in the spotlight when she heard the camera man say, "We have some eye candy today." Her male co-host was charming and welcomed me as he sat down next to me; in striking contrast, she was cold and distant. I handled each one of her questions while my concerned auntie sat nervously in the audience. I guess Lavelle and I were the coming out party to bring healing to our ancestors. It was now time to stop living in secret for fear that some devout Christian would kill us. Immediately, the energy shifted and I knew that the co-anchor wished me no good in the interview. I also knew to use caution with my reactions and responses. Silently, I asked for protection and to block her darkness from touching me. This woman had forgotten that I had just been standing in front of over 100 homicide detectives from various agencies who had put me through big time paces for hours. Apparently, she did not know that I would be able to clearly see through her. I knew how to answer her questions in a direct manner and I would not allow her to intimidate me. To make things worse, her male co-host was very much enthralled with me and had nothing but supportive things to say about me. I was silently thanking my angels for surrounding me with their presence. Walking off the set, I realized I had learned a big lesson about television interviews: never let them rattle you. As we walked out of the station, I was worried Lavelle would lecture me about how she said others wanted to harm us. When we got into the car, Lavelle was fired up and much to my surprise not in the way I was expecting. My sweet little auntie had another side to her that showed her power. "Honey, you handled that horrible woman with style and grace and made her look even more foolish every time she opened her mouth." Her words were like a sword that cut away all the ill intent that had been sent to me. Her eyes flashed as she boldly stated, "She couldn't hurt you." Then looking into my eyes, she gave me a warning, "though, she will try!"

A most empowering feeling filled the car as the two of us drove to my parents' house. It felt like a heavy burden was cast away from our shoulders and hearts. Lavelle made it very apparent that the two of us were not hiding all our wonderful gifts anymore! At least not when she was with me. From that day forward, she was brave and stood ready, by my side. She was my confidant and I was not alone anymore. The two of us arrived at my parents' house, victorious, with the TV station's copy of the show in hand. Mother had made tea and there were cookies waiting on the trays before each one of us. All eyes were upon us. Now we were all gathered around in silence as the segment began. As I looked at each one of them, I was nervous about how they would react! Just by the looks on their faces glued to the television, I knew this was going to open lots of doors for communication or complete silence. Despite the drama and pain in our family, it was and is filled with creative, hardworking, talented, and oh-so-eccentric people. I also discovered other family members who had unusual abilities that would not be spoken of until my life path would force them to be revealed.

After watching the show, there was dead silence for a moment and then it happened! My grandmother (Grandma Hoo-Hoo) suddenly blurted out loudly (she had a bit of hearing issues), "Honey, you know many of your great, great grandmothers and other relations were trance mediums, clairvoyants, and many had healing hands. Honey! People used to come to them for all sorts of things just like they come to you nowadays. That's where you also get those gifts." The room went into shock and dead silence and everyone was looking at her. Auntie Lavelle quickly leaned over to me and excitedly whispered, "keep her talking she has never told us this part." Doing her bid, I responded sweetly and loudly to Grandma, asking her to tell me more! Grandma was in the Queen's chair and ready to have the spotlight shine upon her. She continued to share a bit about the first-born daughters in the family and a few of her own experiences. "One of them could stick her hands in boiling water without pain or a burn! She touched people and they felt better." Lavelle was in shock and awe listening to her mother share our history and so was my father as he stared at his mother.

What a day this was! The house was all a buzz and like never before there was a coming out of the closet party talking about the ancestors and me and then their own experiences. While alone in the dining room, my father came up to me and said, "You know I have those things happen also, never talk about them, I have feelings about things that are going to happen, I call them 'tremors.' They are like a chill going up my arms and the back of my neck. You did a good job on that show." It was the first time he opened up to me in my life. After thanking him for telling me that he also had the same thing since a child, he then walked back into the living room and sat down in his blue chair. I now understood some of the reasons why he drank heavily at times became violent and was angry all our lives. He had PTSD from the Pearl Harbor years and because of his unusual abilities as a sensitive.

It was all coming into to place and halleluiah! I was not crazy; and if I was, I certainly was not alone. Maybe I was leading them all out of "The Closet" at last…even those in our lineage who were persecuted for having such gifts. So, now at last, removing the fear and silence from my grandmother and aunties, there was a new openness and freedom that had arrived and respect for their abilities.

After the television show, in the coming weeks Lavelle started digging into the archives and at a later date shared more about our lineage. She showed me a photo of two of my ancestors in Victorian dresses. Pointing to the one wearing the black dress and a big cross necklace she said, "This one was a very strong trance medium; in later years she would try to deny her abilities and became quite eccentric. She constantly changed the wallpaper in her home." This gave me the chills. Most people are afraid to use wallpaper as it takes a knack to put it up correctly. For some reason, I never hesitated when working with it and would slap it up on the walls in every room. It always felt good to work with it, almost an obsession! Sharing this with my auntie, she nodded and her eyes sparkled. "That is her coming through you!" I now understood and believed that I had been given more than just spiritual gifts from these relatives. What she told me next brought even more shock and amazement. Pointing to the next woman in the worn photograph she whispered, "this one was clairvoyant and a medium and she also had healing come through her hands." There was a glimmer of amazement in her eyes exclaiming, "she could stick her hands in boiling water and nothing would happen to them! People came to her in secret for their ailments." Looking at their faces the chills ran through my body and looking at Auntie, I told her a secret. "I have done the same! I was boiling water for pasta after seeing clients and when I went to stir the pasta my hand accidentally went deeper into the water! I did not feel anything and I thought that strange." I then remembered that I was always able to use very hot water when washing dishes by hand. When working with candles, I could also run my hand through the flame and hold it there longer than most people could without any burns or pain. I felt many times the "presence" of someone near me also. Could it be these two women watching me? So many things would be revealed each time we got together. At last, I understood why I was often nervous when someone would ask me the dreaded question, "What type of work do you do?"

Finally, everyone became more settled with what was happening to me and to themselves. The secret was out of the closet, and after being upset with me, they all calmed down after seeing that I was not dragged off and burned at a stake. Mother, who was a Scorpio, had a touch of gifts herself but chose to dismiss them. Listening to my grandmother and Aunt Lavelle and Lauretta talking with my mother, I was reminded that the four of us were given unusual and very strong abilities that could bring repercussions of attacks by those who feared what they did not understand. There was another time at a family gathering in this home, when a very large piece of butcher's paper had been placed upon Auntie Lavelle's coffee table. It was the family tree that included those who were like us. While everyone was outside in the backyard, she took me inside to speak privately with me. "I want to show you who is on this family tree," she said quietly. "Your cousin, Karen, is helping with the genealogy, and I am passing down this work to her. I want you two girls to support one another with this work." There was a list of names on both sides of the paper building the family tree. Lavelle pointed to a name towards the top of the paper then whispered to me, "She was a first-born daughter and had strong gifts as did these." Her finger moved down the paper to three more who had very strong abilities: clairvoyance, trance mediums, prophecy and healing abilities, all used in a variety of ways. It seems I had received each of my gifts from one of them because they also had touched my grandmother and auntie. Listening to her, I understood the reason why my hands would get so hot when I touched someone in pain and why they said it soothed them as their blood pressure monitors would become very peaceful. There was my ability to see those on the Other Side, at times passing on messages to their loved ones who were sitting before me. Then, there were times when I would know someone was going to die, or seeing/dreaming when world events would happen. They would occur between three and four in the morning.

As her finger moved down the page, there was a last one on the right side. "See this one?" she whispered, looking at me and then moving her hand further down the paper touching my name. "She was very strong like you are becoming. You must be careful so they do not hurt you!"As her hand went up to the top of the paper and moved back down a final time to each one, she told me they were treated unkindly by others because of their abilities. It is the reason we have kept silent about all of this. Then I knew the reason why on many occasions, while I was out socially I felt anxious that someone would ask what type of work I did. While I did not tell my auntie, I'd had a couple of my own radical, hate and fear-filled encounters with devout Christians. I also learned years down the road from my cousin Karen, when we were in North Carolina and Tennessee pouring through the county records, that many of our ancestors not only had small tobacco farms but some were also uplifting ministers while others were pharmacists. I found it to be an interesting combination. As I gazed at the paper on the table, a part of me was sad knowing how the ignorance of others who professed to be "favored by God" would assault those who had spiritual abilities in such cruel ways. "You are the first one to reveal what we have been given…abilities that are called gifts…but they are also a curse," she said quietly. Standing together, as we looked down at that paper on the table, the room was filled with those souls from the past. We two had come full circle with each one that day.

We both knew part of the price that was paid, because our health would be fragile at times and we carried the heavy burden of knowing what was to come. Lavelle, like me, knew when a death was coming. Even then, we were strong and our minds and abilities carried us through the family drama and tragedies. She, like me, was first-born and we both had two sisters whose gifts were not filled with the intensity and responsibility that we had to carry. One of my sisters feared this path and the younger one was curious and open but neither of them had a strong connection with our father's side of the family. The strength of the gifts came through Grandma to Auntie Lavelle and then to me next through my father, who had strong intuition. This also brought a heavy burden at times that came with this lineage. It was a secret kept so no one knew why they had those feelings and experiences. My father, the only son, said he felt it in his bones when something was going to happen. He too, like me, could not shake it off until the event happened. What was interesting is how these abilities jumped to our sons in this unusual family tree. It would be given to her two boys, Chris and Kurt, and my son, Michael who had these intuitive gifts of telepathy and prophecy at times, like we three women did. Chris predicted his own death many years beforehand, telling his brother Kurt that he would die on the day Kurt got married and that's what happened. Our lives would become even more entwined at that moment.

My Auntie Lavelle and Uncle Lloyd's house always felt welcoming and cozy. I had stayed there a few times and we always had so much fun. Uncle Lloyd adored my auntie and always wanted her to be happy! They even came to Reno one time when I was going to do a KOH live remote broadcast in the showroom of the MGM Grand Hotel. The room was packed with listeners from near and far! It was a success, and as people lined up to say hello, many asked if she was my mother. On one occasion Uncle Lloyd and I were chatting in the kitchen where he was making us a martini. He had a big smile on his face. "She is so happy you are here. We wish you were our daughter...the one we never had." Loving words that were a sweet blessing, which I carry in my heart to this day.

Sitting in the living room of this house filled with memories, listening to these three women laughing and talking, brought me comfort. Suddenly, I felt a spirit energy standing by Lavelle. I immediately knew who it was and it did not surprise me when I saw my cousin, Chris, smiling at me. I remembered when I had to knock on the door in the middle of the night with the painful heartbreaking news. As he had predicted, Chris had died in a car accident after leaving his brother's wedding reception. Right before he walked out the door, Chris and I had a conversation sitting on the edge of a bed upstairs away from the crowd. It was so good to spend time together. He was happy his mom and I were spending time together. Then, suddenly he looked me in the eyes and quietly asked, "You know, don't you?" When I asked, "What do you mean?" he just smiled and repeated it again. Suddenly, I felt uneasy, but I did not know why. My mind blocked what the wave of his strange words had sent to me. Then he asked me to keep close to Auntie Lavelle insisting that I promise to do so. I felt a foreboding chill. "What is this about, Chris?" I asked. "You know, Cuz," he said with a smile. He pulled me closer, then looked deep into my eyes and said softly, "You'll see. I need to go now. I love you." He gave me a lingering hug and a little kiss and we went downstairs back to the party. I started towards the outside deck where everyone was gathering for the bride's garter throwing ritual. I turned my head looking back to see if Chris was following. I saw him talking with a few people as he headed outside, his fate awaiting. In a matter of thirty minutes he got into his car, drove down the road and had a fatal accident. No one knew when we were out on the deck and heard the horrible sound of a car crash in the distance, that it would be him. Upon hearing the echo of the crash, Kurt did not know his words would speak truth so close to his heart: "Somebody did not make it out alive with that one!"

Hours later, there would be that late-night phone call at Kurt's house. I was staying there since they had left for their honeymoon. I was chosen to be the one that got the call from the Coroner's Office inquiring about who resided there. Replying it was my cousin's house, and I was the only one there, the coroner replied wearily, "Oh that makes sense why he was wearing a tux." Those words hit me like ice cold water thrown on me! I caught my breath hearing those words we all pray we'll never hear. "I am so sorry to have to tell you, he died tonight and I am so sorry I did not notify you earlier. Such a busy night." Sitting there in the dark, listening to his voice, it seemed like a bad dream turning into a nightmare with each word slowly spoken, turning into so much pain. As my own mind tried to process his words, I felt the sadness in this man and soon found myself gently talking with him about his work and all that he experienced. "It is times like this...it is a tough job even after all the years," he said in a quiet voice. Time stood still as I listened in the dead of night, and at some point I said, "you have very sacred work that you do and you carry a lot of weight on your shoulders," finding myself now giving him comfort. Thanking me, he replied, "I usually don't express myself like this but for some reason I did." "It's okay," I replied, "a lot of people say that to me, and I'm glad you were able to share. It must be lonely at times, just as it is also for the police, who have to notify families when their loved one dies." He apologized again for his late call, he then asked me the most powerful question. "Do you think you can go tell his parents? I feel you are strong and can handle this properly. If not, it will be hours before a police officer can go and notify them because we are all so busy tonight. I feel it will be better coming from you than the police. Please tell his family I send my condolences." The task was accepted and as I hung up the phone, my heart felt so heavy. His request had placed into my hands a most pain-filled and sacred work for me to do. I dressed warmly to go out into the dark of the night. So many hearts were going to be broken. Sitting in the car with my head bowed, part of me felt guilty that I would have to speak those words that the coroner passed onto them through me. Knowing the truth would cut so deep into all those that I loved so much, what would become a familiar prayer would go with me, "Please give me the strength, guide me and be my words when I tell my auntie and uncle." I also whispered prayers for my cousin Kurt and his beautiful bride Susie, "please give them a little bit more time to be happy."

The sound of the ladies' laughter brought me back into the present time on this sunny day at Auntie Lavelle's house and I could still feel and see Chris in this same room. I had done as the coroner requested and this room was never the same for me nor Auntie Lavelle. I also wondered once more if Chris had guided the coroner to me that night and to that conversation. Looking back, I remember him looking deep into my eyes that fateful night and hearing his voice speaking of his mother. "Promise me you will keep close to her. Promise, she needs you!" Now understanding the hidden meaning in that unsettling final conversation between us, I whispered, "I promise." Tears filled my eyes as I silently asked, "Why Chris? How does your brother erase this from their anniversary each year?" Turning my head away so that the ladies did not see my tears, looking towards that front door, the one I had entered that night bringing all that pain, he said, "Tell them not to think about me that day. It's okay to forget about me that night. I want them to live in the hours before, and want them to stay in the happiness and fun." His final words were "Tell my brother I love him and I am sorry." And then, he was gone, taking part of me with him.

The afternoon had flown by and I was suddenly very tired. When at last saying goodbye, Auntie Lavelle had a present for me. She placed a size six dress in my hand that had belonged to her. I was amazed that I had gotten down to that size. Holding the dress up I thought, "When did that happen?" She always dressed so nice. She was beaming and said there would be more of them later. We looked like mother and daughter in ways and she knew that I always needed something new because I was doing television shows and social events.

There were lots of hugs and kisses at the door. It was a wonderful way to end my trip. As we drove back to the house, my mother and I continued to talk about my decision to have the surgery in Reno. We tried to keep the drive upbeat and positive. In the near future, she would be sitting on my couch in Reno, tears of denial falling, as I told her about the fact that I might die. I counseled her as I did so many, only this time it was me who may not live. I would take on dual roles of grief and loss counselor and the one who was seriously ill. It took all my strength to tell her we had to be practical, that I needed her to help plan my funeral, what to do with my things and most important about my beautiful son…just in case the surgery did not have a happy ending. But it was to no avail; she was not open to discussing such things. She would only tearfully echo the heart wrenching words that every parent whispers repeatedly…when faced with the unimaginable.

"No! This can't be! No child should die before their mother."

At last, we were pulling into the driveway of the house with slightly lighter hearts. It felt like on that last night things were improving because at last we had some answers, but there was an unspoken anxiousness about what was to come in the weeks and months ahead. I knew deep down that I was in big trouble and there may not be a way to continue to live. I was like a volcano that could erupt with pain and death at any moment. What little control I had over my life seemed to be slowly slipping away. I just had to hang on long enough to meet with Dr. Smith. He was my lifeline! I knew this was my last night in this familiar house that had so many childhood memories. It was frightening to not know if I ever would return to it again. It was a quiet, pleasant and healing night with my parents, and it gave me strength to take with me back to Reno.

In the morning after breakfast, I finished packing and was ready to leave. I stood on the porch and watched my dad open the trunk of the car. The flowers were blooming on both sides of the porch, whispering a "goodbye." Overwhelming emotions filled me as my mom gave me a big hug and a kiss on the cheek. Breathing in the fresh air as I went down the steps, my heart and soul wanted to be filled with all the beauty a last time. I looked to the left at the familiar cherry, plum and apple trees and remembered my sister and I sitting in the trees laughing with our faces all stained with cherry juice. I recalled lying out on the grass on a warm summer night looking up at the sky counting stars…wondering what was else was out there. I headed for the gate passing the big chestnut tree and those old friends the lilac bushes, breathing in their fragrance and the damp earth a final time. With a final wave to my mother, we headed down the country road past childhood landmarks in a place called Bonney Slope: familiar houses, fields, the little country store that we would walk up to for an ice cream. Soon we passed by the grade school. Turning the corner, a wave of sadness filled me as we passed by Kathy Woods' house, bringing back the memory of that phone call and my grandmother telling me she had died. High on the hill was the cemetery where my grandparents were placed to rest. As we came into Portland, I said another silent "Goodbye" flooded with memories of life passages in this town, not knowing if I would return.

With the airport in view, my dad gave me the verbal list of what I must do when I got back to Reno. He parked the car and took my suitcase out of the trunk and we walked quietly into the airport. Giving me a big hug he said, "Now, when you get back, you find that doctor and let us know." Thanking him again for taking me to his doctor and helping me, with tears in my eyes I said, "I will Daddy." As I walked away, I was overwhelmed with thoughts as to what was waiting for me when I got back to Reno. The trip home was filled with many emotions as we climbed into the sky and I had feelings of deep anxiety about what would be waiting for me when we landed. I prayed that God would continue to guide me to my healers. Looking out the window, there was so much green below us and I felt the trees and mountains were saying goodbye to me. Memories of my life in that town filled me as we climbed higher and higher. Wondering if I would ever see my family again, I thought of my little sister who lived not far from our parents and for some reason had not stopped by to see me. Worry crossed my mind as I closed my eyes. As we climbed into the clouds I drifted off into a peaceful sleep. Time literally flew by and I heard the captain's voice announce that we were preparing for landing. Reaching into my purse, I pulled out my compact and once again saw my weary eyes. I looked at my watch and was relieved that it was almost time to take my medication which would stop the deep pain that was trying to wrap around my left side again.

When I got home, I was filled with those familiar mixed feelings of hope and fear, and I reminded myself to take one day at a time. When you live on what I call "Spiritual Automatic Pilot," magical things can happen out of nowhere even in times like these. They continued to appear. I still called out for the right and perfect doctor to arrive that could see and feel what was happening with me. I knew the surgeon to ask for, tucked safely inside my purse but the first doctor had not arrived yet. I felt as if I was in a holding pattern with the one who never seemed to listen to me and who was always gone. During my constant praying for the right healer to arrive, my mind kept wandering back to someone in the shadows. There had been that tall, young doctor with eyes like a hawk who had been standing at the foot of my bed with the others, when I was in the hospital before my trip to Portland. It seemed that he was starting to appear more often even in the emergency room when I could not stand the deep pain anymore. Turning the key and opening the door to my apartment, I said out loud as I stepped into hallway, "Archangel Raphael please send my healer to me!"

Between Two Worlds

The prior month, somehow a copy of the book "The Dynamic Laws of Healing" by Katherine Ponder fell into my hands. I still continue to use this book when working with people who have life-threatening illness. I had been reading it constantly and would recite out loud the healing affirmations and call out for the healing Archangel Raphael to stay at my side. There were many times I could feel and see their presence around me, and as those weeks and months went by, I felt like I was slowly floating far away from Earth, between two worlds. Before I went to see my parents, between the strong pain medications, loss of weight from not eating, and exhaustion, it was harder for me to work. It seemed like I was spending more time in another world even when I was awake in this one. I had a constant worry and fear about what would happen to me and how I would survive if I had to be in the hospital. I was running out of money and that brought me constant stress. A variety of emotions filled me, just like the stages we go through when a loved one dies. Denial was my constant companion until the time came when I was faced more each day with stronger pain, more trips to the ER, hospitalizations, obvious weight loss, and doctors prescribing stronger and stronger medications. Gradually, my mind's strong denial could not buffer the reality of my serious situation anymore. Each day fear resurfaced more and more in me as my mind processed the seriousness of my situation. I would lie awake at night worrying about my son, Michael who was on a guided missile destroyer out in the gulf. There was the constant battle within. Should I tell him that I could die? If I did, what good would it do? He would suffer and worry since he could not be with me all the time. The thought of his grief if something happened to me broke my heart. Loneliness and depression were my constant companions. Wrapping myself around a pillow was not the same as having loving arms holding me, making me feel safe and comforted.

Occasionally, I endured fleeting thoughts of anger, reminding me of how this whole thing started: all about not signing separation papers that Friday night, being thrown down upon that concrete step. At times, I felt great anger towards this man whose selfishness and temper created my pain, on so many levels. I resented him for hurting me in so many ways. Then, there was anger at myself that I should not have answered the door that night nor been alone with that man. As my pain increased, I realized I needed all my energy to try to heal rather than waste it on being angry about him. Spiritually, I knew that he would weep his karma somewhere, sometime, some lifetime.

I felt regret from time to time. There was so much that I wanted to do in this life. I wanted to spend more time with my son, be a better mother, be more present in his life. As the seriousness of my situation increased, I tried to bargain with God promising I would do even more work with others who suffered. Each day, the problems in this world seemed so silly and so far away. People grow a lot when they are faced with their own mortality, experiencing a variety of emotions: denial, fear, anger, remorse, more denial, then eventually acceptance. Even though I was not lazy, I saw how much time I wasted and realized my heart could have loved so much more. It was like one part of me was struggling along in this world and the rest of me was in another place I could not describe. I was afraid to go back to the doctor who was always out of town. I was hesitant about calling him for the referral I needed to see the surgeon suggested to me by my father's doctor. Did I unconsciously know that I must find help somewhere else? He had ordered the images, looked at them, and said nothing except I should put my affairs in order before he left town. My father's doctor knew immediately what my problem was from the same images. He told me to see the surgeon immediately.

There were days when I felt stronger and was able to do more. I prayed for it to continue. During those times, I worked with others in need and in worse shape than I was. Despite this, I felt that something inside me was horribly wrong. Looking back, I do not know how I did all the things I did. I was constantly…living and working…in the Valley of the Shadow of Death.

One of my clients, named Dee, arrived at my office one day wanting to have me interpret a foreboding, recurring dream she was having. She told me that she saw herself in a casket with a large amethyst in her hand. When I asked about her interpretation of this dream, she looked at me and said, "I am going to die soon." There was a heavy vibration that ran through my bones and I knew that this was not just a dream…it was a prophecy of what was to come. From that day on, I worked with her on a variety of levels to fill her with strength and give her the tools to work on healing herself. We would fight together, to make her dream not come true. Sadly, she would be diagnosed with cancer and in the months to come would undergo chemotherapy. The time came when I was at her bedside at the same hospital where I was later admitted again. I held her in an altered state for hours to keep her pain away until the night shift nurse finally arrived with strong pain medications to soothe her. A busy day with patients had Dee being forgotten by the nurses who should have been attending her, and it seemed that I had been guided to stop by unannounced to say hello. I found her in agony and her hand reaching for mine asking for help. "Oh, Elaina! You are here! I have been praying you would call me but could not get to the phone!" Tears were falling down her beautiful face as I leaned over her to gently hug her petite body. Immediately, the healing gift was activated in my body as I touched her. An hour passed and then another and there was no nurse coming with her medications. I became angry as the call light had been pressed with no response! Dee was still and resting. Heading to the nurses' station I informed them of her condition and that someone needed to get in there and give her the pain meds! They told me that she was not able to have them again until the shift change. My words were filled with frustration, "I have been holding her in an altered state for hours and I cannot leave her until someone gets in there!" Returning to her room, I began working on her, praying I would be given enough strength to continue until a nurse arrived. At last, I could leave! Exhausted, I stopped at the nurses' station to give them an update and shared my frustration about how long it took to give her the injections that would stop her suffering. They too spoke about their frustration and the helplessness they felt when they could do nothing about the med schedule. "It is wonderful what you are able to do for them. We wish the hospital would hire you to do this with others on a regular basis." With their heads all nodding in agreement and thanking me, I said goodbye.

The time came when I was in that hospital. I opened my eyes to find Dee standing at my bedside. After I told her she should not have come because I knew how sick she was, she smiled and placed a vase with a green carnation on the table. "Looks like it is your turn, girl, to have some healing. I could not lie on my fanny at home knowing you were in here after all you do for me," she said with a big smile. "Okay, you told me green is the color of the Divine Physician and thought I had better bring you one this time!" The student had become the teacher for me. This beautiful, fragile, petite woman with a scarf wrapped around her head from the loss of her hair now had a sparkle in her own pain-filled eyes. There was a moment of twisted humor as we both laughed, feeling that deep loving bond of two souls who were walking a tight rope to stay alive. We had a private joke between us that whomever went first would come back and say hello from the Other Side. There would come a time when things turned bad and she would fly me down to Stanford to do pain control on her. I was at the elevator one time and a young doctor was chatting with me. When I told him I was visiting Dee, he smiled and said, "Oh! You! Are the little lady from Reno! We have heard about you!" As we got into the elevator, his words shocked me. "We don't know what it is you are doing with her but keep doing it! Amazing!"

There is more to that story, but let's just say there came a time when she could not fight anymore and certain events arrived in her life that triggered the cancer to come back like a raging fire! She did at last die a few months later. I woke up one morning feeling her presence next to me, seeing her smiling and hearing her whisper to me from the Other Side. And then the phone rang bringing the news that Dee had just died right at the time I felt her in my bedroom. She had insistently asked her family to call me immediately after she died. They told me she was being taken out of the house to the mortuary as we were talking.

It seems that many of those that have become my family in so many pain-filled ways were surrounded by death. I have either walked with them to the end of their life or comforted them in their time of the loss of a loved one. It is a bittersweet path to walk but also very sacred to me. Everybody was sent to me, and I to them…by a Heavenly Presence. Nothing or no one is ever by accident.

The Man of the Cloth

One afternoon a Catholic priest named Father Dave was doing a radio show at KOH radio station. He was a big supporter of mine which I was very surprised about and grateful. I remember crying the first time I heard him defend me on the radio. He happened to be in the studio for one of my segments when a radical Christian minister called in and the topic he wanted to discuss was me. In the typical "zealot fashion" it was not a discussion but a full-blown attack on my work and how people should not follow me because I was an evil witch! Listening to the hate spilling into the studio, my Auntie Lavelle and her warnings crossed my mind. Taking a deep breath and wrapping protection around me I said, "I don't ask people to follow me, and to those who do want to, I say, don't follow me. I have enough work to do on myself in this life. Follow your God and your inner whisperings of how to live life in the Light." Then I said boldly, "Jesus is not pleased with you, Reverend."

Father Dave took the wheel as the minister continued to rant and rave about me. The fanatic hardly let him get a word in, and when he tried the self-righteous minister would not listen and continued to spill words of hatred about me and my work. The energy in the studio was very intense as the show host, Lou Gutenberger, looked me in the eyes. He knew this was going to be a "Hot Topic" segment! Father Dave finally had enough and said firmly, "Okay. You have had your turn to speak. Now it is going to be mine and you have a choice. You can either stay on the air, be still, and listen, or I will have them mute your call so that I can have a chance to speak." The phone was finally silent as Lou Gutenberger took his cue, hit the mute button, and gave us a smile. Father Dave took the mic and firmly put it all on the table. "You are not having a discussion or conversation, Reverend. Your ears are closed to everything except your way and yelling and verbally assassinating this woman is against everything that God tells us about how to live." He talked about the responsibilities of being a minister or priest. Then he said, "I ask you, Reverend, do you know this woman? Have you ever met her? Spent time with her?" The minister replied, "Of course not!" The priest then asked, "If you do not know her, have not spent time talking to her or observing her, how can you say that she is evil and going to hell? Is that not God's decision to make, not yours or mine? Throughout this world people believe in God in many ways. He is called by many names. God is everywhere since the beginning. Does not Jesus ask us to be kind, giving and compassionate towards all people? I also had questions about this woman, but when I got to know her, hear and see how she lives her life, serving those in pain and dark times, I received understanding." The studio was silent as he continued. This priest had taken command of the microphone. "She encourages people to seek God and their places of worship not discourage it; so how is that evil?" the priest asked calmly, adding, "Elaina may not say things in the language that I know as a Catholic, but I believe God speaks and works through her, just like HE does through all of us if we are open to receive it. What about Gandhi, Buddha and others who walked with love and peace and compassion just like Jesus? Were they evil?" Then he wrapped it up and gave his final food for thought to this radical minister. "How can we as ministers and priests spill hatred such as this towards others just because they do not practice their beliefs in God the same way we do?" He calmly asked, "is it not our actions more than our sermons on Sunday that are the Truth and Light?"

The show ended on that note. In a daze, I thanked him for joining us and standing up for me and said goodbye to Lou. I listened on my car radio to his show segment which was after mine as I drove home. I cried humble tears of gratitude that this Catholic priest protected me from this alleged "man of God's" verbal assault. Looking back, I know it was a sign. Long ago, one of the things I wanted to be when I grew up was a Catholic nun. Was this one of the many quiet prophesies whispered to me when I was a young girl and my connection to that faith? Or was the desire to serve humanity and this priest bringing memories to me of a past life? There was the time we talked on the phone about exorcisms. I was in my sick bed and he on his couch resting, before another mass in the evening. Our minds traveled to so many spiritual topics including house cleansings that I did for people. I described the procedure and how the occupants felt a beautiful change in the energy of the dwelling and the personal lives of those who lived there. It is not just waving a sage stick around in the air but a long process that takes time, ability and power to clear and activate the Light. I felt completely comfortable sharing my secrets with Father Dave. "It is interesting, Elaina, that you do this in a very similar way that priests have done it for hundreds of years, blessing homes with holy water and other sacred acts. Yours seem to be on deeper levels, though. Were you taught to do this?" It felt good to be able to share with him on this level. "Not really, Father. These are just things I seem to know how to do. God whispers to me what I need to do." We had wonderful conversations at times about God, life, death and those suffering. I also told him about what comes through me, what I see and feel when I am walking someone to the Other Side. And I shared a new awareness, that it seemed there was another level or frequency given in the last rites. I discovered the ability to go with a person to a certain point and then I could not go any further. I became aware of another fated and karmic event, reaching back through the centuries. I realized that this priest had been destined to be part of the closure to the karmic pain of persecution so many had experienced through time. There was comfort knowing this priest stayed near me as I walked with one foot on Earth and one in Heaven, between two worlds.

Last Rites

The weekend after the eventful radio show with the fanatic minister, I got a phone call from Father Dave asking me if I would do his talk radio show in Carson City, which is about thirty miles south of Reno. He was the priest for the prison and told me that many of the inmates enjoyed listening to me on the radio and would love to hear me on his show. He asked if I would share what I saw for their lives. "It would mean a lot, Elaina, if you could give them some hope for a better way to come. They have worked hard to turn their lives around." He told me they were graduating from some classes and he wanted to give them the hope of a brighter future on the next early morning weekend show. Even though I did not feel well, I gave him an immediate response. "Of course, Father! I would love to reach out to them." I hung up knowing, despite the pain, I must keep my promise. Not to mention that I owed him big time after his defense of me. Pulling the blanket up around me for a nap, I closed my eyes. I knew I would have to be very strong to make that drive. The week passed in a blur and late Saturday afternoon the phone rang. It was Father Dave confirming the show for the next morning. I told myself I would go to bed early that night, so I could be strong enough to make the drive. I had hardly been eating or drinking water and it felt like I was living on air because I had zero appetite. It was getting so bad that my parents would call me and do a phone intervention. "Honey, let's go to the refrigerator and get something to eat. I know you can do it!" Mother would plead over and over with my dad on the other phone agreeing with her. I resisted until their persistence took me to the refrigerator just so they would stop talking about it. The only food I could tolerate was a milkshake I made with ice cream, strawberries and wheat germ. This is an example of the strange things that angels would place in my hand. Sometimes I also added a banana or blueberries. I kept the shake in the refrigerator or freezer and had a teaspoonful on occasion. In the future, I shared this recipe with those who were in similar situations to help them keep up their strength while they were trying to heal. I became a coach for the dying as well as spiritual minister, teacher, counselor, medical intuitive and friend forever.

Getting into bed that night, I suddenly felt so "far away" as if I was up on the ceiling. My mind drifted to many things about life and this world. I could not understand why people on Earth were so concerned with so many silly things. I set the alarm and prayed deeply that I would wake up to a better day. I felt light as a feather as the medication took me to a cozy pain-free place. Time flew by and soon I was waking up to the sound of the alarm. It now was exactly 4:00 a.m., plenty of time to slowly get ready. Sitting on the side of the bed, I felt a grumble of pain starting to run from my stomach around the back of my left side. Knowing I needed to act fast and to calm this thing down before driving, I felt a bath might soothe me. I was so weak from the pain attacks; warm water was one of the rituals that calmed things down. I breathed in the aromatic bath salts as I slowly got into the water. Leaning back in the tub I felt the warm water flow over my abdomen and chest. Closing my eyes, I was guided from within to breathe.

Lately, with my pain attacks, I found myself imagining healing air going into me as I inhaled through my nostrils and slowly exhaled through my mouth. I would "see" all the pain being blown (just like Superman's breath) out into the universe where there was a garbage can with my name written on it. But lately, the warm baths that used to soothe my pain were not as effective and this morning it was hard to get out of the tub. The pain was different now and was a warning of what was to come. Pulling myself out of the bathtub ever so slowly, I prayed that I would not slip and be able to get up and out of the tub safely. As I was drying myself off, I suddenly vomited a black fluid into the toilet. Feeling faint and shaking, I washed myself off, put a cool cloth on my face and brushed my teeth hoping I would not vomit again. Just as I regained composure and had applied some lipstick and blush to look healthier, I had an uncontrollable pressure in my bowels forcing me back to the toilet. What I would see revealed another new symptom of something ominous. There was a black substance with a thick consistency like road tar. I learned later if this happens it usually is old blood that is coming from the upper section of the G. I. Tract…that means from the esophagus, stomach or first section of the small intestine. The tar-like consistency in the stool means the blood has been exposed to digestive juices. While I did not know the exact meaning of this occurrence, it became apparent that something very wrong was happening inside of me that could not be ignored or hidden much longer. Cleaning myself with warm water and putting on my clothes, I sat down on the edge of the bed for a moment. With head bowed, I asked for guidance regarding going to the radio show. Should I attempt to go down to Carson after what had just happened to me? I knew Father Dave and those in prison were waiting for me and I did not want to take away their chance for the message of hope, healing and a new life arriving. Also, I did not want to disappoint this kind priest. In my stillness, there came a knowing that I would be able to do this but I also was told that time was running out!

I headed for the kitchen and took my morning pills with sips of the smoothie. I hoped I could keep them down after what had just happened. I knew it would take all my strength to drive so I focused my mind on arriving safely. It was about a thirty minute drive each way and I vowed not to drive again after this last trip because I did not want to hurt someone. Driving down the highway, I watched as a hint of dawn's light appeared in the darkness. Praying with each mile to the studio, I knew that powerful mind of mine was once again taking over my body. "Jesus take the wheel" was now activated in real life. Angels had to be driving through the valley that morning because I do not remember the drive. Father Dave greeted me at the entrance and took me into the studio. Sitting down, he asked how I was feeling and I tried to keep the conversation light, not wanting to concern him. As I put the headphones on, I sent out a silent call for guidance and asked to bring the healing words needed for those who would be listening. We went on the air. The phone lines lit up and the time flew by quickly. We both felt good about the inspiration that was instilled in the inmates as I shared God's whispers about their life paths and new directions. I felt light as a feather and there was a deep clarity about each soul who called in asking for guidance. After the show, Father Dave escorted me to my car and we saw the sun's early morning light amidst beautiful clouds. With a smile, he gently touched my arm. "Thank you, Elaina, for doing this. I know it was so early in the morning and a long drive on top of it and I am grateful for your help. We all are lost at times, some more than others, and there are times when God asks us to do spiritual work in ways that neither ourselves or others may understand." His next words were such a comfort, "I always say from my knowing you and the work that you do, Holy Spirit has made you a messenger of hope, healing, forgiveness and love that has a wonderful effect upon others." Humbled by his words, I bowed my head and felt a tear falling out of the corner of my eye. He laughed gently. "You just do it in a way that is most unusual." I smiled back at him. "Amen to that, Father!" I replied. As he gave me a goodbye hug, I felt soothed and safe in that brief moment. He walked to his car parked next to mine and we both unlocked our doors. Now standing by our cars, suddenly my heart was pounding and there was the flicker of an ominous feeling running through me. "Father, what you are going to do now?" Looking at me with a big smile he replied, "It's Sunday, Elaina, and I am going to serve mass." I realized I did not even know what day it was because they all were running together. I felt dread within knowing that something was coming that I could not control and I needed to lean on this priest's strength. Feeling my deep pain awakening again, I knew I needed to leave and get back home fast. "Father, will you do me a favor?" That moment was surreal because, just as he smiled, the sky above and behind him now had slivers of golden shafts of light and started turning pink and blue as the shadows on the mountains behind him were becoming lighter. "Would you please pray for me today? Keep me in your prayers, please? I need them." There was a fear in my bones about what was coming and part of me wanted to hang on tight to this man. It was all very clear at that moment at last! I knew neither my body nor my mind could not take much more, and as panic started to fill me it took all my strength to not cry out. "Don't leave me!" With immediate concern in his eyes, I took his words into my heart as he slowly said with a different tone in his voice, "You've got it!" Immediately, I felt him assessing my ominous request. Then in a most serious tone he said, "Of course I will, Elaina, and you are never forgotten." He blessed me at that moment and as I looked into his eyes I did not want to leave him. I was very afraid of the unknown but felt this priest's love and prayers surrounding me. We said goodbye again and I got into my car and watched as he gave me one last concerned look as he drove away. My hands on the steering wheel started to tremble. At that moment, I felt a shift within me. As I headed out to the highway I realized that, even though I was not Catholic, it felt like a priest had just given me last rites in the parking lot. I found comfort knowing I was not alone and would be with him while he was serving mass. As the sky was turning blue, pink and gold it was apparent that Heaven was very close and time was running out for me. With each turn in the road, I was aware of the heavenly gift that had been given to me. This dear priest had been sent to me by the angels. He was kind and compassionate towards me when others attacked me. He was now with me in my darkest hours.

Knowing I must get home fast, calling for angels to help me do so safely, I was comforted that there was a priest performing a mass and praying for me. I now accepted the truth. My time was running out!

Time Running Out

Part of me was numb from the bombardment of feelings of what had just happened and my new awareness of what was coming to me. I could no longer deny or bravely tell myself "it will all go away." Driving home with each mile I felt a wave of acceptance…a quiet grace and dignity as I held on to those last words Father Dave spoke to me. I had a feeling deep within as I saw those beautiful shafts of light coming down from the early dawn sky, touching us with their heavenly beauty. I carry that moment with me to this very day, my heart and soul holding that profound moment in time, forever. As I parked my car, I gave thanks for arriving home safely. I knew the woman in the black velvet cape would be standing in my hallway. Gathering my strength at the bottom of the stairs, I looked at the green grass and noticed there was a lilac bush right below my place. I slowly climbed up the apartment stairs and it took every bit of my energy to do so. Upon entering, I went straight to my bedroom, took some medication, put on my pajamas, and prayed for pain-free sleep. I felt cold even though it was a sunny, hot day and pulled the covers up and around me. I told myself I just needed to sleep for a while then figure out what to do. I was so ill and felt so vulnerable, and there was no one there to help me think clearly about all that was happening. Promising myself I would call my friend Joanna after I rested, I said to myself, "one thing at a time, Elaina. Just rest now." Exhausted from the drive and the early start of the day, I knew that I would have to call the doctor Monday because this was the weekend and the only alternative was the ER. I fell into a deep sleep as medication started to flow through my body. Time stood still, bringing me quiet and peace at last.

The next morning was spent in bed because I found a comfortable position and did not want to move and wake up the pain. I called the doctor's office and was told that he was out of town for the week, leaving me once again in limbo. An unseen presence seemed to keep separating me from this doctor. The only alternative would be the emergency room if I was in severe pain. I knew it was just a matter of time before I would be at the ER. In the meantime, I tried to keep pain free. The days to come were a blur. Certain events and conversations are very clear and not forgotten while other times are a fog all running together.

This is what I remember.

Memorial Day weekend was approaching. At some point, I was torn from my soothing sleep by a pain so hard it ripped through my body and literally forced me to sit up. The dresser mirror at the end of my bed showed a woman with her eyes bulging out and the veins in her neck protruding. Then even stronger, deeper pain hit me harder than ever before, ripping through my abdomen, throwing me back down on the bed. I tried to center myself and breathe out the pain; it slowly eased for some time, or maybe I passed out, because when I looked at the clock again, it was late afternoon and time for more medication. My shaky hand grasped the water glass and the two pills and crackers next to it. After taking them, I grabbed my book "The Dynamic Laws of Healing" and frantically read a passage or two. Lying there, waiting for the medication to take effect, I heard voices below outside my open window. It took all my strength to get up and look out the window. Down below, I saw two women who were talking and laughing on a late sunny afternoon by the lilac bush. Immediately, I had to get back to my bed as I felt so dizzy. I was so weak that the women talking below my window could not hear my feeble cries for help. Soon, I heard them saying goodbye to one another and then there was only silence. As the medication started to take effect, I felt my body relax at last. My sleepy eyes caught the lady in the black velvet cape from the hallway. She seemed to be standing closer to the doorway.

At some point, another strong pain ripped through my body across my abdomen and wrapped around my left side again. It felt like my life-force was being knocked out of me! I started crying out for helpers because *this* attack was like nothing I had experienced before. Alone and frightened, I asked God for the strength to get help. At this point, I was so disoriented I did not even see the phone on my nightstand and didn't have the mental clarity to know a number to dial. There was only one way to make a final attempt to get help. I knew I had to get out of that apartment! With great effort, I got off the bed and slowly crawled to my door in the dark hallway. It took forever to reach up to the door knob because the pain in my abdomen was overwhelming. Somehow, I got out onto the landing and crawled to the neighbor's door. Finally, they heard my feeble knocking.

Off to the hospital I went, but how I got there, I do not even remember.

Fred Fricke M.D. G. I. Specialist –Dr. Lindsay Smith, Surgeon

Words cannot express my gratitude. May you both be blessed always. I would like to thank God and my two amazing doctors who, with God's guidance, saved my life. I believe Archangel Raphael works through healers and they always arrive at the right time: Dr. Fred Fricke, M.D., Specialist Gastroenterology, Northern Nevada Medical Center, who never gave up on this frail woman, so exhausted from the off-the-chart pain thresholds. I feel it was Divine Intervention when I would arrive at the ER for months on end, and even on prior hospitalizations, that he was most times on call. I am so grateful I had enough strength in the ER that late afternoon just before sunset, knowing that time was running out, to ask him to legally become my doctor so he could help me. And, second so thankful that I was able to hold on to consciousness long enough to tell him, "I want Lindsay Smith, General Surgeon (Retired) Northern Nevada Medical Center as my surgeon," bringing this incredible doctor also to my bedside. How he arrived at that critical moment whispers to us that "God does truly work in strange and wondrous ways."

The End of the Road

"Though one may be overpowered, two can defend themselves. A Cord of three strands is not quickly broken." Ecclesiastics 4:12

Life was becoming a blur; pain has a way of making that happen. With a strong mind, there is the ability to dismiss or hold at bay those signals of pain, warning that something very bad is happening. Those who are not surrounded by family and friends on a regular basis have no one to monitor them or translate what appears to be something very serious happening to their external body that is not being addressed. Lying in the cubical of the emergency room at Northern Nevada Medical Center, I heard the familiar voice of the doctor who had been there for me so many times before and who was now saying to a nurse in what seemed an angry voice, "She is here again?" Then there were a couple of swear words. I felt awful. He was from another hospital and had to drive to this side of town to see me all the time because my doctor was always out of town. Now, I was afraid of him coming to my bedside, then startled when suddenly the curtain opened and there he stood. This tall slender man's eyes seemed to be scanning me on many levels. As he came closer to me, there was a spark of golden light emanating from them for just a moment. There was also frustration on his face as he looked at me. Starting to cry, I apologized for bothering him again, bravely letting him know that I heard what he said on the other side of the curtain. The confusion on his face changed as he realized what I was saying. Shaking his head, calmly said, "No, that's not why I am angry. It's not you." Then in his very direct manner, he said it was about the other doctor who had not done anything for me all these months. I listened as he explained to me that he was not my doctor and could not treat me the way that he felt should be done. "I think I know what is happening to you, but my hands are tied because you are his patient not mine, although I am always treating you on call due to his absence." His voice was filled with frustration and there was concern in his eyes as he looked at me. It must have been an overwhelming moment for him, after all the critical time that had been wasted to still not know what was erupting inside my body. He now had to work very swiftly to discover the way to diagnose my condition and formulate a plan to move forward. At last, the final realization came to me lying there, looking up at this man. I was dying…in agony with the most horrible pain I have ever felt. Even that heavenly presence that had taught me an altered state technique to get out of my body to rest, heal and function was fading away. My weight loss was so great that I felt weak and drained of all my energy. I had become totally disinterested in food and was not even drinking water to hydrate. These are sign posts along the path to dying. I had finally arrived at the end of the road. At last the healer had arrived! His name was Fred Fricke. I knew there was very little time left and my strength to continue was exhausted. It was Thursday evening, May 22nd, and I knew that there would not be too many more days for me. Looking up at him prophetic words were spoken. "Will you be my doctor? Cause if you do not help me, I will be dead in three days if something is not done fast!" His eyes filled with compassion; then that flicker of golden light once again confirmed for me that Archangel Raphael was working through this new doctor. As he took my hand he said, "You've got it!" There were tears in his eyes. "You are not going to be hurting like this anymore and now we must get to work!" At last, I was able to let go and gave my pain-ravaged body over to him. "I am going to admit you and give you very strong drugs, Elaina, that will make you pain free. I am going to set up some tests at the other hospital for you and then we will know what's going on!" His words gave me hope. "I promise this will get done, and in the meantime I am going to keep you as comfortable as possible and tell you soon what is happening. I have had a feeling I know what is going on since the last time you were in the hospital, but now you are my patient and we are going to get this B.S. done!" In the weeks and months to come I learned this doctor called it like he saw it and held no words back with his colorful manner of speaking. Along with his other patients, I discovered this strong man was not afraid to shed a tear also. Pausing a moment at the doorway he added, "And we are going to have to get you a surgeon. Just know that." As he started to leave to admit me and order pain medication, I heard the voice within me saying repeatedly, "Tell him the name! Tell him the name quickly!" With all my strength, I spoke the surgeon's name I had been given in Portland. Just as I had promised myself, it was still embedded in my mind no matter how much pain I was in or how many drugs I had to take. A second of panic filled me knowing I must speak his name quickly and loudly in case I became unconscious at some point. "Lindsay Smith." My new healer looked surprised as he heard that name being spoken "What did you say?" It took all my strength to reply "Please! I want Lindsay Smith to operate on me," repeating it twice just in case he did not hear it the first time. There was a surprised look on his face. "How did you know about him?" I told him how my father's young doctor in Portland told us that the best surgeon in the country for the pancreas was here in Reno. He replied, "Well then, that is the one you will have." As he headed out the door, I finally started letting go of everything I had carried on my shoulders and in my heart for so long. Angels had arrived at last! My new healer, who now had my life literally in his hands said he would get this surgeon for me.

Lying there in the ER waiting for him to return, I felt so cold even after I pulled the hospital blanket up tighter to get warm. Lately, it seemed I could never get warm enough and there was always a chill around me. The memories of sleeping in my old room as a child, and that wonderful smell of my clean sheets and warm blankets as I had pulled them up over me, comforted me. I thought about my grandparents appearing before me with those worried looks on their faces on my recent trip to Portland. I now knew my time was short; there were those lilacs blooming outside my window and something else I could not quite remember.

Soon the doctor was back with the injection he promised would give me more relief. There was a different mood in the ER this time. Nurses were swiftly hooking up IVs into my fragile thin arms. The powerful narcotics soon took me to a warm and soothing place. "Now let's get you to a room and get you comfortable. Don't worry now, Elaina, just let me take over." Feeling my fear about him going away after all the time alone with no doctor to care for me, his words brought me comfort. "I will see you later, I promise!" I felt his hand gently touch my shoulder as they were wheeling me out into the hallway. Looking up at him, I remembered the Bible Verse Ecclesiastic 4:12 that I had read days before arriving in the ER when pleading for help and for a message of what was to come. "Though one may be overpowered, two can defend themselves. A Cord of three strands is not quickly broken." The second cord of the strand had arrived! A bond was created between us that day that would last through this lifetime. I felt myself starting to let go of all that I had been through as I heard his voice say that he would come see me in a bit and I was not alone now. As they were pushing the bed through what seemed to be a hallway filled with shadows, I saw a flash of the lady with the short red hair and the black velvet hooded cape watching as they were moving me to the elevator. My mind was fuzzy from the strong drugs but even then I had clarity that she had come for me even here, now, in the hallway. I was to the point I did not

234

care anymore because my will to fight was almost nonexistent. It was now in the hands of God completely, this Healer and the surgeon, who would soon walk me to the next step. As the nurses tucked me into bed in a peaceful room, I was drifting off to someplace ever so far away. My last words were whispered prayers, asking to be kept in the white blue Christ Light of protection. I slipped comfortably into the black velvet darkness once more.

Archangel Gabriel

It is said that Archangel Gabriel is the bringer of news and heralds the revealing of answers. He is chosen by God to deliver very important messages. After months of pain and no answers, at last His Presence had arrived. The next morning the nurse got me ready for the trip across town. They had planned it so that I was given my pain med injections just before being wheeled downstairs so I would be comfortable while having the tests. Soon, I was whisked away in an ambulance to Washoe Medical Center across town for cat scans. As I was being prepared to go through the imaging machine, a young man with deep blue eyes was looking down at me. He mentioned that he always listened to me on the radio. "We knew you were coming, so you just be strong and know that we all are batting for you and we will find out what is happening to you!" We looked at each other a final time before the scan and I heard him say, "Don't be afraid, hold real still." I realized there was so much love being sent to me. The powerful pain medications were now running through my veins and I had no sense of time, drifting in an out of my body during various diagnostic tests. At last, they were completed. At some point, I was pulled out of the scanner, and while I was lying there, across the room was a group of doctors wearing white jackets standing in a room with large windows looking at what appeared to be black and white images on a screen. They had such intense, somber energy around them that it felt like you could cut it with a knife. Drifting in an out, I was startled awake again when suddenly I heard a loud cheer through the glass and I saw them all giving each other high fives. The young man came out of the room and came in where I was and leaned over me and whispered, "you will know soon. What we found. I can't tell you but it is better than what we thought we would find. Hang on!" As I was wheeled out of the room heading for the ambulance ride back to the hospital, they all waved goodbye, still jubilant about something. In my drugged haze, I thought they looked like angels... and for me they really were.

During my ride back to Sparks, I was surprised the whole town seemed to know that "Reno's favorite Psychic" (as Lou called me on the air) was seriously ill. Near and far, they had listened to me on the Lou Gutenberger Show on KOH radio and he had mentioned that I was hospitalized. Lou told me that there were calls flooding the station, asking which hospital I was in. He said he did not disclose that information for my privacy. Lou became a link for listeners to get updates on me. He enjoyed being the messenger and told me enthusiastically the whole town was buzzing. So many prayers! God has blessed me in so many ways. Privacy was hard to keep at times. Upon being hospitalized in April, I had to go under my married name because there were many people who wanted to visit me. But even a different name didn't stop them from finding me. Many were curious to see what I looked like. Medical staff, cafeteria workers, and others would sometimes be at my door in the days to come, wishing me well and telling me they listened to me on the radio. Some even asked me, "can you tell me something about what is coming for me?" At one point two listeners, Doris and Steve Kresoja, who were very much into the metaphysical life, found their way into my room. Steve had healing gifts and offered to work on me. I accepted, of course, because somehow they had entered the room. While this also is a blur, I do remember him standing at the end of the bed sending healing energy through my feet, while Doris stood by my side smiling. They became part of my close spiritual family from that day forward.

Some of us die with crowds of people around us. Others die more alone or with strangers. It was the latter one for me, except for a few clients, medical personnel, and others that I had also been helping who were also dying and preparing for their crossing. We were a strange, wonderful group who helped each other in such a variety of ways during the dark nights of our souls. And then there were so many others in my new town who were also praying for me, people I did not know, becoming my family. Strange how life is and who is there in these times and who is not. While it was not the way I would have expected it to be, everyone and everything was in Divine order. If you have faith and trust, you will find that all will be given, and some things taken away, forever.

Since that cold night when the man I loved threw me down on the concrete step and walked away leaving me on the ground, there was never a communication from him. No card, no phone call. Only silence. I was too weak to even care.

The Third Strand of the Cord

At some point when floating in and out of my body, I opened my eyes to see a man entering the room. Sitting down next to my bed he introduced himself. "I am Lindsay Smith, the surgeon you requested." I immediately noticed his hands and knew he was the one to operate on me. He had those long, delicate fingers that are known in palmistry as "The Philosopher's Hand" and are found to belong to many brilliant surgeons. At last! He was not just a name spoken in Portland or that sacred piece of paper my mom had placed in my billfold. He was here in my room and I breathed a sigh of relief. He was pleasantly surprised to hear how I was referred to him by the young doctor in Portland. We discussed the operation, and while most of it is now a blur, I do remember him drawing a line on a paper napkin of the incision he would be making. And then he gently asked, "do you think you can make it until tomorrow? I don't usually ask that question to a patient, but your doctor told me what you said…that in three days you would be dead. I always take words like that very seriously. The reason I'm asking, is that the operating rooms are jammed since it is the Memorial Day weekend. But if you cannot hang on, I will get you in, I promise. So, don't worry about that."

Closing my eyes briefly, I asked my angels for the answer to his question. I heard a "yes," then replied, "I will try to hang on and wait until then." As he said goodbye, I saw that flicker of golden light coming through his eyes revealing that Archangel Raphael was with us at that moment. Both the doctor and the surgeon had arrived at last! These two would walk these final steps with me. I knew all those prayers were answered and now a new door was opening to the unknown. I was not alone anymore! I knew both of their names and faces and held onto the words of the one in the ER who was not afraid to use a swear word or two or shed a tear and who took charge fast. Dr. Fred Fricke promised to give me relief from the violent pain taking over my body. I held on to his strong words of comfort to me. "You are not going to hurt like this anymore!" My weary mind could relax and not worry anymore. The light outside my window cast a soft golden shimmer as the May twilight arrived. Everyone had arrived and for a while no one was at my bedside, only the air filled with a stillness that permeated every corner of the room. At some point, I opened my eyes to see a nurse with syringes and new IV bags filled with the potions to keep the pain away. I felt only the desire to be peaceful and pain free with a simple request to the nurse, "So cold, more blankets please."

The room was dark except for a soft light above the bed. At some point, someone placed more warm blankets over me and left me to my solitude. Lying their quietly in prayer, as I waited for sleep to take me, I felt a Holy Presence with me in the room that did not leave. As I closed my eyes and let go, I heard a voice whisper.

"The cord is now completed. Just rest now, you are not alone."

No Turning Back

At last the day of surgery had arrived. I had made it to the third day! There was activity in my room as the nurses were preparing me for the surgery. Today I was alone, no one there with me, just a message from my friend Donna assuring me that she and Johanna would be waiting outside the operating room later that day. As the noon hour arrived, the steps were finished for prepping me to go to the operating room. Feeling like a vulnerable child again, I heard echoes of my childhood prayers running through my head. I asked that God would be with me this day and for my doctor to be blessed and guided. I humbly asked if I did not live that I wanted to go to that beautiful place called Heaven. I do remember having fleeting moments of panic, knowing that soon I would be wheeled into the operating room and have no control over what would happen. Truth be, I never did have any control over what was happening inside me. There is a time and place for traditional medicine and this one was of those times. I implored the sacred Presence in my room for healing Light to wrap all around me as I drifted in and out, and the nurses completed their work. I could not fight to live anymore, feeling like I was hanging on to what is called "life," as if my hand was holding the string of a balloon floating higher and higher away from this world becoming light as a feather heading towards the Unknown. My weakened, emaciated body could not take any more. I made peace with my God asking forgiveness for any trespasses I had made. I began sending blessings to my loved ones and to my son, asking that he be blessed in his life and know he is loved so much.

Then at last I was wheeled down the halls and into the operating room. Lying on the table, there was no one in sight. Only the sound of my heart beating on the monitor next to me keeping me company. Suddenly, I had another feeling of panic running through me because at this stage of the journey it was just me and I knew that; I was alone no matter how many more people would arrive. I realized that the surgeon is truly the last person you will see before going to sleep, not knowing if you will ever wake up again. I reminded myself that I had to trust because Dr. Fricke had arrived on that final visit to the ER. He was the one that got me ready, setting the stage for the next step, bringing all his team's discoveries to this room. Now he had turned the wheel over to this surgeon, handing him all the maps he would need. Dr. Fricke would be waiting for the results, so he could take over the next steps with my care. I scanned both sides of the table, hoping I would see him in the room. Days were a blur but I remembered he had said he would come by before I was put to sleep; it seemed like forever. Then, there he was, standing in the doorway with files in his hand and said, "it's my day off but I thought I would come by and see you as I promised and catch up on some work. I will see you later, Elaina!" His presence and words comforted me.

Such a powerful task now given to Dr. Smith. He was the captain of the ship and at the wheel of this operating room and all those who were with him. My father's doctor in Portland flashed before me, the three of us sitting in the office after he reviewed all my medical files, hearing him say, "You happen to have the top surgeon in this country that does surgery on the pancreas right in Reno. His name is Lindsay Smith and truthfully many of us admire him and his abilities, for the pancreas is a very high risk surgery." I took comfort in knowing Dr. Smith and Dr. Fricke had been given to me, that Archangel Raphael had arranged it through my father and his doctor, and that Dr. Fricke had kept all his promises, making me feel safe at last. I felt cold, and I heard someone entering the room. It was the anesthesiologist behind me, preparing my cocktail of sedatives that would be administered in stages through my IVs. Something that "took the edge off" started running through my veins. There were potions being prepared that soon would be administered carefully in stages; my own "special brews" that function as sedatives, pain relievers, and hypnotics for when it was time for the "putting me to sleep" phase of general anesthesia. I was all "hooked up." EKG stickers were in place and monitors operating to observe my blood pressure and oxygen levels. I was finally at the end of a long, pain-filled road, searching for the right doctors to help me and hopefully save me. I had tried my best to be healthy and strong but was losing the battle. I was exhausted from agonizing pain, no nourishment and no rest. Still hanging by a thread, the only question running through my mind now was, "Will I wake up?" As the energy in the room shifted while I was still awake, I said a final prayer asking once more that my son be protected in life and that I had walked in a good way with all that I had done in life up to this moment. Thoughts passed swiftly through my mind, scenes and feelings flowing through me: playing at the beach with my sister Janice as young children, living with my grandparents out in the country, my grandfather teaching me to dance in the living room, him preparing an apple for me with his pocket knife, carrying my baby sister Lynn on my hip...so much it felt like she lived there. Scenes floated by of playing in the large yard eating cherries and apples from the trees, smelling the scent of the lilac bushes in the yard and in the vases throughout the house. The scenes continued. Sitting in Sunday school and church singing "Yes, Jesus Loves Me" and sitting in the Buddhist Monastery before dawn. Visions of all the places I had traveled in the world came alive as though I was there once more: Paris, my marriage, then the birth of my son, seeing myself smiling when I got to see and hold him for the first time. It was as if a slide show filled with deep feelings appeared before me, from years ago, and up to present day. My parents playing the piano and singing. I was standing by the piano, singing in harmony with my mother. A happy time, at my Auntie Lavelle and Uncle Lloyd's house. Then suddenly shape shifting into the darkness and deep sadness of another visit when in the dark of night, I had to knock on the door to tell her and my Uncle Lloyd that their son had been killed in that accident. Seeing once again that helpless look in their eyes in the darkness, the words I had prayed to come in the right way arriving at last spilling slowly out to give them time to adjust to what I was saying. Once again, hearing and feeling her agony as I stood by her bed as she called out her son's name. "No! Chris! Oh, my Chris," In the dark of night asking, "Why? Why?"As our tears flowed. his presence there with us and an angelic presence bringing a luminous light into the room. Taking one pain-filled second at a time, united in sorrow.

As if I was watching a movie playing on fast forward, one life passage after another was floating through my mind, some parts dark and painful, other parts filled with joy, and all experienced deeply and on so many levels. There was no stopping the flow. All I could do was lie there and go with the waves of each one of them. At some point, I saw myself lying in bed at my apartment, knowing time was running out and hearing, "You will be dead in three days if something is not done" then finally back to the operating room in the present. Now, the last step was being taken, knowing it would bring the outcome of those words, and something would be done. No need to ask for the Light since it had remained with me and that unseen presence was in this room. I felt comforted, knowing this was the end at last. Coming full circle from that painful first night when the event occurred, and the journey I had traveled emotionally, mentally, spiritually and physically, everything bringing me to this doctor and this room.

It seemed like an eternity and then my kind surgeon was standing by my side, taking my hand assuring me all would be good. I heard his voice and the sound of my heart in sync with the beeping of monitors. "I want you to just relax now and not worry. You have been through a lot, Elaina. I am going to put you to sleep and you will get some much needed rest. I will see you later, okay?" Then I saw the shimmer of golden light in his eyes and knew it was that Heavenly Presence guiding him. Lying on that table, the only thing I could whisper was, "God be with your hands." He smiled, thanking me. My last words to him would be prophetic. "Well, I think when you open me up, you are going to have a big surprise! I hope to see you again, but we shall see." His demeanor changed as he looked over to someone behind me that I could not see, reminding me we were not alone on many levels. Giving the nod to put me to sleep, I felt his hand touching my forehead gently. He looked down at me and said softly, "I don't want you to worry about a thing. Just sleep now, Elaina." A moment of fear ran through me, knowing this could be my last awareness of all this life. There was no going back now as I was barely in my body. I had put all the mental control that I had held so tightly all those months and placed it into his and God's hands. I looked up at my doctor one last time and saw his eyes were filled with golden light! Archangel Raphael was with him! Intuitively, it started to feel as if I was standing on a very high cliff and soon I would have to jump into the unknown. The beeps of the heart monitors whispered to me, "get ready to go!" A shimmer of light was in the room as I felt more powerful sedatives flowing through my veins. The faces of my family loved ones flying in front of me; I sent them love and a last goodbye. Countdown was arriving, it was the last ticket to ride and there was no other way to go but into that black velvet that was taking me. Just as when I was a child and I was afraid, I now heard my inner child asking Jesus to help me. A brief feeling of panic filled me with the desire to jump off that table and run out of the operating room. It was overwhelming and silly and I knew I could not do that nor did I have the strength to do so. I must surrender! Again, one of my last thoughts was, "Where am I going?" I made a feeble weak attempt to call for protective Light around me for wherever I would be going. And then, it arrived! That warm feeling of those powerful drugs running through my veins, slowly starting to take over my body and mind. Inside me I heard my inner child whispering, "Now I lay me down to sleep. I pray the Lord my soul to keep. If I should die…"

Time had run out as I let go of this world and was soon wrapped in a warm blanket of black velvet unconsciousness.

The Journey into the Light

"They can tell you it is only because the brain is shutting down, the powerful anesthesia and drugs, but in truth you are undergoing an out-of-body experience, stepping into another dimension that so many call Heaven. Just like others who have taken this journey, I have no time reference and it is hard to associate a word or description to what I experienced. Even now, my rational, reasoning mind still has a hard time assimilating the experience. I understand that this is quite common for those who have had an NDE, and most find it hard to share this event fearing it was just their imagination, but at the same time they have a deep lingering feeling, a knowing, that something very real happened."
-Elaina Deva Proffitt

Knocking on Heaven's Door

"We are born naked into this world and so shall it be in death" -Elaina Deva Proffitt

Many of us know what it is like to be lying in an operating room, one minute conscious, then in what seems just like a few moments, we wake up not remembering a thing. For me, after months filled with high thresholds of pain and emotional trauma, I left my body and had gone to a place that the mind would find hard to comprehend. Standing before me was a doorway that opened into a black velvet room with no walls or ceiling. In the center of the room was a beautiful soft white light coming down from what could have been a high ceiling. I was feeling very drawn to its Essence, wanting to go into the room or space or whatever it was and get closer. I felt disoriented and it seemed to take a while to enter. I was drawn to this Light and its luminous glow as it ever so slowly seemed to move closer to the floor, if there had been one. I felt compelled to reach out my hands and walked into this place, feeling an indescribable desire to do so, as if something was pulling me. My hands were shimmering with light. I was mesmerized by the way they looked as I stretched them out in front of me turning them palms up then palms down. Stretching my fingers apart, observing light flowing through them, gave me the most soothing and delicious sensual feelings. I felt energy moving through me just like it does when I perform touch healing work on others who are in pain. Looking up, it seemed that I was moving further into this place where the Light was glowing. There was not a sound, only pure silence, as a strange stillness filled me. Turning my head in all directions, there was nothing but that perception of a black velvet space. Noticing the light, which seemed to have dropped down lower from above, I was drawn to my hands once again then to my body of shimmering silver golden sparkles and I had the most wondrous feeling, as if I was turning into what seemed to be stardust. In awe, I watched the pulsating light sparkle. The feeling it gave me was hypnotizing until I suddenly realized I was naked! Startled, I looked to the right and left and I heard myself cry out, "What the hell?" at the same time covering my mouth with those light-filled hands. I quickly looked around in that black velvet place and heard myself humbly say, "I am sorry" because at that moment, I felt a most powerful unseen Presence was there with me. I found myself rubbing my hands together because it felt so good and was calming me! Such a sensual, soothing feeling and I had no pain at last! Could this be true? Where was I? Where were my clothes? I could not remember anything about who I was or how I got there! My whole being was focused only upon the Light and the golden sparkle of my naked body. Now I was underneath this pulsating light and I raised my hands and tried to touch it. I had a very strong feeling of impatience wanting it to come closer. I was now filled with anticipation and eagerness because I was so close to reaching it and my attention was totally focused on doing so without knowing why.

Then I heard someone calling to me in the distance. After numerous times hearing this voice, I was drawn to turn back towards the invisible opening and see who it was. In a microsecond, I found myself in what felt like a swimming pool, under water, at its side, pushing off, kicking my feet, heading back towards this voice. I lifted my head out of the water and there was a portal or peep hole in front of my eyes. Was this Alice in Wonderland? I was so disoriented, accompanied by a feeling of irritation, because it felt like I had been interrupted from something very important. The female voice was very insistent and I felt like I was being pulled in two directions. How do I describe this event? Words cannot explain the depth of this experience, but I do have these vivid flashes of recall that have left their imprint on me.

It was as if I was looking from the inside of a coke bottle or a fish eye lens. I saw a woman with brown eyes and another with a shower cap on her head looking down at me with great concern. I remember being irritated at her and questioning her telepathically. "Who is this person that keeps interrupting me?" I had no clue why I was in this important place only that my being there was amazing and I wanted to stay with that beautiful Light! I could not resist the pull of that strange place where I felt so good. Suddenly, I was back in the pool, kicking off, under the water, arms by my sides, swimming like a dolphin, heading back to the entry way of the room with the big glowing light. I tried numerous times to enter completely, and just as I would get close, I would hear a voice calling my name loudly. Each time, I returned through the deep water and saw her worried face again. The last time standing before the entryway to the room with the Light, I heard the echoing voice again calling out "Elaina" and "No!" There was no looking back as something inside me let go once again as I stood at the entrance to the luminous Light.

All at once I had no control over my feet as I took soft floating steps deep into that space. Now I was driven to move closer to the Light, noticing that it was very low and I had a feeling I could touch it. Lifting my hands up higher, the Light enveloped me softly and I was floating as though I was a cloud. Ahead of me was what looked like a tunnel and I effortlessly entered it without fear. Multicolored prisms of rainbow lights started to slowly shimmer and float towards me. An uncontrollable feeling of curiosity drew me deeper into this place and what was beyond. Suddenly, there was a high pitched whirring sound that accelerated rapidly. I had a feeling like I was in an elevator going very fast. The lights were flashing and dancing at a rapid speed in front of and around me taking me higher and deeper into an unknown destination. Ahead of me in a cavern was a soft, round doorway of a satiny, creamy light. Passing through the doorway, I was propelled into another soft velvet darkness, now standing by a little creek or babbling brook. The water was liquid gold, shimmering as it ran past in front of me. Looking down at the stream, I had the flickering feeling that I had been here before. My bare feet were at the very edge of its banks. It was so close that I could see and feel the golden water droplets splashing my toes. It felt so soothing and I knew that there would be no more pain or suffering ever again. Looking across the stream, there were shadows of what appeared to be a group of people walking towards me. It was black velvet on the other side of this babbling brook, but there was a shaft of beautiful golden light coming down behind these silent souls who seemed to be patiently and lovingly waiting for me. We were quietly looking at one another in this stillness and I knew my grandparents were there in the front. I felt like I could recognize them by that familiar warmth filling my heart with such a loving feeling being sent to me from across the babbling brook. It was as if I was a young girl again, surrounded by their love and protection. Standing next to them was a young girl holding the reins of a horse. I heard my voice whisper, "Kathy."

I do not know who the other ones were, but I had a feeling of familiarity, so much love and a knowing they were waiting for my arrival to greet me. I could see the shadows of adults and even younger people and a few children that seemed to know me. I put my toes into the gold stream and started to cross over to them but then something stopped me. Was it that quiet nagging? A pull to be somewhere else that was becoming a slight irritation and distraction? There was no time to ponder because in the next moment I found myself turning around. I was now standing in a doorway looking into a room with shiny hardwood floors that felt warm under my bare feet as wisps of clouds quickly dissolved. Across the room there was a beautiful woman with her back to me in a high neck ecru lace Victorian dress. Her auburn brown hair was swept up with a beautiful comb holding it in place and soft curls against her neck. She was sitting on a window bench looking out of a big bay window at the most beautiful clouds passing by. As if feeling my presence, she slowly turned around with a welcoming smile, then looked deeply into my eyes. A feeling of shock ran through me when I realized…her eyes were mine!

In another instant, I turned around again, finding myself being drawn to an unseen destination as if someone was waiting for me.

The Nursery

I heard the sound of a lullaby and I felt drawn to it. In the blink of an eye my bare feet were gliding along the beautiful wood floor in what appeared to be a hallway with many beautifully carved doors. It also sounded like little children somewhere close by and down the hall on the right there was a light coming out of an open doorway. My feet were pulled in that direction. Soon, I was standing still, looking into a cozy room with beautiful beveled glass windows that cast a beautiful light on everything that was in this lovely place. The walls had lovely old-fashioned Victorian cherub blue and gold wallpaper. Tears of absolute joy filled my eyes as I saw little cribs and beds filled with children of all ages and different colors. There were mobiles twirling above them with soothing pulsating twinkling stars. These babies were so content and peaceful with a soft luminous light behind them. The sweet scent of babies and the fragrance of rosewater filled the room. Sitting on a beautiful well-worn carpet, there were other toddlers quietly playing with what appeared to be old-fashion blocks that had lovely carvings and were painted. To the right was a woman with her back to me wearing a long white gown with an apron. She had a Victorian nurse maid's cap on her head with lace around the edges. There was a baby that she was lovingly rocking in her arms, standing in front of the little ones playing on the carpet. Feeling my presence, she slowly turned around and smiled at me and said telepathically to me, "This is one of the Heavenly places the little children are taken, who have been so horribly abused on so many levels and lost their earthly lives in unspeakable ways." Her eyes captured mine with so much love and compassion as she spoke to me. "This is their healing chamber after crossing over, where their innocence is restored and the impact of all the cruelty they experienced is washed away once more." I felt tears on my face and bowed my head for a moment in humble thankfulness for her words. Moving closer to me as I looked up, she had a beautiful smile on her face as she showed me the child cradled in her arms that appeared to be around seven months old, wrapped in a cozy swaddling blanket. There was a shimmer of luminous, soft light in the cloth and when I looked at the toddler children playing on the floor, I noticed they all had their blankets next to them. Motioning me to follow her, we slowly walked by all the cribs and those who were sitting on the carpet. "Everyone has their swaddling blanket; it is their comfort for it also has the scent of their mother in every thread, that will never fade until they are reunited." She then continued to heal me with her gentle voice. "This is one of the Heavenly nurseries where they are all safe and loved. No one can, nor will, ever hurt them again. At times, the older children here, who are healed from the violence, torture, drug overdoses and other painful things that happened to them, also come to visit the nurseries. They love to help with these little ones. It is healing for all of them." Then she told me how children of all ages have a special place where they heal, and then move to different levels of Heaven just like in school on Earth. "Mothers or fathers who died with their children in traumatic ways also are in healing chambers, and when they are ready, they come to visit their little ones until the time they are able to take them with them to another part of this Heavenly realm." Looking around the room, seeing all the little children playing quietly and the babies in the little Victorian ornate cribs and bassinets with their lace-trimmed canopy shades, filled me with awe and so much comfort. It was as if I was in a beautiful dream. I had such a great feeling of relief and it was as if she read my mind, for immediately she smiled then softly answered my unspoken question. "At the moment of their dying, an angel is sent to be with them and take them immediately. Whether they are left in some remote area or hidden deep, they are not alone and in truth they have gone to Heaven with their angelic guide. Even when their flesh suffered, a part of them is not in that body while it is happening. There is no remembrance of this event. Upon the discovery of their remains, there is an unseen Presence that may be felt by those kind detectives and others who never gave up searching for them." As I walked towards the wall, it appeared to dissolve and opened into another beautiful room revealing countless children and young people at various earthly ages when they lost their lives. The final room that we entered was filled with sleeping children that were suspended in cocoons of pulsating Light. Angelic doctors were working on them and I was told this is the place where the new arrivals are first taken by the angel that was with them. This was the space where the shifting, cleansing and karmic healing of all their bodies occurs on many deep levels: emotionally, mentally, physically and spiritually. Healing is activated, preparing them to go into their nursery or the Heavenly dorms for the older ones.

I felt her hand touch mine as she said, "For some reason you have found us and it is important for you to see this and other rooms in this healing chamber. You will know why, dear Elaina, when it is time. Come, let us go to other rooms now." As I followed her, my heart was full of joy. There was so much love in that heavenly nursery!

Prayers Up

The next moment I was standing on a very high mountain top that felt like Tibet. I could see what felt like eternity and it was the most amazing view, filling my whole being with a powerful energy of exhilaration! There was a breeze blowing through my hair as I tried to resist the urge to step off the mountain top and walk onto those fluffy white clouds and float over those snowcapped mountains below into what was waiting for me beyond. Despite my earthly fear of heights, this was now not the case because the urge to step out on them was pulling me to the beyond. My eyes were soaking up the view to eternity. I could not get enough! There was a perfect peaceful stillness like no other. Such an exhilarating feeling! I was completely within each microsecond of the moment and the clouds and mountains felt so alive and part of me! I should have been freezing cold but for some reason there was no sensation of temperature. I was neither warm nor cold. I felt the Life Force of the snowcapped Himalayas that surrounded me, and heard a Tibetan bowl softly singing. I felt like at last it was confirmed what I had always believed since I was a child. That our prayers do float up into the sky and they are heard.

I felt like I was an observer of a living slide show presentation that took me to so many different places, each with unique sensations and feelings.

After all my pain on so many levels, I finally felt that at last I was free, living completely in the moment. The meaning of the word "time" did not exist anymore. The meaning of "pain" and the events causing it did not exist anymore on any level. If there were words to describe this feeling they would be Holy, Sacred, Eternity, Awe, Compassion and Pure Love. I could now see and feel even more deeply on so many levels. Looking down, I watched as the nonstop prayers sent by all faiths were floating up to the Beyond like beautiful iridescent bubbles from Earth. There were the whispers and cries of voices speaking many languages with many feelings expressed; as hope, joy, gratefulness, pain and sorrow. I knew the Heavenly Presence did not exclude anyone from this sacred place. The intent and actions of love and compassion were the only "key" to open this door. No religion held an exclusive passcode to this most sacred world. It was much deeper and more far reaching than any requirements to enter this sacred place. I realized that many books throughout the world spoke of same truth and the passcode which is: *"love one another."* Reading this on Earth was one thing but experiencing the profound totality of that message brought a very deep emotion that now filled my whole being as I stood there seeing the doorway to eternity. I experienced a flood of awareness like no other. God was not a "He" nor a "She" separately, and was not to be feared. This was all One God, One Goddess, a loving, living Divine Presence that at that moment was sending messages in many languages that were floating up in prayers. I knew that Divine Essence was within each soul praying and not separate nor outside of us. There was a comfort in knowing that a wonderful sign post was left in each part of this world. A most powerful truth that all rang the same bell, just in a different way. From that mountain top, it was revealed that getting to this wondrous place was not just for those who use their beliefs in self-righteous ways of alleged "Holiness." Religions instilling fear in congregants, with the claim it was only "their path" that was the right way and everyone else was excluded, was now shown to be false. The truth; love is kindness and compassion recorded from ancient times; truth spoken by Jesus of Nazareth and the other Masters and Prophets. The rest being only words made of paper that continues to be altered and rewritten to this day to fit the needs of others to control and for some to feed their greed. God's chosen ones are All of us and it is Our responsibility to find that Essence that rests within, not in a building or house of fear and separateness. It was so soothing, feeling the waves of prayers, sacred songs, even the drum circles in the Native American lodge, calling out to the Creator as they climbed high up to where I was standing. There were also those humble churches and temples speaking and practicing love and compassion. This was not in a building. It was simply a most sacred essence <u>within us all</u>. We must be open and look deep within for the answers and the path to walk. While listening and taking into my complete being the various languages and the feelings that were whispered from so many souls, I heard from within, "*In my Father's house there are many mansions.*" This filled me with a newer, deeper understanding of those words channeled by Jesus. Bowing my head, becoming one with all that was given and revealed in this most sacred moment, there was a shimmering aura surrounding me of what had been my fragile body. Appearing before me were faces and voices praying and wishing good things for me. It all blended together, those in my own life who remained on Earth and those who had departed. WE were, and all are, ONE in Heaven and on Earth.

I was wrapped in a comforting blanket with all those prayers floating upwards to me. The big puffy, white clouds moved gently towards my bare feet swirling ever so lightly around them. Now, I was light as a feather, feeling my feet start to slip from that highest mountain peak. There was no fear of heights, only peaceful surrender to all that I had become, which seemed to be only an emptiness that was at the same time Fullness of Being. What is called "Samadhi." Woven into this thread was a familiar, deep harmonic frequency, the sacred sound chanted by the monks and I during our meditations so many years ago. I was not only hearing it, it felt as if I was being filled up with that sacred sound, becoming the sacred Amen "the Om or Aum" as if I was riding a wave that was taking me to the "Mahâsamâdhi," known as the complete absorption of the individual consciousness in the self at the time of death. Visions of invisible doors were opening and mysteries started being revealed in incomprehensible ways. My rational, reasoning mind was being bombarded with bursts of microcosmic flashes of light into that complete and unbroken union with the Divine. I was free at last from the limitations of my weary body.

Back to the Garden

I found myself in a beautiful garden not knowing how I got there. A small waterfall was to my right that emanated lovely tones as the drops fell into the pool. There was such stillness and peace, with the intoxicating scent of flowers flickering with light. Their vibrant, psychedelic and monochromatic colors of magenta, blue, purple, pink, yellow and peach were pulsating with glowing Life Force. Looking down at myself, I saw a long, sleeveless sheer gown on my body. It had silver and gold threads at the bottom that sparkled. It was so light weight it felt like a feather. My bare feet were slowly walking on an emerald green grassy path, leading to the right towards a waterfall and its crystal clear pool. The tones and harmonics of the water drops spilling down to the pool were hypnotizing, and I found myself sitting on a smooth, large rock. I did not see myself when I looked down into the water, only the outline of sparkling lights around my shape and my eyes filled with wonder. I was compelled to gently place my feet into the water. I immediately felt a soothing elixir moving up my legs and throughout my being. The sensation was like no other and I can't easily put it into words, it just felt healing. I had no recollection of time or how long I was there, but at some point I felt a pull to stand up and return to the path. Something was drawing me deeper into this place. I had no fear, only peace, and the sound of the melodic waterfall was now behind me. The petals of the flowers were pulsating, filled with the nectar of sweet Life Force and it was as if they were silently communicating, welcoming me to this secret garden. I had a feeling that this was like a house with many rooms. I felt someone was up ahead of me, waiting, although I couldn't see anyone at that moment. Somehow, I knew that I was not alone and not to be afraid. I had the urge to keep walking and listening, and became aware that I was now on the threshold of crossing into the unknown once again. I paused for a moment, closed my eyes, and breathed in deeply as the familiar scent of lilacs permeated my being. I heard the voice of my grandmother calling out to me. I turned around to see her and my grandfather whom I called "Fader" standing on the porch with big smiles upon their faces. The imprint of our lives together had returned in a most joyful way. What it took to get there did not matter anymore, nor could I remember exactly "how" I had arrived there. I had always felt safe and loved in their home. All that mattered was that we were together again at last. With our arms wrapped around one another, my grandmother then whispered to me, "I am sorry, honey, that I was not there when you came home from Paris. Remember, when I said goodbye the night before you left and I told you I did not feel I would see you again? That's why I had to come back another time before you went into the house to give you an extra hug before getting into the car." Her words brought that specific event back to me with the memory of her funeral bringing a moment of sadness and then confusion for she was standing before me alive and well. "Michael was such a beautiful baby. I know your heart was hurting because you so wanted me to see him, and I did honey just in a different way." Happiness filled my heart hearing her words. I wanted this moment to last forever and then I felt Fader's arms around me with a heavenly hug and breathed in the familiar scent of his aftershave cologne. "Just know we always visit him and that your grandmother and I still do watch over him. We see Michael has such a kind heart." His words filled me with peace, seeing their loving smiles and hearing my grandfather's words of reassurance. A heavenly breeze touched my face and there was the scent of those purple and white lilacs once more. I knew that there was no time, nor worldly concerns here, only love. And while I wanted to stay with them, something was pulling me away once more. My grandparents smiled and my grandfather nodded in silent agreement to our parting. There was a knowing that we would see each other again.

Gradually, I was suspended in time again as my bare feet left their yard. When I opened my eyes once more, I found myself standing before three angelic beings who were greeting me. They were dressed in soft, flowing robes that gently touched their bodies. There was not a halo on top of their heads but there was an aura of pure Light wrapped around them from head to toe. There were indescribable feelings of such peace and a beauty that cannot be put it into words. Behind them the path continued and I was drawn to follow it because there were beautiful lilac bushes at its entrance. A telepathic communication was now guiding me to turn in another direction. The view was amazing. I saw the Earth out in space, a big blue marble turning around and around. I felt a connectedness to this object but the reasons why were fading so quickly.

I saw the Sun and the Moon with galaxies in the distance and the Aurora Borealis above Earth. Then in the twinkling of an eye, I was shown many things coming…what would be powerful times and changes…that would happen on that big, blue marble, events happening to this day. There were glimmers of many things to come and revealed about in my own life, that I saw at warp speed but I cannot remember all of them. I can only recall things at specific times in my life. Sometimes when I have recall, my body and whole being release the unconscious tensions deep within. "Shaking it off my bones" would bring a confirmation. Other times, I will get a feeling about a location and where I am to travel, and get whispers about why I am being sent there or suddenly find myself meeting strangers who in a matter of hours have me making plans to go to some faraway place to work with people in need. Also, events to come can be revealed in a deep, dream state and appear as visions at 3:00 a.m. in the dark of night. There would come a time when a television show on the Northern Lights would repeat again and again. No matter what time of day. Soon the Aurora Borealis would fill my dreams and whisper to me, "There is work for you to do with us." Within a matter of months, a man from Norway came into my life, and gave me a ticket to come to Tromso at the top of the world. It was there I would chase the lights and have them dance above me on dark cold nights. I was filled with their light activation and felt it run through my body, out my hands and fingers, being sent to all I knew.

Looking out at the vastness of space, these angelic beings told me why and how I had arrived in this most sacred place. As I turned and looked at them, one of them spoke. "You may stay, Elaina. But we would like you to go back, as there is still much work for you to do." The voice that spoke those words was neither male nor female. It was emanating the most peaceful vibration and said, "This time you have a choice. It is up to you as to which direction to go, but know there is still much work to do." The thought of leaving here was a shock; how could I leave this most beautiful place? Oh, how I wanted to stay in this sanctuary of tranquility filled with such pure love! There was so much to explore in this place, it was filled with the presence of sacred beings, love and peace. I felt so good and safe and I knew that no one could ever hurt me again!

The grass under my bare feet was delicious. I was pain free and alive like never before. I had a feeling of such peace even though I still felt something stirring inside that I could not explain. Once again, it seemed as if I had to make another decision. In the distance, somewhere out there in the unknown, I heard what seemed to be a familiar voice calling my name again.

There was that woman with the worried brown eyes looking at me again. I was confused as to how she got to this beautiful place. My vision was distorted and it was like I was looking through a fish eye camera lens or I was standing inside a glass coke bottle. Looking up at her, I asked myself, "do I go through it?" Everything around me in the beautiful garden was dissolving and once again I was turning around, seeing that black velvet room with the light that was still there waiting for me. I heard my name being called out, echoing through me, and I wanted to shut my ears. Strange…I did not recall agreeing to leave that most sacred garden where those angelic beings were. I was not finished there because I was curious to see where that path lined with lilacs led, but something was pulling me in another direction. A brief moment of clarity arrived, and I remembered how I could get back to the garden. I just had to enter the black velvet room before me once more. I floated in the direction of the doorway and arrived at that familiar entrance accompanied by the distraction of a soft voice calling my name. I chose to ignore it and with great effort turned around. As I tried to go through the entrance a final time, I found myself hitting some sort of shield that felt like a strong slap in the face, throwing me backwards. I felt my body jerk, the way it does while you're in a dream state out of body. It was as if I had been forcefully dropped down onto something hard. I heard a "pop" and instantly felt a searing, burning pain running deep across my abdomen and throughout my body. I heard voices talking in what seemed a loud and concerned manner. There was that oddly familiar woman's voice, "Please get her something for pain!" Suddenly, all was quiet as I left my body once more and fell into a deep sleep.

Welcome Back

There was no time or day as I was drifting in and out of my body, finally coming back to the earth plane. The first thing I saw when I opened my eyes were those beautiful hands with the long, delicate fingers. My surgeon was sitting by my bed in what seemed like a meditative state. His first soft words were, "Welcome back." It was hard to respond because my throat hurt. I didn't know there was a tube in there making it difficult to talk. As I started to drift off again, his voice brought me back once again, and I will never forget what he said. "You told me in the operating room that when I opened you up I would have a big surprise! Well, I did. Your body cavity was filled with blood clots stuck together, your spleen was embedded into your pancreas and you were devouring your stomach and intestines. You had a blood clot about the size of a baseball on the tail of your pancreas. I removed it and part of your intestine. It seems you had hemorrhaged inside for quite a while. It took hours for my assistant and I to pick the blood clots out of your body cavity before we could even get to your organs to do the surgery. It was the most challenging surgery of my career," he said calmly.

I must have gone into a deep sleep again, traveling out of body once more because I don't remember anything else he may have said. My prediction had come true and so had the palm reader's in the tea room all those years ago: "Something to do with loss of blood. I see lots of blood!" In the days to come, drifting in and out of consciousness, my room was filled with shimmering pink, lavender, blue and gold light. I saw my guides and a small child standing by my bedside. I would slip in and out of my body so gracefully, just like a dancer, into those lights. At some point, Michael Alukas was sitting at the foot of my bed, his prayer mala in his hand. "I am here," he said softly with tears in his eyes, "If you want to go, it is okay. I am here for you. You have had enough pain. Do you want to? Or do you want to stay?" Once again, the room filled with beautiful soft colored lights that mesmerized me as I watched them dancing by the side of my bed. I heard myself whisper, "I guess I will stay." And I drifted into a deep sleep once again. From that moment on, new life was slowly returning and finally at some point it was time to go home.

It was strange how I found myself at last becoming aware of where I was at that moment and the world around me. During this period, time had stood still and it felt like my life was a blank slate about how long time had passed and what exactly had happened. One of my most vivid memories was the day I knew it was time to get out of the hospital. Nurses were standing over me discussing where to insert the new IV as I had become a pin cushion with track marks all over my scrawny little arms while my veins were collapsing. A nurse was probing near my collarbone and my wakeup call had arrived! "Are you going to put that in my neck?" I asked as loud as I could. "No! I don't want any more needles. I want my doctor!" They tried to calm me down to no avail. "That needle is not going in my neck. I want to see my doctor and go home." After he came and examined me, the decision was made. "Never mind, take it away," he said, telling me that I would have to keep myself hydrated and follow his orders or he would put me right back in the hospital. Freedom had arrived at last! He was going to release me! My mind was a blank as to where my home exactly was or how I would get there. What had happened to me was a blur and would continue to be for a while until I got more permanently stable once again.

Home at Last

When I walked in the front door of my apartment I was overwhelmed. Everything felt so different to me and it was a bit unsettling. I was happy to be there, but I felt confused because my mind was having a hard time grasping that this was where I lived. It is a common experience after a heavy passage of serious medical trauma, all the medications, anesthesia and being close to death. These are also the symptoms of what is called a "walk-in." A "walk-in" is the term for someone who has left their body due to trauma or other out-of-body experiences. If they return to their body, it feels "foreign" to them. It is as if they are a new spirit entering their old body. It was as if I was in a strange place and in someone else's home. Maybe excruciating pain and the strong narcotics filling my body also contributed to this newness. All I knew is that I felt fragile and reborn, like a phoenix rising from the ashes. When I stepped into the hallway and again at my bedroom door, I felt so much physical pain and sadness in this place. I also felt a Zen stillness throughout each room. Everything appeared attractive and in perfect order. I was filled with a curiosity as I wandered very slowly from room to room, looking into the closets and examining objects placed on a table. I remember opening the refrigerator door and noticing that it was almost empty. There was only a jar of wheat germ, a couple of cans of 7-Up, and a small pint of ice cream in the freezer. In a kitchen cabinet, there was a full bottle of Ballantine's Scotch and Captain Morgan Rum. I opened the bottles and breathed in the scent of each and shook my head wondering why I would have this in my cupboard! Did I like this strong-smelling stuff? My eyes scanned each room, activating all my sensory perception. It felt as though I had returned to a place where someone had died or suddenly disappeared, a situation all of us will experience at some time in our lives upon entering a departed family member's home. It was the same feeling of emptiness as when viewing a lost loved one's chair or empty bedroom, standing there knowing that the loved one had left this Earth, never to return. An overwhelming stillness permeated every room and brought a feeling that I was in someone else's place. There was also the indescribable faint odor of death throughout this attractive apartment, something my olfactory senses had become very sensitive to, that gave me the ability to identify when someone was dying, even if it does not look like it on the outside. In times-past, I had walked with a detective into a house that had been a crime scene, but was now clean and neat. My clairsentient abilities would activate all my senses including the olfactory, whispering death had visited this place and I'd be drawn to a specific room. Every investigator will tell you it is a smell you never forget, no matter how faint or strong the odor. My body cavity had been filling up with blood clots all those months here in my apartment, and my highly sensitive olfactory sense must have been picking up that scent. What was predicted by the beautiful lady in the tea room was still long forgotten, but it had come to full fruition. The prophetic events had arrived in my life in the months past, exactly like the reader had told me that day so long ago: "I see lots of blood!" Now, inside my own home I had an underlying feeling that things had happened in this place. Bombarded with flashes of strange scenes, I was too tired and weak to dive deeper for their meaning right then, or maybe I just did not want to experience it all again. I had to go lie down. I felt very weak and truthfully I was exhausted. It seemed like I was experiencing a trauma. Being unsettled in my own apartment. I walked into my bedroom and looking in the dresser mirror, I saw a pale, thin woman with the weary, pain-filled eyes of someone who has suffered deeply. Was this me? I did not look nor feel the same. Like others who have had this type of experience, I knew that something serious had happened to me but it takes time for the mind to accept it. Turning around slowly, I saw my bed that still had the imprint of my body on the bedspread. Also on the bed was the book, "The Dynamic Laws of Healing" by Katherine Ponder, which I had been reading with its well-worn pages and my Bible. The room seemed to pulse with a variety of feelings, flashes of images and thoughts that I chose to ignore. I sat down on the bed and touched the book's worn pages. My psychometry ability kicked in (the sense or ability to read the history of objects), a spiritual gift I had used many times doing investigative work. I saw scenes of me in this room reading this book as I was lying on the bed so fragile, frightened, weak and in agony, praying for help. Opening the book, it was turned to page 29 and there was a lightly underlined quote:*"If you can put a thing out of your mind, you can put it out of your body."* I felt like I was transported back to the moment my eyes first fell upon this line, seeing my thin fingers shaking as I held the pen to underline what I believed to be an angelic whisper from Archangel Raphael. Without thought, my hands went to other pages that had been underlined in green ink, pages 39 and 41, and I wondered how long it had taken to read 12 pages. I could feel the fading life force that had touched these few pages, so delicate, fragile and ever so weak. Tears came to my eyes as I bowed my head, holding on to that vision. It was so overwhelming. I had to lie down for a while. I crawled under the covers and rested my head upon my pillow. I whispered thank you to God and the angels that watched over me and brought my healers and all those kind strangers to help me. Drifting off to sleep in my own bed, my hand was still resting on the book.

Even to this day when I touch the book "The Dynamic Laws of Healing" and my old Bible, I can feel myself so alone and in so much pain. I can also feel the Heavenly Presence that was with me. My hands feel an energy running through them from those pages that I touched. Now, I see and feel that there truly was and is a Higher Power that was in my bedroom and each room of my apartment. I can still feel it when I look at or hold the laws of healing book, going back to those months of April and May when I turned the pages to that time when at last, I could not hold on any longer. It would be years later that I would rediscover a Heavenly letter resting between the pages channeled through my weak hand. *"Elaina I bless you with Divine Desire and with Divine Fulfillment. You are satisfied with Divine Love now. Health and Harmony are now established in your mind, body, and affairs."*

I know this was from Archangel Raphael. He had brought the right and perfect doctors to me and it would be He that would guide me in the years to come, when I was working with those who were suffering deep emotional pain and serious illness, and doing so to this day. I also realized throughout the years, how Saint Michael had also protected me so many times in my life, and since that dark November night when I was thrown down upon the ground and onto that concrete step. In the years that followed, Archangel Michael brought events into my life that were his realms of work and his Presence remains with me to this day. Gabriel the messenger always brings the needed answers to me at the right and perfect time. He will for you also if you ask. It would take over a year before I returned completely to my body. I was 5'7" and wore a size six dress. For months, foods that I used to enjoy tasted foreign to me. It would take time before I felt more grounded. One day Johanna Wilson looked at me strangely. When I asked her what was wrong, she just stated in a very direct manner, "Your eyes, they are different now. There is something in them that shows that you have been to a place that none of us has seen, nor will we until it is our time." There are photos taken of me after this near-death experience that reveal eyes that appear to be filled with pools of infinity. I call them Angel Eyes.

When the sword of suffering is impaled into your heart and you feel that you have lost your way, fear not because truth be…you are not lost. Life is just different now…as are you. It is in your eyes; they tell the story of your journey to that Heavenly place and it will remain with you.

Clarity

I found out two months later from a friend who had visited me in the Intensive Care Unit what had happened from the earthly side of the world. When I returned home, I experienced disconnected flashes of strange images and feelings. At times, when I was drifting off to sleep, scenes paraded in front of me as if I was watching a movie, flashes of being in the operating room and my surgeon looking down at me. Other times, I saw a hospital room where I was lying in a bed in what looked like a clear plastic tent from my chest up. There were monitors beeping slowly, tubes attached to my nose and IV drips. I felt as if I was above the bed looking down at the scene. I looked so still and was surrounded by a beautiful pink, blue and purple mist. There were people standing by my bed looking at me. One of them was a dark curly-haired little girl about two years old, and a very tall male dressed in a white robe wearing a turban. His eyes were very loving and I felt he was protecting me. I also saw my deceased grandparents standing next to me. They seemed to be waiting for something. I also saw other different faces that felt familiar, all of them not of this world. It was fascinating. I seemed to slip in and out of my body, leaping gracefully in slow motion like a ballet dancer. It felt so good to be enveloped in those beautiful soothing colors of pure love. When I was back home and going to bed each night, I kept hoping to have that experience again. The light felt so good and seemed to be the best sleeping pill I could have. Always at the end of the bed there was a blond-haired Nordic-looking man sitting there quietly with Tibetan prayer beads in his hand. I remembered the time he whispered to me, "it's okay. You don't have to stay here anymore if you don't want to." At some point, I realized it was my friend Michael Alukas whispering those words each night in my dream state. Each morning as I started my day, I carried this feeling of the dream world that I walked in each night. There also was Donna Lombardi, whom I had met when I first came to Reno and who had set up the first radio show I did there. She was the person who waited outside the Operating Room for so many hours that long afternoon. She told me she could be with me in ICU shortly thereafter. I don't even remember her being there, but later she would have quite the story to tell me.

There was a time as my healing began that Michael, Donna and a friend of hers took me to Lake Tahoe and the Truckee River for a picnic celebration and a short rafting ride out to a little island in the river. I was covered with a big hat, strong sun block and sleeves to protect me from the sun because of the powerful antibiotics I was taking. I remember the sun was glistening on the water and the trees were so beautiful. Everything was so alive like never before! Sitting under some trees with water surrounding us, the blankets and pillows were spread out. There was fine china, gold silverware, crystal glasses, fruits and cheeses, Perrier water and a bottle of Moet champagne. I still did not have much of an appetite so this was perfect. A wonderful experience I will never forget! As we were relaxing, the mood turned somber when Donna asked me if I remembered what happened in the hospital. I said I did not; it was all a haze and everything including me felt different with all that had happened to me. Confused, I looked at Michael for assurance. "It's okay, Elaina, just listen to what she says." The story unfolded as Donna began fighting back tears. Pausing for a moment, there was only the sound of the river passing by and I knew there was more to this story. "I was allowed to be in the recovery room with you. The nurse left me alone with you and a short time later I saw your closed eyes moving as if you were seeing someone and talking with them. At that moment, I had a gut feeling that you were going to leave because the vital signs on the monitor lines changed and it started beeping. Your eyes continued to move as if you were communicating with someone. A chill came over me and I knew you were going to die." Now crying and shaking her head, "I do not know what came over me, but I yelled out your name and I said, *you are not going to leave us! We need you here!*" Then she confessed, "I slapped you and your heartbeat started to change as the nurse came quickly back into the room." Wiping tears from her eyes, she said softly, "I am so sorry I slapped you Elaina, but so many of us need you. I could not bear the thought of you leaving." Then it all came back to me, sitting under the tree with the Truckee River passing us by on a summer day. All those silent feelings and questions were answered, verified and confirmed. Flashes of light, scenes, voices and that black velvet room, trying to reenter and the feeling of a strong, forceful, unseen hand in front of my face blocking my way into that black velvet room...one final time. Today, I still believe that when I returned that last time to enter the soft black velvet room with the glowing light, it was Donna slapping me that blocked me from going back to that deep sleep, and at that point I felt myself slam down on to the bed and back into my body. I heard voices giving orders and the hazy image of a woman with a shower cap on her head, and brown eyes filled with concern, calling my name. Donna's brown eyes!

Throughout the coming months, pieces of the puzzle came together as I was healing and my mind started to accept that something powerful had happened to me other than the bleeding inside for months. A peaceful feeling began to replace my uncertainty. The month of May was and is when I historically have had health issues. I used to have quite a bit of anxiety when that time of the year arrived. My memories of the pain and drama made me anxious it might happen again. Two years later I started to become ill again. I was becoming bloated and had a feeling of burning or inflammation inside and my skin color was pale. My doctor was going to capture some images and I was supposed to drink a reflective solution prior to scans. One day, my dear friend Don O'Gorman made a request. "I want you to trust me on what I am going to ask you to do. I have set up an appointment with a Homeopathic Physician, Dr. Katrina Tang. I have paid for this visit so do not worry about the cost. Just try this before you do the other testing." I did as Don suggested and went to the clinic. Dr. Tang performed some tests on me and gave me some homeopathic intravenous injections. I will never forget that cool soothing balm that filled my veins. "You should be feeling better soon Elaina," she said with a smile as she walked me to the door. I went home and laid down on the couch, praying that this would heal whatever was happening inside me. When I woke up a couple of hours later, the fire I'd felt in my abdomen was gone! Never to return. Angels had arrived once again and Don O'Gorman was one for me that day. I always trusted his wisdom and I am so grateful I listened to him. I have discovered that the archangels work through all of us at times and it was apparent by the tone of his request, Don was guided by them that day. To this day, he is my mentor and counselor at times.

There was a woman named Mara who owned a store called Country Health. She was a friend of Michael Alukas. I visited her quite often and unknowingly there would always be something placed into my hand as a wandered through the aisles of products. Angels even helped me shop. Mara was a very good medical intuitive and kept watch over me from near or far from the start of this heavy passage. She intuitively scanned me and assessed my energy. "As you say dear, you still have one foot on Earth and another still in Heaven." As the months and years progressed, it soon shifted to easier times. I still had a foot on Earth another in Heaven but it was on another level. It remains that way and I use that state when working as a medium and grief and loss counselor. God brings gifts to us in strange ways. It got easier to just trust and be open, knowing helpers always arrive. In the future, it would be my turn to help others in their time of serious health issues and even their time to cross over. Heaven revealed each day, there is a never-ending circle of help for us all that continues every day.

My life changed in many ways after that experience. I have always loved nature but now when I see clouds, I am mesmerized by their beauty and feel that same strange pull looking out into eternity. My experience of the afterlife is sometimes triggered when I look at certain mountains. They remind me of standing on top of that peak in Tibet and are accompanied by a feeling of homesickness. My out-of-body experience has brought so much to my life. Strong energy still runs through me when I am healing and soothing others in pain, with my clairvoyance and intuitive abilities having been enhanced even more. I still have that feeling of remaining with one foot on Earth another in Heaven when I bring deceased loved ones into contact with their grieving families and friends. After this experience, I became even more empathic, even more open to those suffering, and felt even deeper compassion and understanding. The warm, soothing energy that flows through me becomes even stronger now. To this day there are times when, in a microsecond, I return to that beautiful place and hear those words, "there is still much work for you to do." And then someone new will enter my life who is suffering physically or grieving deeply, and I gain access to new abilities and understanding for each one of them. I have always had the ability to see and feel the souls of others, but now I get whispers offering deeper guidance as to why they have arrived and our mutual connection.

I know from firsthand experience that when we endure a serious, life-threatening event, we must never completely surrender the total healing process to another, even though they may have the word "Doctor" before their name. It is important to activate complete body-mind-soul-spirit and actively participate in your own healing by observing and asking questions. Then you will be given the answers that these elements are to be your healers. You do not have to keep seeing someone if they are not fully present and engaged in your situation. Another medical professional will arrive if you ask Archangel Raphael to guide you to the right and perfect healer. In retrospect, I realized that the reason the other doctor was never "there" was because he was not supposed to be. My prayers were answered by the two that DID walk with me. Everything occurs in Divine Order when we have faith and trust knowing all will arrive at the perfect time. I also discovered that our inner circle of friends serve as messengers that archangels speak through at times becoming instruments for our healing at just the right time.

"And in the end, when you take that final breath, there is only what has been your truth and the Holy Presence". —Elaina Deva Proffitt
5/26/1986

Quan Yin, Goddess of Compassion

Ancient texts tell the story of a Goddess of Mercy and Compassion. Quan Yin (She Who Hears The Prayers Of The World) attained enlightenment. As she was about to enter Heaven, she paused at the doorway when she heard the cries of the world, "we need you here!" She decided to return to help humankind find the right path to ease their pain and suffering, reincarnating wherever she is needed.

There was a time in Sacramento when I was at a Chinese restaurant and I held that first statue of Her. It was given to me by the owner's son who told me, "You like Quan Yin." Quickly, this Goddess of Mercy and Compassion was in every room of my house. Some part of me probably knew that a powerful passage filled with suffering was waiting for me on the horizon. This Goddess came alive within me and my life soon mirrored hers. I too, had a choice to make while standing at that doorway. "You may stay but we would like you to go back for there is still much work for you to do." I remember saying telepathically, "But it feels so good to be here." I remember being blocked from reentering that black velvet room with the beautiful light and plunging into my ever so fragile body, hearing my dear friend Michael say, "Do you want to go or do you want to stay?" and my reply, "I guess I'll stay," then slipping back into the shadows for a while longer.

Throughout the years, I have seen much chaos and pain on this earthly plane, and I often wonder why I chose to remain here. I must have been hearing the cries of the world…the prayers of love, faith, hope, gratefulness, suffering, and pain all floating up simultaneously from Earth while I was standing on that heavenly mountain top watching the big clouds floating into eternity. Somehow deep within me I knew I had more to do, and I decided. While the prediction by the beautiful lady in the tea room so many years prior to this event was long forgotten, years later my dear friend, Fran, reminded me about that reading when she came for a visit. I realized that the reader's prophesies occurred in my life exactly like she spoke them that day. There were also my own words spoken as a child, when I watched my grandmother arrange those purple lilacs in the crystal vase on the table because…It was May and the Lilacs were blooming.

"Every once-in-awhile, we get lucky. This time we did."

Those words were spoken a few years later at a private campaign event for the Attorney General when I was sitting in a lawn chair chatting with Dr. Fricke and another doctor. I had mentioned to the other doctor the medical drama I had been through and how Dr Fricke had been a major part of saving my life. As the two then talked about what he had discovered and the surgery involved, Dr Fricke also talked about the severity of the situation. There are many close calls with death at times in their profession, and I was one of them. Turning towards me with a smile he said humbly, *"Every once-in-awhile, we get lucky. This time we did."* His words filled me with gratefulness.

Epilogue

No matter what people believe about near-death experiences, this most mysterious event has touched people. Some call it a hallucination. I will agree to the extent that it is a "trip". It seems to leave a permanent impression on how one views life and brings a new purpose to most. Of course, there are physical manifestations when the body dies, becomes unconscious through trauma, or suffers a serious physical disease. Yes, the shutting down of the brain and body triggers reactions. Strong drugs or anesthetics given during surgery may have a similar effect, but the experience goes beyond those factors. Often, there were no drugs present in those who were in fatal accidents and left their bodies at the scene. Those calling it a hallucination were not in those bodies at that moment nor did they physically endure the trauma or illness triggered by such an experience. The NDE debate will likely continue for millennia to come. But until one has undergone this profound experience (as millions have worldwide), it is like a child saying they do not a like a food they have never tasted. Knowledge is one thing, but having this experience becomes Wisdom. (The natural ability to understand things that most other people cannot. It is gained by having the experience). It is like graduating with the first Ph.D. in dying, knowing that down the road at some point in life a final breath will be taken and the final graduation arrives. We must be open to the fact that there are many dimensions of what we call "life" and "death." How can we say a near-death experience is not a reality? Maybe the hallucination is our life upon Earth? Once I adjusted to life after all that I had been through, my life changed quickly in ways I was not expecting. Sometimes, I felt compelled to talk to others about my experience. I struggled to put this otherworldly experience into words, and I got frustrated when I tried to bring this event into "Earth time and Earth words." Bits and pieces, fragments of what happened, left an imprint upon me for the rest of my life. All I know is that I had been gravely ill and my pain so extreme that the threshold of it climbed higher each month, then each week, and then each day, until I knew I was going to die without intervention. My body was wasting away and the medications were no longer effective. Little did I know that I would learn a wonderful pain control technique at that most powerful agonizing time in my life. Thinking back on those pain-filled months and the end of the journey, I cannot recall who took me home. I remember the moment my doctor finally agreed to release me, being wheeled out of the hospital, but I don't remember who was there to pick me up. I recall pieces of the events like watching a movie and then suddenly, what happened next is a blank screen. A chunk of time in my life is gone, lost deep within my subconscious. Occasionally, I'll get a flash or see an event or place where I traveled triggered by something going on around me. It is as if I am walking in two separate realities. I have come to believe that NDEs resemble a form of PTSD.

When I opened the door to my home, it was filled with mystery and I felt a sacred presence. I was overcome with a variety of feelings hitting me: curiosity, uncertainty, fear, sadness and loneliness. A part of me did not feel completely earthbound. I had been in such fragile condition, after months of excruciating pain, little nourishment and the constant battle to live. So much had happened to me that I barely recognized myself physically, mentally or emotionally. Constant visits to the ER and numerous hospitalizations prior to the final admission, led me not only to exhaustion but I also felt a desire to surrender to the unknown. I wandered in and out of my rational mind. I heard whispers in my head that something was different about me. I have strong memories of certain events during those long months, and writing about them has been like reliving them once again. I clearly remember certain conversations with doctors, family and friends, but time was a hazy blur regarding other things. I remember voices in ICU, and at some point a visual flash when someone was trying to wake me up, but I then descended back in unconsciousness. In a recent conversation with my surgeon Dr. Lindsay Smith, I told him I vividly remember him sitting by my bedside and pieces of what he told me. I also felt that I woke up in one or two days to which he then replied, "It was not a couple of days. How about a week or two, even three, with the type of surgery that was needed for such a trauma? It takes time for the body to awaken and adjust to the physical changes that were created." I then recalled that my father's doctor told us that the hospitalization would be lengthy.

If you have had a near-death experience, I know you are probably filled with many overwhelming emotions and may even at times feel quite alone until you find others who have also taken the journey. This amazing experience can come in many ways. For example, I have had others tell me that they experienced it when they were very sick as a child and saw what they described as an angel. People of all ages and cultures no matter under what circumstances, whether they were in a hospital or involved in a serious accident, have spoken of seeing a beautiful light, and/or deceased loved one coming for them…even speaking to them…or what appeared to be a kind stranger. The light seems to be a common link for those who have had this experience. I know it was for me, and so were many of the other experiences I had, which were described by NDE Author Dr. Raymond

Moody. Seeing his words, it is comforting to read consistent documentation confirming that you are not alone.

"One of the nine elements that generally occur during NDEs is the tunnel experience. This involves being drawn into darkness through a tunnel, at an extremely high speed, until reaching a realm of radiant golden-white light. Also, although they sometimes report feeling scared, they do not sense that they were on the way to hell or that they fell." (Dr. Raymond Moody)

Religion and NDEs

I found out at an early age when my beloved grandfather died that many ministers have very little true awareness of how to communicate with those who have lost a loved one. Just because someone goes to Heaven does not mean that the families will stop grieving. So many clergy are also uncomfortable with ones who are grieving, and despite their beliefs, are fearful of the process of dying. We all are human, and death (the most powerful final passage from what we call life), is beyond comprehension. Today, many ministers are taking courses in grief and loss and how to communicate with ones grieving at funeral services.

People who have undergone an NDE often find it hard to put into words until they become more relaxed and feel safe from judgment or ridicule. When religion is added to this topic, I cannot begin to count the individuals who have admitted to suppressing, hiding, or even denying their NDE because the experience conflicted with the faith in which they were raised. While there are more open-minded ministers today, it has not always been the case. In years past, as more survivors brought their NDE stories into mainstream consciousness, such discussions sparked uproar in traditional religious communities. NDEs were viewed as a threat to traditional beliefs of what constituted Heaven and even God. In those days, many survivors told me that when they tried to talk to their minister or other religious authority about their experience, they would encounter resistance and even contempt. Personally, on more than one occasion, I experienced an alleged "man of the cloth" spouting his hate and poison at me, insisting that someone like me could not go to Heaven. As the minister preached, it was the devil giving the illusion that I had gone to Heaven and any such experience (my NDE) was just part of Satan's work. Going to church and accepting more traditional religious dogma was the only way to Heaven. Even as a child who attended church regularly, I questioned these religious beliefs and philosophies. As a clairvoyant with strong medium and empathic abilities, I felt the subject was so much deeper than they could understand. Their religious beliefs did not make sense and seemed to contradict what I and others had experienced. If there is a loving God, wouldn't this Divine Presence bring us messages from those on the Other Side? If, as the minister preaches, there is a Heaven, then why would it be "evil" to be able to communicate with those who have gone before us? In this crazy world of uncertainty in which we live, I personally find it comforting to know that there is a place we go when we die. It seems to me that we just step into another dimension of "life." In the spiritual community, there are many levels of life upon Earth. What we see in front of us is not the only true reality. When one lives with a new, deeper awareness of life and death, one's spiritual path opens, revealing many new worlds and ways of living. We discover the truth; our reality has simply shifted. It seems we are constantly shape shifting, every cell in our body is living, breathing, dying and reborn.

As time has gone by and individuals have become more enlightened and knowledgeable about what is called God and the Other Side, I have noticed religious television programs making greater use of the word supernatural. This word has historically been directed towards others in a persecuting manner. TV evangelists and religious zealots are now professing authority on the subject. Their new-found interest in the supernatural seems ironic to me since at one time these religious experts lumped that term into the same taboo categories with soothsayer, astrologer or witch, including "gifted" individuals like myself. Many bibles have been rewritten and now claim that only a man can be a prophet. This claim is contradictory to past versions of the Bible which did not distinguish between the prophetic ministry of women and men, and in which there are numerous references to women who prophesized. A Prophet or Prophetess is chosen by God and is a person who opens their spiritual ears and eyes and speaks a message. "Channeling" is another word used for receiving messages. For example, Acts 2:17-18 states, "And it shall come to pass, in the last days, says God, I will pour out My Spirit upon all flesh, and your sons and your daughters shall prophesy."

"Supernatural" is now the trendy word that is being exploited by many as another means to fulfill their own private agendas and basically to keep the flow of monetary donations coming into their dial-a-prayer networks. It has become acceptable to have prophetic dreams, visions of the future, and near-death experiences as long as they relate to a church's agenda. For years now, people have been turning away from the narrow path of religion finding that God and the Temple are everywhere on this Earth, just as Jesus said. Archeological documents have been discovered that recorded Jesus' true words and included a description of how he lived his daily life.

I must also acknowledge that there are many ministers who have higher spiritual awareness of this subject and do recognize that some people are gifted with prophecy, sight and healing abilities. I admire these preachers who have embraced a nice blend between the traditional and the spiritual, encouraging a well-rounded, inclusive and inspiring church experience. Since the activation of higher consciousness in the '70s, many individuals turned their back on traditional religion but not the pure essence of its meaning. We have now arrived at a time on this Earth where more people are reexamining their own religious beliefs. It is as if angelic intervention has entered the pulpit. There's more to this story, so dig deep and have an open mind.

With new documentation surfacing about NDEs on almost a daily basis, combined with the changes in the lives of those who experience them, their existence and the occurrences of this journey can no longer be denied. Whether one is involved in an accident, had a serious illness, endured surgery, laid in the ICU, had cardiac arrest, or a variety of other possibilities, leaving one's body occurs throughout the world in amazing and often similar ways. There is no age requirement for such an experience. Old or young, people all over the world have reported similar experiences in some manner. For most survivors, they describe a place of Light and a family member or friend who has died, who appears before them. They describe sights and experiences that the rational reasoning mind has a hard time assimilating. Even some who consider themselves atheists with no belief in a "Heaven" have found themselves in such a place. We become an ever-growing "Family of the Light."

NDEs happened to people long before the arrival of the Internet and access to information that could contaminate statements and facts regarding this mysterious experience. Individuals often report an overwhelming feeling of awe and a deep knowing that no matter what anyone else believes, they have been touched. For so many, the feeling of being totally wrapped in love and becoming divinely connected to all life force brings a new reverence of life and humanity. Many individuals who have gone to the Other Side find that their whole belief system changes in radical ways. What seemed important before no longer is a priority now. Having this experience awakens many survivors who were raised in the fog of unbending traditional religion to a more open, spiritual way of not just believing but knowing there is an afterlife. When sharing with others throughout the years, I discovered the experience most often changes the traditional believer's perception of what we call life and can even answer some of the questions about the mystery of death and dying. Some survivors are drawn towards a greater spiritual path or more holistic lifestyle. They often seek out someone like myself for guidance in that regard, to assist them in discovering their natural abilities. For myself, having grown up with unusual gifts prior to my own experience, this powerful event ended up enhancing some of my gifts. My ability to do absent-healing work or pain control when thousands of miles away from clients was suddenly accelerated after this event. Another technique I also use to assist individuals who are dying, experiencing severe pain, or suffering deep emotional trauma is the soothing warm energy flowing from my hands. Countless clients have told me that it helps take away their pain, allowing them to relax and have a more peaceful feeling.

Years later, when I was at a hospital working on someone dying in ICU, the nurse standing at the doorway stated she felt a burning heat all the way across the room from where I was at the bedside of the patient. "My God, it's so hot in here!" Walking over to her and touching her arm, she experienced my soothing mysterious gift. She said, "I have never felt anything like this, how does this happen?" After my out-of-body experience, I noticed that the soothing energy had grown much more intense as had my general psychic sensory abilities. For a while, the increased intensity proved very discomforting to me until I got used to it. Many other survivors have also reported enhanced intuitive abilities of one sort or another following their out-of-body experiences. One of these survivors was a woman who came into my life and had an amazing story to share with me. We would become Sisters of the Light!

NDE Friends

Pam Reynolds Lowery, "my old friend" as she called me, was a survivor of one of the most extreme near-death experience ever recorded. I have always known that my life was filled with fated encounters and this amazing woman was one of them in a most powerful way. Pam became my friend on the social networking site Myspace and from the start we had a special connection. At last, I had found a very special kindred spirit bringing me validation. An immediate bond was created between us as we shared our similar experiences with one another. We could see and feel the soul of each other from the first time we met. We were like two "old friends", as she called us, who had found one another again. We found a gold mine in each other from our first "hello." Our meeting helped us validate that we were not crazy nor alone, and that something had happened to each of us but just a little differently. In our private conversations, we both revealed that we felt like we were outside our body at times, as if part of us was still in another place. There was always a sacred feeling when we talked about how we never forgot the feeling we both had, that there was the presence of something or someone very powerful that had been with us when we hovered between life and death. The similarities in certain parts of our mysterious experiences were amazing.

Pam's NDE was a very rare event and one of the most famous in the medical world. Due to a giant basilar artery aneurysm that could not be removed in the typical fashion, she was referred to Dr. Robert F. Spätzle at the Barrow Neurological Institute in Phoenix, Arizona. Dr. Spätzle had pioneered a very daring radical surgery which is called Hyperthermia Cardiac Arrest. In a nutshell, they dropped her body temperature to sixty degrees, shut down her entire system including her brain and heart, and put her at death's door. Then they operated on her brain. Pam had no brainwave activity and no blood flowing in her brain, which rendered her clinically dead. Once her surgery was completed, her doctors restored her to life! In a conversation one time, she spoke of the moment when they started to cut through her skull with a surgical saw and feeling herself pop outside her body and hover above the operating table. She got a kick out of the fact that she was hovering over the surgeons in the operating room and would be able to tell them what they had been doing and what they were talking about.

I told Pam about the empathic overloads I experienced from time to time. Pam also struggled, feeling people so empathically that she too, would have to step away from them. It was amazing because we both had increases in hearing things more clearly and distinctly than ever before. She also sensed a Presence and Light at the end of a vortex which was pulling her away from her earthly body. It was also the reason we called each other "Sisters of the Light." What was interesting is that we had not known about each other's experiences prior to our meeting. When we talked, we were amazed at how similar some of our experiences had been, such as looking down at our hands, mesmerized at how they shimmered with sparkling light, and the fact we felt no pain. Our experiences, the colors of the various lights and even the tones and harmonics of sounds were very similar. We both had our grandparents coming for us and others we could not recognize but knew we had some sort of a deep connection with. We also had an audio experience when out of body, Pam hearing a sound like a musical "D" and me hearing a high-pitched whirring sound, accelerating rapidly! The sound she heard seemed to pull her out of her body just as mine did. I had also heard a "pop", and this was the first time that someone else said it had happened to them, too. We also had similar experiences reentering our bodies.

We two knew that something powerful and real had happened to us. and that was all that mattered. "They all will have their turn at some point," she would say. We knew we were "Sisters of the Light," as she called us many times on the phone. Pam also was a guest on my Blog Talk radio show and we enjoyed spending the time sharing our experiences. You can go to my website and listen to one of our conversations. We felt like we were in a closed club that brought us comfort.

Pam's NDE and what happened to her during the surgery were very powerful. I loved and respected her for her strength and faith to go through those operations and recovery. My journey prior to my surgery was a painful one and I also had a "not the norm" operation only not as extreme. We did not know each other during those times but found out we had very similar events occur on what we call the Other Side. At times, she would ask me to use the gifts to look at her and see how her life force was doing. She knew each day was a gift and her time may be short. We made a pact: *"whoever goes first will send a message."*

****

By 2009 I was more settled. Pam and I talked about my coming to see her so we could spend some time together. She had been feeling better, but then her health took a downturn. She called me and left a message that she was going to the doctor again because she was having some problems. She asked for me to please send her healing and we would talk soon. Regrettably, our time with one another upon this Earth plane was brief. Pam said "goodbye" first, and for many months I didn't know that she was gone. She'd cross my mind from time to time and I'd try to call her, but each time I called I could never get through. It never occurred to me that she was gone. The mind does not want to think of the worst, and tries to distract us from painful realities. Pam continued to come into my thoughts and I found myself talking out loud to her, "Pam where are you? I called you!"

Then I was compelled to search for her name on the Internet, feeling her presence around me. In a matter of minutes, there on my screen I saw the announcement of Pam Reynolds' death. At that moment, I knew that she had been visiting me, trying to let me know she was gone. I remembered the time we had laughed and made our pact...whichever one of us went first would contact the other. She was communicating with me through Heavenly whispers, just as we had planned to do when one of us crossed over. I felt a deep sadness and I did not want to accept that I would not hear her voice one last time. We would not get to meet in person as we planned, because it was time for Pam to take flight to Heaven. She was an amazing woman, and loved her family deeply!

Pam Reynolds died from heart failure at Emory University Hospital in Atlanta, Georgia, going into the light one final time on Saturday, May 22, 2010. At some point months later, I felt her presence again pulling me to look at her date and month of crossing. There it was, giving me chills up and down my body! I knew she had sent me a most powerful message, seeing her smile and hearing her whisper *"Goodbye my Old friend."*

My NDE occurred May 26,1986

We two know that we will see each other again!

Her last written message to me was:

"Hi Sweetie, it's been awhile since I've written. Hope this finds you well and happy. I've been in and out of hospital with pulmonary embolisms but have declared my body a bummer-free zone so we'll see what happens. Glad to hear your move went well and hope you'll be content there. Stop by once in awhile, old friend!!!! Hugs," - Pam Reynolds

That was the last time I heard from Pam. Her words of determination despite the challenges of her body were, and still are, such an inspiration to so many. It saddens me that we were unable to have a final conversation on the phone here on Earth or see one another as planned. I cared deeply about her from the day I first met her. As I read her message it was bittersweet because she was gone but also not suffering anymore.

I will see you down the road, my beautiful "Sister of the Light!"

Bob Campbell

Angels protect many of us by guiding us to the place that can help most: an ER. One person who experienced this mysterious event is my new NDE friend, Bob Campbell of Dallas, Texas who shared his amazing experience with me. A blood clot entered Bob's heart triggering a heart attack. During this episode, Bob flat-lined on the heart monitor. He had played golf earlier that day and then gone to lunch. After lunch he felt like he had indigestion, so he drove home thinking a nap would help. When he pulled in the driveway he thought, "Hmmm, maybe I should drive myself to the hospital."As he explained to me, "I walked into the hospital, immediately dropped to the floor with a heart attack, and then just walked 'Into a Light' as I flat-lined." When I asked if he saw or felt anything, his reply was, "All I knew when I walked into it (the Light) was that everything would be okay. When walking back out of that Light, it felt as if I had done a full 180-degree turn. From that moment on, I had a complete feeling of peace that I've never ever experienced before and still have not to this day. It was truly a spiritual awakening like no other." Prior to this incident, Bob had always been very ambitious, driven, and hardworking in the business world. While he is a successful man to this day, since he went into that Light, he has found his true wealth. He is more empathetic, nonjudgmental of others and the path they walk, filled with compassion, not concerned with worldly things and more forgiving and giving to those in need.

When I first visited them, his wife Nancy and I were in the kitchen talking when Bob walked through the door. One of the first things I noticed about him was that "look" in his eyes that some NDEs have. He had not told me of his experience but there was something in those "crystal blue eyes" when he first said hello to me. When he finally shared his story with me, it verified what I had "felt" about this man the first moment I saw him.

In his eyes, I saw deep soul Light looking back at me. I call them "Angel Eyes"…the same phrase that friends and clients have said to me. "There is something different about your eyes. It is like you have seen something and been somewhere that none of us will be allowed to go until we leave this Earth." Bob Campbell has those eyes. It is a wonderful experience to see that soul Light in someone's eyes and the comforting feeling it brings.

Nancy Campbell

I wrote Nancy an email asking if she would share what she had walked into that day at the hospital. She graciously replied.

"I remember it like it was yesterday. Before I even started reading what you wrote, I remember Bob's crystal, clear blue eyes. March 3, 2003... It was a typical day at work when I received a phone call from a social worker at Presbyterian Hospital. She said that my husband was in the ER. I said I would be right there and she said, 'I think that is a good idea'. I raced out of the office, got to the ER and raced through the hospital. The social worker met me in the hallway and took me to Bob. He was in a room waiting to be taken into surgery. It was so surreal. There were at least 6 people standing around him. I walked in and stood by his side. He looked at me and smiled and his eyes were literally crystal clear and as blue as I have ever seen them. One of the nurses wiggled his feet and said, 'Bob, do you know who that is'. Bob said, 'Yes, that's my wife but I remember her being taller' and then started laughing out loud with his wonderful infectious laugh. I am only 5'2" and Bob has always made 'short jokes'. Then he looked at me and said he was sorry repeatedly. I have no idea what he was referring to. I kept telling him it was okay. I remember the ER doctor standing next to me and saying, 'We had a tough time bringing him back.' I kept thinking, what is he talking about? I learned later that the doctors had to paddle Bob back to life. I thank God every day for not taking my husband that day and am grateful for every day we have together."

Nancy continued:

"** Interesting note: My cousin Tom passed away several years ago, and one of his favorite songs was 'The wind beneath my wings'. Whenever something is wrong in our immediate family, we hear that song and know that everything will be okay. My mom and dad came to the ER that day and when Bob was in surgery, my mom looked at me and she said, 'Stop crying, it is going to be okay.' I just looked at her and she said, 'listen.' The song in the ER waiting room was 'The wind beneath my wings'. I knew then that it would be okay. Of course, he took the golf clubs inside the house FIRST and then drove himself to the ER. He had enough time to walk in, get his name out and flat-line. Boy, did he have angels watching over him!!!!! One red light and things would be different."

-Nancy Campbell, Dallas Texas

Grief and Loss

I still reflect upon the "why?" having seen so many good people suffer so much because of murder or loss of a child. When I reenact a crime, I know what it felt like as the victim was being killed. After my near-death experience in 1986, I know what it feels like to be dying in a most painful manner. The difference is, for many reasons, God sent me back to Earth. I can still hear that indescribable heavenly voice saying to me in that oh-so-beautiful place that I had entered, "You can stay or you can go back. It is your choice. We would like you to go back as there is still much more work for you to do." While I don't remember doing so, I chose to come back and you are reading this book as a result. I rarely questioned God about my returning or my very mysterious life, but sometimes when life was hard, lonely and filled with challenges and loss, I too, whispered, "Why?" As each year passes, I have learned that we are given many of the answers to that one little word, which are filled with so much power and meaning. Time and the road we have traveled bring us many of the answers we need. We see what and how our trials and tribulations have given us strength, enhanced our growth, and brought many good things into our lives…if we just open our eyes. We still carry the wounds in our hearts from the swords that cut so deep, but we survive and must carry on with this life. Many times, we discover a new work given to us and it cannot be denied.

Grieving the Loss of a Child

We all grieve differently. There is no set time or way to do it. When a loved one dies, we do not stop feeling the powerful impact that they had upon our lives. The history that souls created together is still there and will remain all through life. It takes time to adjust to the loss and deep pain that overpowers one's daily life when someone dies. Spiritual beliefs and practices can bring more comfort for moments during the loss of a loved one; still the pain takes hold of life. Grieving is a process that each person experiences in a unique way. It is something that we never get over and each day we find it difficult to move forward; we keep wanting to stay in the past, all alive and together. The loss of a child is one of the deepest cuts. As my mother's words spoken to me when my life was fading, *"No child should leave before a parent,"* this cry is the same for any parent who has lost or is facing the loss of a child.

A future together sharing life's passages is taken away in a matter of a few breaths! For some, there is a period to prepare for the goodbye that will ultimately arrive with a child's lingering illness, giving the mind a chance to adjust somewhat to the coming reality. Then, there are those who have lost children who were taken in a sudden and often times violent manner. Regardless, there is always a deep wound to the heart. Life and the daily process of trying to stay strong, watching one's child die and not being able to take away their pain, is a living nightmare. No one's grief is more important or special; there are just different events leading up to that final breath. We all suffer and feel the pain. People grieve in many different ways. Death also knocks at our door in a variety of ways.

Grieving the Loss of a Child

Whispers from Heaven

Fawn O'Jeay is a mother who stood at the door watching her two teenage children step off the porch, get into a car, and head down the Louisiana country road. It would be the last time she would see her son and daughter alive. They would be killed in a car accident in a matter of hours. Fawn has had numerous visitations from them throughout the years since they died. One day as she was showing me paintings of them in her bedroom, they suddenly filled the room with their presence. It was as if I was meeting them when they were alive. I also felt their presence one day when she was having a cup of tea at my place sharing her story. Suddenly, there was a curtain of light, playful energy moving towards her shoulder. When I described to her what I was feeling and seeing and commented that the energy was filled with their playfulness, she smiled and said it was the anniversary of their death. She often had visitations from them in the manner that I described. They even moved objects from one place to another with a "whisper" that they were always near. Death brings a sudden horrific shock to the mind with a deep cut to the heart and soul. It can come as the result of accidents or from the dark, heinous act of murder, ending precious innocent lives and shattering the dreams of the victim's parents and family.

Murder never leaves you where it found you.

Dayna Herroz and her husband, Roy lost their daughter, Tori Vienneau and their 10-month old grandson, Dean in a most horrific homicide. It creates another living hell on Earth because there is a perpetrator to face in court (in the months and years to come) bringing even more trauma to the heart and soul. When we are open and more peaceful, there can come a moment in time when one feels the presence of a loved one. They will come when least expected, in a moment when one's sight is clearer. Whispers from heaven can arrive in many forms: a breeze, a shimmer before the eyes, a feeling of peace and comfort, their scent or even a hummingbird sitting on a wire looking down at you. Dayna Herroz experienced such signs from heaven just when she seemed to need them the most. And there were the whispers that emerged through me to her. It is a very sacred experience for me to be a Heavenly messenger and then to get confirmation from their family of information which only their family would know.

The Humming Bird

Tori Marie Vienneau 3/17/1984-7/26/2006

Dean Robert Springstube 9/26/2005-7/26/2006

"I sat outside on Friday and this hummingbird sat on a wire staring at me. I started talking to it as if it were Tori. I said something like I hope she was proud of the work I am trying to do and she flew so close to my head and stopped right in front of my face and did a little flutter dance. I could feel the breeze from those tiny wings she was so close to me. If I said something that may be one of my deepest regrets or where I felt like I failed; the hummingbird just sat on the wire staring at me again. Changed it up to a positive and how they are doing in Heaven and she flew all around me again. I said I was sorry for not filling the feeder but it would be filled by this morning. When I woke up, there she was on the wire looking right at the feeder I had not filled up; just like Tori would have done. I felt so at peace and knew I was in my daughter's presence which brought great comfort. I told her, 'thanks for visiting and come as often as you can'."
August 2015

Dayna Herroz

Angel with a Baby in a Rocking Chair

-Dayna Herroz

I lost everything the day my daughter, Tori (22) and grandson, Dean (10 months) were murdered in July of 2006. I can honestly say that I was all consumed with finding them "earthly" justice; knowing that he would also have to face the ultimate justice when he stands before God, I have always taken comfort in that. After the verdict and sentence were handed down (2 life sentences without the possibility of parole), I was happy to have that process over.

Yet there was still something bothering me. I needed to know that my daughter didn't see what the murderer did to Dean (hung by a noose in his crib). Elaina explained to me that when a person is murdered their souls are ripped from the physical body so quickly that not only do they not know they are dead, nor do they feel the physical pain, but many are still able to see what is happening on earth. Such was the case with my daughter.

So, that added to the questions I had: did they go to Heaven together? Are they still together? How was Tori doing now, etc. Elaina suddenly started sharing what she was seeing and feeling from the Other Side then describing where she was standing and what appeared before her. The description of where Tori's soul was (in a pale pink & white glistening room where she was resting). She was surrounded by angels and a special angel was sitting in a rocking chair with a baby in her arms. That made the hair on the back of my neck rise because I had just received an angel with a baby in her arms in a rocking chair that rocks and plays "Did you ever know that you're my hero?" In my heart and my mind, I took great comfort in the words Elaina shared with me and the answers she gave me brought a measure of peace to my heart.

Had I not met Elaina, I would still be struggling with this but she put my mind at ease. She is the real deal, someone I trust with my loved one's memories here on Earth, and someone I can turn to when I am confused or need some direction. I am eternally grateful to her.

Sincerely,
Dayna Herroz
Peer Advocate/Violent Loss
The Citizens of Courage Award 2016
San Diego, CA 92143

Trinity of Angels

-Dayna Herroz

The first major sign I got from Tori was from a necklace and matching bracelet called the Trinity of Angels. Inside each were 3 Angels: Peace, Promise and Protection. When the set arrived Tori just laughed and laughed because the necklace looked like a dog collar. I had given strict instructions that that necklace was to be wrapped around her hand in the casket. When we went to see them for the first time (after 5 days) we also brought what they would need to have them ready in the casket. We had their clothes with us and instructions that I wanted the Trinity of Angels necklace wrapped around her hand. Here is where the sign came in:

As I was getting her clothes and jewelry together I put the necklace with all 3 Angels in the box on the necklace in her bag. When I woke up the next morning there were 2 angels on the kitchen table. I checked the bracelet I was going to wear and all 3 angels were there. I checked inside the bag at the necklace and 2 angels were missing(Peace & Protection). 4 different people had checked to see if everything was in each of their bags the night before and the Angels were there then, but when we woke up they were on the table and not in the bag. Roy carries those Angels with him and I have my 3 from the bracelet.

"She had left them for me because she didn't need them anymore."

My coolest and most memorable sign came about 3 months into this journey. Roy's daughter had brought me dinner and we were in my home office talking, computer was turned off. I was crying and saying I didn't know who I was anymore. I prided myself on being a mother and grandmother and I felt like that was gone now. We were both teary-eyed and there was this moment of silence. Then suddenly my computer turned on and a song I had never heard of came on blaring through my speakers. By the time the song was over the computer turned itself off. We were on the floor sobbing and I said "what the hell was that?" my stepdaughter said "that song was from Josh Groban but I can't remember the name." We looked it up on the computer and the song was called "You're Still You" I lost it. The words were so right on and the way it came through could only be explained as divine intervention. She wanted me to know I was still me. I play that song all the time now when I feel like I am nobody anymore.

Dayna Herroz (mother and grandmother) has taken her pain and turned it into a powerful light for others who have had a violent loss of a loved one. She has a busy schedule these days reaching out to others who have suffered a violent loss.

Peer Advocate/Violent Loss: works with families who have had a violent loss, providing support, court accompaniment, and support groups.

San Diego County Citizen of Courage Award 2016

Dayna is also a contributing writer in the Murder Survivors Handbook by Author Connie Saindon. She also is one of the eight survivor writers using the pen name Rose; Tori was Victoria, and Dean was Louis.

On the Board of Directors for San Diego Crime Stoppers, Keynote speaker at the California Conference.

On the Board of Directors for Victims Assistance Coordinating Council.

She also facilitates a Violent Loss Support Group at the Center for Compassionate Care of Elizabeth Hospice at the Liberty Station office.

Acknowledgments

Law Enforcement Acknowledgments

Victor Calzaretta, (Rest in Peace) Criminal Attorney and former Clark County Chief Criminal Deputy, Vancouver, Washington, who planted the seed and once again turned my life in a new direction. You and Rod Englert walked with me into the shadow and guided me upon the forensic path that first time. You always inspired me and expected the highest ethical behavior from me when working in the investigative world. Thank you for being in my life.

(Retired) Detective Chief Deputy Rod Englert, (Retired) Commander of Operations Multnomah County Sherriff Department, Portland, Oregon, currently a consultant on high profile murder cases across the country, expertise in homicide crime scene interpretation and blood spatter interpretation who guided me in the ways to use my abilities as a forensic tool.

(Retired) Chief Richard Kirkland for opening the door for me to work on very interesting cases in Reno, Nevada.

Former Detectives; (Retired) Chief Steve Pitts/former Detective, (Retired) Detective Ben Africa, (Retired) Bob Boginson, (Retired) Kevin Cassinelli, (Retired) Joe Depczynski, (Retired) Gary Eubanks, (Retired) Ron Dreher, (Retired) Allen Fox, (Retired) Randy Houston, (Retired) Duane Isenberg, (Retired) Dave Jenkins, (Retired) Dave Keller, (Retired) Dave Larson, (Retired) Dave Ramsey, (Retired) Troy Shipley, and Floyd Soristo (Rest in Peace)

Sandra Cavanagh, Crime Analysis, Reno Police Department

(Retired) Pam Engle, Reno Police Department

Keith Hashimoto, Reno Police Department (Rest in Peace)

Cathy Bradly, Police Technician, Robbery Homicide Division, Reno Police Department (Rest in Peace)

(Retired) Richard Putnam, Polygraph, Washoe County Sheriff's Office

Kathleen Bishop, Deputy, Washoe County Sherriff's Office

(Retired) Undersheriff Curtis Kull, Humboldt County

(Retired) Dave Spencer, FBI Agent, Reno Office

(Retired) Steve Pitts, Chief of Police/Homicide Detective, Reno Police Department for reviewing the Investigative chapters.

I worked with incredible leadership, investigative talent and committed personnel at the Reno Police Department from 1985 into the 2000s. Please know, because of the tremendous outpouring of effort provided in their relationship with me, their families and our community throughout the years, I am unable to mention everyone. Thank you also to the various Law Enforcement Agencies Statewide, Federal Agencies, too many to name, who have allowed me the opportunity to grow on this fascinating level through the years. I am honored to have walked this path with so many of you.

Journalists and Reporters Reno NV

-Ed Pearce Senior Correspondent and Investigative Secret Witness Journalist. Reporter KOLO News Channel 8, Reno and a founding member of the board of Secret Witness, past chairman, current longtime cochairman for rewards, honored as the first recipient of the Crime stopper of the Year award which is now named for him. Emmy nominated, he is a two-time winner of the Prestigious Edward R Murrow award.

Thank you for the wisdom that you passed on to me and your professionalism when covering the investigative work I was part of regarding homicide and missing person cases. Blessings for your dedication to helping find the lost, helping uncover the answers, and helping apprehend those who have committed heinous crimes against the innocent.

-Bill Brown Anchor (Retired), KTVN Ch 2, Reno
-Victoria Campbell, Veteran Crime Reporter (Retired), KRNV News 4, Reno, for your ethical reporting throughout the years.
-Terri Hendry Reporter (Retired), KRNV News 4, Reno
-Terri Russell Chief Reporter, KOLO News Channel 8, Reno

-Lou Gutenberger, Talk Show Host (Retired), KOH Radio
-Ross Mitchell, KOH Radio

Mike Boyd, Veteran Investigative Reporter, Live at Noon, KCRA Ch 3, Sacramento, who was my mentor in the world of television.
(Rest in Peace)

-Bob Carroll a Pioneer in Television and Radio Broadcasting, Reno Nevada

Friends and Family

Bob Vaughn for believing in me and helping me in so many ways these past years. The Vaughn Family. Michael Alukas, who came into my life just at the right time and helped me in this most pain-filled time. Longtime dear friend and mentor, Don O'Gorman who sent me to Dr. Katrina Tang with whom I had amazing results when I started failing in health again and had amazing results. D.J. O'Gorman, for your love and kindness.

Lorna Bevan, Joyce Blake, Sandy Cavanaugh, Candy Greene, Jim Eaglesmith, Nancy Eklof, Pam Engle, Amy Fambrough, Sondra Frances, Margaret Graham, Frank and Pat Gross, Robin Manteris, Steve and Tamara Pitts, Laura Smith, Mary Thompson and so many more, in so many places, who came into my life becoming family.

World Renown Tattoo Artist and Author Madame Chinchilla, who inspired me to start writing while living by the ocean in Fort Bragg, California. I soon found myself being asked to write a piece for her book Electric Tattooing by Women 1900-2003 (Triangle Tattoo & Museum Series) about Olive Oatman, who was, at the age of 14 kidnapped by the Southwest Indians and her chin was tattooed with ink made from cactus. The second beloved artist, dancer and poet, Vali Meyers. With Chinchilla's guidance, I found my myself entering the world of tattoo freelance writing for Skin Deep Magazine U.K. Thank you for your support.

My son, Michael Cernin, who since birth has been more places than most people travel in a lifetime. Thank you for your patience, understanding and strength having a mother who walks such an unusual path in life. His children, Amanda and Maxwell and nephew Travis.

Shawna Larsen Mefford, my daughter from another mother. I appreciate all your support. Thank you, Pat Larsen, (Rest in Peace) for sharing her with me.

Karen VanLoo Stamps to whom Auntie Lavelle passed down our family history. Thank you for taking me to the South to experience the most interesting history of the Proffitt's and the resting place of our ancestors. To all the cousins who will have this book. Another part of our family's history.

Rest in Peace Family and Dear Friends

Mother and Father, Shirley & Robert Proffitt; Grandparents Elmer & Jenny Tyler Frey, Grandmother Lethal Cross Proffitt, Aunt Elsie Kipling Tyler Richardson, Uncle Lloyd & Aunt Lavelle, Chris Sauvola, Auntie's; Loretta & Gerrie, Fran Cotner, Irene Morros, Patricia Larsen, Johanna Wilson, Sabrina Wheeler, Thelma & Kendall Vaughn, Kelly Lott, Steve Kresoja, Kathleen "Kathy" Woods, Victor A Calzaretta, and so many more. You are not forgotten.

Appreciation

Doctors are those who dedicate their lives to healing others daily, often dealing with suffering and pain, confronting death as well as new life. Always nice to say a "Thank you" to them. I am blessed to have had the following doctors care for me in Texas:

Dr. Rebecca Mayol Sharp, Internist, Internal Medicine NE Tarrant Internal Medicine Associates who was my Primary Care Physician.

Dr. Sam Abdul-Rahim, Oculoplastic Surgery/Neuro-Ophthalmology, Ophthalmology Associates, Fort Worth and Dr. Mark A. Alford, Ophthalmic plastic and reconstructive surgery, Grapevine Texas. You restored my vision and I cannot thank you enough.

Dr. Stephen C. Hurlburt, Neurologist, Texas Health Harris Methodist Hospital, for your help and for sharing with me about the brain of someone such as myself with these usual gifts. "Yes there are people with these types of abilities and we are still trying to understand this fascinating subject."

Dr. Victoria W. Serralta, Dermatologist, Arlington Texas for your encouragement to write this book.

About the Author

Elaina Deva Proffitt has been a nationally and internationally recognized spiritual counselor, life coach and consultant since 1983. Using her intuitive abilities to help people from all walks of life, she is frequently sought out for her accuracy as a clairvoyant, clairaudient and clairsentient medium. Her empowering message of love, hope and healing also brings clarity and peace to those who are walking through the dark night of the soul. Her work includes spiritual life coaching, grief and loss counseling for families of violent crimes and those who have been assaulted, to assist them in restoring balance and peace, and counseling military veterans to help them ease and handle their PTSD. After her own near-death experience in 1986, she found herself having a large grief and loss practice. Elaina has also worked with hospice patients to help soothe and assist them in their crossing. She enjoys sharing her experience with hospice workers, doctors, nurses and other medical professionals.

As a spiritual counselor, she assists a wide variety of clients who are going through life changes, bringing clarity, confidence and harmony. Working in conjunction with traditional therapists, Elaina has also counseled ministers, priests, nuns and those of all faiths. Many have called her the "Teacher's Teacher" the "Healer's Healer" Her spiritual name is Deva.

Law Enforcement Consultant/Speaker since 1983 (Documented)

Due to her professional ethics and confidentiality when working as a Consultant for Law Enforcement on murder cases over the years, families (including the wives of fallen officers) who had lost a loved one to violent death were referred to her for spiritual grief & loss counseling and support. Working with them, she became aware of a world the public does not see and the reality of what it takes to solve a crime. Spending years with those brave men and women, she saw and felt deeply the heavy responsibility placed upon their shoulders in a most dangerous and pain-filled world…as they walked daily into the line-of-fire as a police officer. She shares part of that world, in her book *"It's May and the Lilacs are Blooming" One foot on Earth and one in Heaven.* The world of death, dying, and homicide, including police officers is uncomfortable to most people. Elaina was often asked the same question regarding this unusual work. "How can you do that type of work?" Immediately, she heard the whisper of the woman warrior resting within her heart-soul…the answer that would be spoken to this day "How could I not?"

With her diverse background, she has been a popular radio and television guest throughout the country for over 30 years. In addition, she has done public speaking for various organizations. She has had a high-profile clientele including those in the public; music artists, media, producers, politicians, medical profession and those in all walks of life.

PASSIONS:

Protecting the Rights of Animals and the Environment
Stopping Child Abuse and Human Trafficking
Loves music and the arts
Loves Helping Souls become empowered

TRAVEL:

Lived and traveled to many places in the world
Magical Journey workshops to Beautiful Places

Law Enforcement Associations and Seminars

University of Nevada Reno July 21 1984

Department of Criminal Justice

Multnomah County Sheriff's Office October 4 1984

"Psychics as Investigative Resources"

University of Nevada Reno Criminal Justice Department

"Psychic Awareness an Investigative tool" 1984

Truckee Meadows C.C. Criminal Justice Dept.

Principals of Investigation 1986

"Parapsychology and Criminal Investigation"

American Polygraph Association Reno NV 1984

24th Annual Seminar Advanced Polygraph Instrumentation & Techniques

Lectured: *"Unconventional Investigations"*

National American Polygraph Association August 1989

California Association of Polygraph Examiners

Character Profiling and Analysis

C.A.P.E.

California Association of Polygraph Examiners Feb.1991

Newport Beach California

National Training Seminar Lecture 10 HRS:

"Character Profiling Methodology Application in Investigative Setting"

American Society of Law Enforcement Trainers

Milwaukie Wisconsin January 7-11th 1992

California Homicide Investigators Association 1992-1993

California Homicide Investigators Associate 1993-94

CHIA Conference Reno Nevada March 3-5-1993

www.ingramcontent.com/pod-product-compliance
Lightning Source LLC
Chambersburg PA
CBHW070339090426
42733CB00009B/1232